W9-DEK-129

DRUGS, CLUBS AND YOUNG PEOPLE

For Chez, whom I met in the club

Drugs, Clubs and Young People
Sociological and Public Health Perspectives

Edited by

BILL SANDERS
University of Southern California, USA

ASHGATE

Published by
Ashgate Publishing Limited
Gower House
Croft Road
Aldershot
Hampshire GU11 3HR
England

Ashgate Publishing Company
Suite 420
101 Cherry Street
Burlington, VT 05401-4405
USA

Ashgate website: http://www.ashgate.com

British Library Cataloguing in Publication Data
Drugs, clubs and young people : sociological and public
  health perspectives
  1. Subculture 2. Youth - Drug use 3. Nightclubs 4. Psychotropic
  drugs 5. Drug traffic
  I. Sanders, Bill, 1972-
  306.1

Library of Congress Cataloging-in-Publication Data
Drugs, clubs and young people : sociological and public health perspectives / edited by Bill Sanders.
     p. cm.
  Includes bibliographical references and index.
  ISBN 0-7546-4699-8
  1. Youth--Drug use. 2. Young adults--Drug use. 3. Youth--Social life and customs.
4. Young adults--Social life and customs. 5. Nightclubs. 6. Raves (Parties) 7. Drug abuse. I. Sanders, Bill, 1972-

  HV5824.Y68D773 2006
  306'.1--dc22
                                                                    2006003903
ISBN 0 7546 4699 8

Printed and bound by Athenaeum Press Ltd,
Gateshead, Tyne & Wear.

Contents

List of Figures and Tables

About the Authors

Kristin Evans has a B.A. in sociology from the University of California at Berkeley. Ms. Evans was the project manager on a National Institute on Drug Abuse-funded project on club drugs and the dance scene in the San Francisco Bay Area and is currently project manager on the Asian American youth, club drugs and the dance scene project also funded by NIDA. Ms. Evans has published three articles with Dr. Hunt.

Adam Isaiah Green, PhD, is an Assistant Professor of sociology at York University, Toronto, Canada. Green's research is situated at the intersection of the sociology of sexuality and medical sociology, and aims to develop new theory relevant to both areas of study. His primary research draws from the insights of Bourdieu and Goffman to re-conceptualize the relationship of power and social status in modern erotic worlds. Currently, Dr. Green is supported by the Canadian Foundation for AIDS Research (CANFAR) for a study on the relationship of sexual status structures to sexual decision-making processes among Toronto gay and bisexual men. A second project, supported by a Faculty of Arts Research Grant, examines the new phenomenon of Canadian same-sex marriage.

Geoffrey Hunt, PhD, is a social anthropologist, who has done extensive ethnographic research in West Africa, England and most recently in the United States. He received his doctorate in Social Anthropology at the University of Kent, England. Currently, Dr. Hunt is the Principal Investigator on a National Institute on Drug Abuse (NIDA) funded research project on Asian American youth, club drugs and the dance scene. Prior to commencing this study, he was the Principal Investigator on three other National Institute on Health projects on gangs, and one project on club drugs and the dance scene in the San Francisco Bay Area. From research data gleaned from these studies and the current work, Dr. Hunt and his research team have published over 30 articles focusing on youth, drugs, and gangs.

Karen Joe Laidler, PhD, is an Associate Professor in the department of sociology at the University of Hong Kong. She received her doctorate in sociology at the University of California at Davis. Dr. Joe Laidler has been involved in criminal justice research for the past 20 years. For the past ten years, her research and writing has focused primarily on ethnic youth gangs and violence, and drug use and problems concentrating specifically on issues associated with young women. Currently, Dr. Joe Laidler is Principal Investigator of the Hong Kong Drug Market study which is part of the UNDCP's study on The Global Drug Market and co-investigator with Dr. Hunt on the Asian American youth, club drugs and the dance scene project. Dr. Joe

Laidler has published extensively on drug use in Hong Kong, Asian American issues as well as on youth gangs.

Brian C. Kelly, PhD, is a medical anthropologist, educated as an undergraduate at Fordham University and as a graduate at Columbia University's Department of Sociomedical Sciences. He currently is Assistant Professor at Purdue University in the Department of Sociology & Anthropology. He also collaborates with the Center for HIV Educational Studies & Training (CHEST) at the City University of New York. His topical areas of research interest include drug use, sexual health, and youth cultures. He continues to conduct research in the New York City metropolitan area. The foci of his current projects include club drug use among New York area youth and drug dealing among suburban youth.

Stephen E. Lankenau, PhD, is an Assistant Professor at the University of Southern California, Keck School of Medicine, Departments of Pediatrics and Preventative Medicine. Trained as a sociologist, he has studied street-involved and other high-risk populations for the past ten years, including ethnographic projects researching homeless panhandlers, prisoners, sex workers, and injection drug users. Currently, he is Principal Investigator of a four-year NIH study researching ketamine injection practices among young IDUs in New York, New Orleans, and Los Angeles.

Kathleen MacKenzie received her MA in anthropology at San Jose State University. Currently, she is project manager on an NIH funded research project on street gangs, motherhood and violence. Ms. MacKenzie has published, with Dr. Geoffrey Hunt, four articles on street gangs.

Fiona Measham, PhD, RPHEA, is a Senior Lecturer in Criminology and Director of Studies for the BA honors program in Criminology within the Department of Applied Social Science. Dr. Measham has over 15 years' experience in the field of drug and alcohol studies, gender, licensed leisure and cultural criminology. She is co-author of *Illegal Leisure* (1998) and *Dancing on Drugs* (2001), based on two large scale studies of young people's drug and alcohol use, for both of which she was lead researcher, and is co-editor of *Swimming with Crocodiles* (forthcoming). Her theoretical interests span cultural criminology, gender studies and the sociology of intoxication, with a particular interest in the boundaries of transgression, the criminalisation of leisure, and the problematic-recreational interface in leisure time consumption. Her most recent and current research includes a study of 'binge drinking', bounded consumption and the new 'culture of intoxication'; an historical analysis of the attempted criminalisation of English barmaids; the emergence of recreational ketamine use and the role of insider knowledge in the research process; and the changing nature of 'mature' British dance drug communities.

Karenza Moore, PhD, is a Lecturer in Criminology and the University of Lancaster, UK, where she is currently looking at women's experiences of working in the information technology industry. She has undertaken mainly qualitative research on young people, substance use, and club culture for the past six years, most of which has been conducted in her spare time. Recent research projects include an ongoing study on recreational ketamine use amongst clubbers in the North-West of England with Dr Fiona Measham. She is an avid clubber, club promoter and trance DJ.

Dina Perrone, PhDc, received a University Grant for her dissertation project on New York City 'club kids' at the School of Criminal Justice at Rutgers University-Newark. She is also a Behavioral Sciences Training Pre-Doctoral Fellow at the National Development Research Institute funded by the National Institute of Drug Abuse. While she has written various articles within the criminal justice field – topics including the privatization of prisons and self-control theory – her primary areas of research interest include drug use, drug policy and deviance. She has published in *The Prison Journal* and *The International Journal of Offender Therapy and Comparative Criminology*.

Bill Sanders, PhD, is an Assistant Professor in the Department of Pediatrics at the University of Southern California. He works within the Community Health Outcomes and Intervention Research Program at the Saban Research Institute and the Division of Research on Children, Youth and Families at Childrens Hospital Los Angeles. He is currently a researcher and analyst on a nationwide project examining health risks related to the injection of ketamine amongst young people and is the Principal Investigator of a study examining negative health outcomes, including HIV risk, related to sexual behavior, drug use and violence amongst gang-identified youth in Los Angeles. Both projects are funded by the National Institute of Drug Abuse.

Daniel Silverstone, PhD, is a Senior lecturer at the University of Portsmouth, UK. He is also currently researching the subject of gun crime and has co-authored two reports for the Home Office and the Borough of Brent on the subject. His first book, titled *Night-clubbing: Drugs, Clubs and Regulation* is forthcoming under Willan Press.

Zhao Helen Wu, PhD is an Assistant Professor in Obstetrics and Gynaecology at the University of Texas Medical Branch. She completed a Masters in Sociology at Utah State University in 1993 and a doctorate in Sociomedical Sciences and Health Outcomes Research through UTMB's Graduate Program in Preventive Medicine and Community Health in 1998. She also completed a Post-Doctoral Fellowship at UTMB in PMCH and the Sealy Center on Aging. She also teaches medical students and graduate students. Dr. Wu's principal area of clinical research is the drug addiction process and related health consequences.

Editor's Foreword

I attended my first rave on New Year's Eve 1992 in Los Angeles. I was 20. Around 11 in the evening somewhere in downtown LA, several friends and I entered a nondescript looking building with no signs and no line. The space inside had been transformed from what appeared to be a vacant building into a celebration. Black lights lit up a field of fluorescent designs and symbols, which also outlined a bar selling fruit drinks, water, and soda. Flashing lights and lasers, a distinct pounding, rhythmic music, people dancing, socializing and standing around were heard and observed in this setting. As the night went on, various walls were removed, revealing additional areas of the venue, other levels. Music played in some, while others were dimly lit, quieter 'chill out' zones, a couple with beds. Another room housed a small art collection. People danced in many places. Others lounged on the couches that lined the walls of the main bar area, or stood and swayed and talked. Some people were well-dressed. Several donned cartoon character costumes. We wore t-shirts and jeans. About 300 people attended. Many had a lot of energy, dancing non-stop for hours, very active, lots of smiles. Two individuals selling drugs were observed: one selling ecstasy in large wafer doses and another selling 'tabs' of LSD. We left around seven in the morning as the party continued.

Flash forward to the year 2000 and I work as a security guard or 'bouncer' at a large nightclub in South London. On the first Saturday of every month, the club hosted a night where renowned DJs spun jungle/drum and bass music, and every one of these nights was filled beyond capacity. In a space where the legal limit was 750 people, these Saturday nights often topped 1000, sometimes even as high as 1200 in attendance. Some people wore t-shirt and jeans, others wore expensive designer clothes. The use of ecstasy and cocaine was blatant. 'Pills' could often be found on the ground, and fellow staff members jokingly referred to the cloak room as the 'coke room', as the area contained a small room where the 'bosses' brought 'VIPs' to drink, chat, and snort cocaine. On the dance floor, people are 'having it large': hands in the air, whooping and yelling, boogieing in a sweaty drug fueled mass. Others are dancing on the upper level, on couches, in the hall way, and anywhere they can. Drug sellers circle both rooms, with 'wraps' of cocaine for £50 and ecstasy tablets for £5 each or 5 for a 'score' (£20). A couple of these sellers actually work for the heads of security. I usually left around 7 in the morning, as it took about an hour for the bouncers to get everyone out of the club after the DJ's last record.

Rave and club culture partially define a generation. Going out to underground raves and regulated nightclubs have been activities millions of young people have been doing since the early 1990s in many major cities around the world. The music is electronic, many people come to these events to dance, and many will engage in recreational usage of 'club' or 'dance' drugs, particularly ecstasy. As this culture has blossomed, academia has slowly taken note of the state of these youth. The majority of such research is from the UK, where aspects of rave and club culture permeate popular culture in general. The US, with its handful of studies, has been relatively late to the game. As an American who pursued his graduate degrees in England, the dearth of studies that move beyond flat statistical presentations of club drug users is surprising. While personal experience attests to raving and clubbing not being as popular in the US as with British youth, many young Americans go clubbing every weekend. A quick look in any nightclub in any major city is evidence of this. Unfortunately, academic investigations that contextualize club drug use in the lives of these young people are largely absent. This serves as an impetus for this volume.

What was observed that New Year's Eve night in Los Angeles in the early 1990s was, in many ways, typical of behaviors observed during my tenure as a bouncer at that London club at the turn of the millennium: lights, music, drugs, energetic dancing, and socializing. Clubbing and using club drugs are common recreational activities for many youth in Western societies. This recurring combination of music, youth, dancing and drugs invites exciting and important sociological and public health explorations. The disciplines of sociology and public health have a long history of collaboration. Sociology's impact and image within the field of public health is apparent within epidemiology, which may be broadly defined as the study of the distribution of disease and health. Drug use and violence, for instance, are health behavioral concerns, which may be framed epidemiologically (see Bhopal 2002; Syme 2000). Sociological research, with its emphasis on context and meaning, is able to complement epidemiological concerns, particularly by placing the environment back into the forefront of the 'host'-'agent'-'environment' equation (Agar 1996; see also Clatts, Welle & Goldsamt 2001; Lankenau & Clatts 2004; Lankenau et al. 2004; Lankenau & Sanders 2004).

The overall aim of *Drugs, Clubs and Young People* is to explore and analyze behaviors common at raves and nightclubs through sociological and public health perspectives. This volume examines and contributes to methodological, theoretical and pragmatic considerations within the fields of sociology and public health. The collected chapters have been written by authors from several universities and research institutions, utilizing data collected from the US, UK and Hong Kong. A few of these chapters are based on data gathered in investigations funded by national and federal grant governing bodies. Overall, these studies apply sociological and/or public health approaches towards original data, much of it collected *in situ* and over time. All are based on solid empirical research, not allegory and analogy. As such, these investigations allow for the demystification of stereotypical presentations and the illumination of real concerns surrounding young people who attend clubs and/or use 'club drugs.' Data on behaviors at clubs and raves from different countries permits cross-cultural comparisons to emerge. In addition, the chapters included in this volume offer many theoretical insights related to illicit club drug use and supply, which aims, in part, to challenge current orthodoxies on the role of drug use within young peoples' lives. An overall greater understanding of youthful drug use may promote heretofore perspectives and polices that have been unimagined or underutilized.

*

Drugs, Clubs, and Young People is broken down into four somewhat distinguishable sections. The first two chapters are introductory. In the opening chapter, I offer a brief overview of raving, clubbing, club drugs, and the responses their intersection has generated. The overall aim of the chapter is to underscore the importance of examining such phenomena from sociological and public health perspectives.

Next, Fiona Measham and Karenza Moore explore the early origins of rave research in the UK, and discuss the ramifications of personal experience in the course of researching young people, clubs, and drugs as professionals. Here, the authors address important questions, including: What is 'insider' status in the club, and how can this be beneficial in research?

The next three chapters comprise the second section, which primarily concern club drug use amongst young people in New York City. In the third chapter, Dina Perrone offers a contextual analysis of club drug use amongst New York City 'club kids'. Through in-depth interviews and prolonged observations in various cities on the East Coast of the US, she explores the meaning of club drug use in different aspects of the lives of a relatively affluent sample.

Next, Brian C. Kelly examines how 'Bridge and Tunnel' youth – a term for young people who commute from the suburbs outside New York City – use ecstasy and understand the health risks associated with their ecstasy use. Kelly's comparison of 'folk' and professional models of risk associated with ecstasy underscore important decisions youth make regarding their consumption of the drug.

Adam Isaiah Green concludes the New York trilogy by exploring the intersection of sex, community and club drug use at establishments frequented by men who have sex with men, such as bars, dance clubs, sex parties and bathhouses. Green's interviews reveal the significant role clubs drugs have in facilitating social and sexual relations in particular semi-public environments.

The next two chapters discuss the use of club drugs outside of club settings. First, Stephen E. Lankenau offers an overview of ketamine. Lankenau discusses the history and various uses of the drug, and offers some insights from more than five years of his own research on the drug, including interview excerpts from young users.

Then, Zhao Helen Wu examines ecstasy use amongst young, low-income women – an under represented population within studies on club drugs. Wu explores various aspects of ecstasy use within these women's lives, including their overall knowledge of ecstasy, risky sexual behaviors, and levels of stress associated with ecstasy use.

The final three chapters explore clubbing, club drug use, and various night-time economies in cities outside the US. In Chapter Eight, Karen Joe Laidler, Geoffrey Hunt, Kristin Evans, and Kathleen MacKenzie examine clubbing and club drug use in Hong Kong. They trace the emergence of both clubbing and club drugs, particularly ecstasy and ketamine, as well as perspectives on clubbing and club drug use from Hong Kong youth.

Next, based on my complete participant role as a club security guard or 'bouncer' within a large London nightclub, I offer a contextualized account of ecstasy use, and the operational processes a small group of bouncers employed to control the sales of ecstasy and cocaine. This manuscript is an expanded version on an earlier piece of work, and I further discus my role as a bouncer in the club, as well as some contexts of violence, hence the jocular addition of 'redux' in the title.

Finally, Danny Silverstone, based on his experiences as a bouncer and from researching gun crime, examines alcohol, club drugs (primarily ecstasy), and violence within clubs in the UK. Essentially, Silverstone suggests at least three relatively distinct night-time economies exist within the country, which revolve around pub space, club space, and urban space and catering to different crowds with particular tastes.

While this book is designed to be read from beginning to end for those unfamiliar with the topics of clubs, drugs and young people, all chapters are complete in themselves. None of the manuscripts in this edited volume claim to be representative. They offer, however, critical insights into very popular youthful behaviors, which are relatively unexplored. With luck, this book will provide a foundation from which future sociological and public health studies on young people, clubs and drugs, as well as the young people themselves, will benefit.

Bill Sanders
Los Angeles 2005

Chapter 1

Young People, Clubs and Drugs[1]

Bill Sanders

Why study young people, clubs and drugs? A number of social trends have emerged in recent years that are worthy of social science and public health investigations. For one, contemporary clubbing and 'raving' are activities that have been and continue to be enjoyed by millions of young people around the world. The behaviors and styles associated with raves and clubs define a new youth culture. Raves and clubs are also important to study because of their relationship with illicit drug use. Youthful drug use in the US, Australia and many countries in Europe has generally increased since the early 1990s, and the popularity of raves and nightclubs amongst young people has paralleled this rise. The terms 'club drugs' or 'dance drugs' emerged in relation to the apparent ubiquity of illicit substances, mainly ecstasy, used within rave and contemporary club settings. Raves and clubs have also generated a considerable response, particularly in terms of public health initiatives and the law. For instance, national organizations in the US, such as *DanceSafe*, have been established, in part, to help promote safer clubbing. The Home Office in the UK has published material to these effects as well (e.g. Webster, Goodman & Whalley 2002). Perhaps more profoundly, raves and/or clubs have been threatened at a legal level, such as the Criminal Justice and Public Order Act of 1994 in the UK and the Illicit Drug Anti-Proliferation Act of 2003 in the US. This introductory chapter explores these incentives to study the intersections of young people, drug use, and clubbing.

A New Youth Culture

Every decade since the post-World War II era has witnessed the rise of 'spectacular' youth cultures within Western societies. In the 1950s, 'greasers', Teddy Boys, and other rebellious youth listening to rock and roll existed. In the 1960s, the mods, rockers, 'rudies' and skinheads emerged. And in the 1970s hippies and punks came to the fore. Each of these youth cultures was somewhat distinguishable in terms of race/ethnicity, socio-economic status, 'style', and, of course, age. 'Style' here not only refers to the clothes worn, but also drugs used and music preferred. For instance, mods were known to listen to jazz, dress in clean cut, fashionable, perhaps somewhat androgynous attire, ride scooters, and use amphetamines. Alternatively,

---

1   Thanks to Jennifer Jackson Bloom and George Weiss for comments on an earlier draft of this chapter.

hippies were known to favor loose fit clothes with ethnic and psychedelic prints, have long or big hair, smoke cannabis and use LSD, and enjoy music with lyrics that promoted peace, love, and social consciousness. However, outside of their overall style (and in some cases ethnicity), spectacular youth cultures have been remarkably similar: fashionably distinct in their time and interpreted by the general population as somewhat 'outlaw' youth. Indeed, the application of 'deviant' youth cultures to these groups of young people, particularly within the media (and academia), appears primarily due to the 'different' way they looked, their use of drugs, and their occasional bouts of violence or protest. Outside of these characteristics, however, scant evidence exists to suggest these young people were remarkably distinct from everyone else. These youth cultures, no doubt, collectively represented something much more profound at the time (e.g. rise of an affluent teenage culture for the mods; equal rights and anti-war movements for the hippies). Nonetheless, youth's participation within these spectacular cultures was often a temporary phase young people went through who, upon becoming older, blended back in to society desiring the same things as everyone else. In the end, these youth were not much fundamentally different from the general population.[2]

'Ravers' or 'clubbers' might be the best way to capture young people part of a cultural phenomenon that commenced in the mid to late 1980s. Essentially, raves are large dance parties characterized by the loud, bass-heavy music played within, such as house, garage, techno, jungle and the many derivatives of such music. Raves were once held in abandoned buildings, warehouses, fields, and other unique venues (Collin & Godfrey 1997; Thornton 1995; Tomlinson 1998; West & Hager 1993). The practice of holding dance parties in such unconventional venues eventually declined, and clubbing[3] began to replace raving. In the UK, this shift from raving to clubbing was due to legislature that criminalized unlicensed raves and the growth of a night time economy around established clubbing venues (see Hobbs et al. 2003; Measham 2004c; Reynolds 1997). In the US, by the time the law caught up with quasi-illegal outdoor raves, the practice of raving had largely moved to legitimate venues, burgeoning into commercial enterprise. Reports continue to emerge regarding 'underground' raves or those with their original 'flavor' in the US and UK,[4] for instance, but the practice of raving in general has become commoditized and institutionalized (cf. Thornton 1995). While the 'vibe' created by the original raves

---

2   For more on the youth cultures described in this paragraph in terms of appearance, behaviors, societal reactions, and overall outcome of the young people who participated within them see Brake 1985; Burke and Sunley 1998; Cashmore 1984; P. Cohen 1972; S. Cohen 1972; Fyvel 1963; Hall and Jefferson 1976; Moore 1994; Mungham and Pearson 1976; Nuttal 1970; Robins and Cohen 1978; Pearson 1983; Willis 1977, 1978; Yablonsky 1968.

3   The term 'clubbing' can relate to a variety of clubs, such as jazz clubs, comedy clubs, etc. Clubbing here refers to attending night clubs that are characterized by house, techno, jungle, and the various offshoots of these types of music – music that has been associated with 'raves'.

4   For instance, during a current research project examining health risk behaviors amongst young injecting drug users (e.g. Lankenau et al. 2005), ethnographers in both New

may be distinct from that in clubs, and others will no doubt attest to how 'different' raves of yesteryear are from clubbing today, raves and clubs are remarkably similar. The music and accompanying behaviors once typical at raves are now commonly found at established, regulated nightclubs, or held on occasion at convention centers, stadiums, sports arenas, and similar such venues. In the early years of the 21st century, millions of young people around the world attend clubs or clubbing events on a regular basis. For instance, reports from the UK indicate around four million people each weekend attend nightclubs (Webster, Goodman & Whalley 2002).

Raving and clubbing may be captured as particular youth cultures, not necessarily as youth *sub*cultures (Thornton 1995). 'Subculture' may be simply defined as a 'culture within a culture', and, as such, capture raving and clubbing fine. However, within the social science literature, the term 'subculture' – particularly in relation to young people involved in 'deviant' or 'delinquent' activities – has been used to suggest a group of individuals with more profound distinctions from individuals within general society. For instance, both the concepts of 'delinquent subculture' or 'subculture of violence' indicate that people who were 'part' of these subcultures not only behaved in ways that differed from most people, but also how such individuals had deep-seated values that were in sharp contrast to everyone else's (e.g. Cloward & Ohlin 1960; A. Cohen 1955; Wolfgang & Ferracuti 1967). Interview and observational data from several research investigations do not suggest that young people who attend raves and/or clubs are consistent in regards to dress and drug use, nor that these young people – whether they use illicit drugs or not – possess values profoundly distinct from everyone else (cf. Hammersley et al. 1999; Kelly this volume; Measham, Parker & Aldridge 2001; Thornton 1995; Sanders this volume). Other conceptualizations of 'subculture' do not capture raving or clubbing well either. For instance, the neo-Marxist 'magical resistance' thesis offered by the 'Birmingham School' (e.g. Hall & Jefferson 1976) to explain the emergence of 'deviant' youth (sub)cultures in post-war UK is too class-based to be applicable to the practice of raving and clubbing, whereas, alternatively, 'postmodern' theories of rave as subculture (e.g. Melechi 1993; Rietveld 1993) fail to incorporate social structures and portray young clubbers as hollow caricatures of themselves (see Blackman 2005; Hesmondhalgh 2005). Even the term 'counterculture' (Sloan 2001) seems a bit heavy handed when discussing raves and clubs in that it suggests a group with more in difference than in common with the general population. When the night is over, young people who attend raves and/or clubs, in the main, appear to go home, eventually recover from the all the fun, and blend back into mainstream society with relative ease because, essentially, they never left it.

While raving and clubbing fit within the spectrum of previous 'spectacular' youth cultures, they remain distinct in several ways. For one, young people from a variety of ethnic/racial and socio-economic backgrounds attend raves and clubs.

York City and Los Angeles reported young people discussing 'underground' raves not held in established venues. See Thornton (1995) for a discussion on 'underground' raves in the UK.

Race and class may shape the 'type' of rave or club attended (e.g. more 'black'[5] young people in attendance during jungle/drum and bass nights (cf. O'Hagan 1999; Sanders this volume); more affluent young people in attendance at clubs with high entry fees; more 'street youth' in attendance at 'underground' raves), but raving and clubbing in general are activities that transcend such distinctions. The style of ravers and clubbers, generally speaking, is also relatively ambiguous. Unlike the Edwardian suits donned by the Teddy Boys in the 1950s or leather jacket and jeans wardrobe of the rockers in the 1960s, young people who attend raves and clubs do not appropriate a uniform which would easily identify them as being part of a youth culture. When raves first emerged, certain clothing symbols, such as smiley faces, Cat-in-the-Hat large hats, oversized white Mickey Mouse-style gloves, and baby pacifiers (dummies), and general 'types' of clothing could be found, including baggy clothing, a 'retro' 1970s look, neon and other clothing that illuminated under fluorescent 'black' lights were popular and indicated participation in rave culture (e.g. West & Hager 1993). Visual elements of these styles may still be found, and, indeed, such styles have been mentioned in our recent (2005) research on young injection drug users in Los Angeles and New York (Lankenau et al. 2005). Clubbing, however, has become 'mainstream' and the fashions of people who attend them generally reflect this (cf. Perrone this volume; Thornton 1995; Sanders this volume). Also, raving and clubbing are distinct from previous youth cultures in the sense that such cultures are not entirely comprised of 'youth'. While 'young people' in their late teens and early twenties clearly dominate this culture, it would not be surprising to see older individuals, including a few well into their thirties and forties, attending raves and/or clubs.

Rave and club cultures are further distinct from previous youth cultures due to the centrality of music. Without music, 'rave' and 'club' culture do not exist. The music played at raves and clubs acts as the gel that binds the entire event together. Another indicator of how 'mainstream' rave and club culture has become relates to the rise of music once particular to underground raves and clubs into the mainstream. Where young people who desired to listen to 'rave type music' previously had to follow a series of directions and map points to locate the event, tune into pirate radio stations, or borrow mixed tapes from friends, such music can now be enjoyed on tap in many cities, whether at the clubs, pubs, bars, on the radio, or on the television. Moreover, clubs nowadays cater to a variety of crowds coming to hear a particular offshoot of house, techno, garage, or jungle music. To this degree, the culture of raving and clubbing contains a series of smaller cultures oriented around different tastes in music, which, in turn, may relate to different 'styles' (cf. Thornton 1995; O'Hagan 1999; Sanders this volume). All the music played at clubs and raves has similarities: repetitive, high-energy, bass heavy thumps, containing a variety of looped electronic sounds and samples. The booming music, the lights and lasers, psychedelia and smoke: raves and clubs not only cater to young people who like to dance, but also those who enjoy the use of particular drugs.

---

5   'Black' people here refer to Afro-Caribbean youth.

Drugs in Clubs

Significant trends have emerged within youthful drug use in the West since the early 1990s. For one, there has been an overall increase in the amount of young people who report lifetime rates of use (Chivite-Matthews et al. 2005; EMCDDA 2004; Johnston & O'Malley 2005; NDSHS 2002; SAMHSA 2005). Several drugs which were relatively unheard of twenty years ago, such as ecstasy, are now of great concern (e.g. UNODC 2003). The non-medical (recreational) use of prescription drugs, including Ritalin, Oxycontin, Vicodin, and Adderall is now facilitated by the Internet, where individuals without a prescription can mail-order these drugs from hundreds of companies (CASA 2002, 2005). Many of these drugs mimic the effects of illicit 'street' drugs (Sanders et al. 2005). Also, the use of hallucinogens, such as LSD and psilocybin mushrooms, was on the rise (Hunt 2004), and these mushrooms may now be bought legally in the UK (see Measham & Moore this volume). Other hallucinogens called tryptamines (e.g. AMT, DMT) and phenethylamines (2C-B (Nexus); 5-MEO-DiPT (Foxy)) have debuted within popular culture (cf. Kelly this volume; Measham 2004c). Crystal methamphetamine use has spread east from the Southwest of the US, only recently showing up in the 'heartland' and the Northeast (NIJ 2003; DAWN 2004), prompting US congressmen to suggest that "Meth is the biggest threat to the United States, maybe even including al-Qaida [sic]" Barnett 2005). Crystal methamphetamine has been problematic in Australia and New Zealand as well for several years (UNODC 2003; Degenhardt & Topp 2003; Topp et al. 2002). Another noticeable trend is the shift in ways that young people can administer illicit drugs. Drugs which young people have predominately sniffed or smoked, such as powder cocaine, crack, and crystal methamphetamine, are also being injected intravenously (Clatts et al. 2001; Lankenau et al. 2004). Youth are also injecting ketamine both intravenously and intramuscularly – the latter being a relatively unique administration for any recreationally used drug (Lankenau & Clatts 2004, 2005; Lankenau & Sanders 2004). Finally, young people no longer need to smoke, sniff, or inject 'hard' drugs in order to administer them. Drugs such as ecstasy are predominately swallowed in a tablet or pill form, and oral administrations of any illicit substance are, perhaps, the easiest and least stigmatizing type of administration.

While not suggesting any causal relationship, the rise of raving and clubbing as popular youthful activities are somewhat associated with the increase in youthful drug use. For instance, the general increase in overall youthful drug use has paralleled the rise of raving and clubbing within popular youth culture. The terms 'club drugs' and 'dance drugs' have emerged, relatively recently, to indicate a variety of drugs with stimulant and/or hallucinogenic properties commonly used within raves and clubs. More directly, British Crime Survey data noted that "lifestyle differences" help account for differential rates of drug use, indicating that youth "aged 16-29 who had visited clubs or discos in the past month were almost twice as likely to have used drugs in the past year as those who had not" – a difference which was even more pronounced for ecstasy and cocaine (Chivite-Matthews et al. 2005 p. 7;

cf. Bellis et al. 2003). Laws have also been written specifically to criminalize raves because of their association with illicit drug use. For instance, US legislatures who penned the RAVE Act clearly understood there to be a connection between ecstasy and 'rave parties'; RAVE stands for Reducing Americans Vulnerability to Ecstasy. While certainly not all young people who attend raves and clubs use drugs, the use of certain 'dance' or 'club' drugs within these settings can almost be guaranteed.

But what are 'club drugs?' A review of the literature reveals no clear definitions other than drugs which have been found to be largely used in club settings (cf. Fendrich & Johnson 2005). As they pertain to young people, illicit 'club drugs' may be broken down into various categories: drugs whose use first became popular within club and rave settings (ecstasy, GHB, ketamine); drugs which enjoyed a type of renaissance within such settings (LSD, psilocybin mushrooms); and drugs with a long history of abuse that also became common in raves and clubs (cocaine, crystal methamphetamine). Many of these drugs have been used in various combinations at raves and clubs for general desired effects. For instance, within rave and club argot, the co-use of LSD and ecstasy is known as 'candy flipping', the co-use of mushrooms and ecstasy as 'hippy flipping', and the intranasal co-use of cocaine and ketamine as 'CK 1'. Within 'circuit party' club culture, the intranasal co-use of cocaine, ketamine, crystal methamphetamine, and powdered ecstasy in various combinations is known as 'trail mix' (Green this volume; Navarez 2001). Observations in various raves and clubs also indicate that inhalants, such as Nitrous Oxide (whippets, balloons) and Amyl and Butyl Nitrate (poppers, rush), are also widely used in such settings (see also Green this volume). Indeed, polydrug use –simultaneously using two or more substances (including cigarettes and alcohol) and/or using a variety of substances throughout the evening – within rave and club settings is common (e.g. Degenhardt, Copeland & Dillon 2005; Lankenau & Clatts 2005; Measham 2004c).

Many of the illicit drugs used within raves and clubs have hallucinogenic and/or stimulant properties and somewhat 'fit' with the overall atmosphere of raves and clubs.[6] Clubs and raves are contemporary youthful leisure outlets, 'wild zones', and liminal spaces where the use of certain illicit drugs may be defined as somewhat 'acceptable' (Hobbs et al. 2003; Measham, Parker & Aldridge 2001; Thornton 1995). In certain respects, both the music and club/rave environments may be constructed in order to accommodate the use of these 'club' drugs. For instance, the effects of these drugs work well with the bouncy music, displays of light, and general party atmosphere of rave and club venues. A punter can work off the effects of these drugs in a main dance area by listening to the energetic music, go and cool down and

---

6   However, opiate based drugs such as heroin, and 'date rape' drugs, such as Rohypnol, have been found to be used in clubs (Joe-Laidler 2005; Maxwell 2005). While the effects of these drugs are in contrast to the other discussed 'club drugs' their use in combination with such substances may produce the desired effect. Indeed, polydrug use involving drugs from various categories (e.g. stimulants, hallucinogens, depressants) is common at raves and clubs.

relax in a 'chill out room' playing soothing ambient music, and repeat this process throughout the length of the event.

Ecstasy is the club drug *par excellence* and its use has been considered, for good reason, to go hand in glove with raves and clubs (Shapiro 1999). In fact, it would be difficult to discuss the phenomena of raving or clubbing within the past fifteen years without mentioning ecstasy (Redhead 1993). In this respect, drug use in rave and club culture differs from drug use amongst young people within previous popular youth cultures. For instance, the Teddy Boys and greasers in the 1950s, mods, rockers, and skinheads in the 1960s, and hippies in the 1970s have all been somewhat associated with using certain illicit drugs. Drug use, however, was only one aspect of these previous youth cultures; it remains a *defining* aspect of rave and club cultures. At the 2002 American Society of Criminology Annual meeting in Chicago, I presented a preliminary manuscript on my experiences as a club security guard in a London nightclub. When I discussed the ubiquity of ecstasy in the club, someone raised their hand and said: 'But drugs have always been in clubs'. This point is undeniable. However, when you read up on drug use in clubs during the disco years, for instance, the use of amphetamines and cocaine is mentioned in passing, not as a central activity many people engaged in. Gilmour's (1979) *Saturday Night Fever* – a fictional account of young people who attended discos – mentions amphetamine usage only in a couple of instances.[7] Tomlinson (1998 p.196) compares raves in the US in the early 1990s to disco in the 1970s and says "ecstasy has replaced cocaine as the drug of choice", but offers no empirical support to suggest that cocaine was as prominent in the disco era as ecstasy has been and continues to be in raves and clubs. Anecdotal and journalistic evidence of generous amounts of cocaine used during the disco era exists – at Studio 54 in New York City, for instance, and Woody Allen parodied such use in the film *Annie Hall*. But these instances are particular, not general, and information about cocaine use during the days of disco is limited. Were as many people in the club using cocaine and/or amphetamines in the disco era as ravers and clubbers have been and continue to do so with ecstasy and other club drugs over the last 15 years? The scant available evidence does not suggest this.

As youthful drug use has generally increased, social scientists and public health researchers have begun to think differently about such use. Some reports reveal that youth who have never used any drug are *amongst the minority* in their age group.[8] No longer can it be entertained that drug use is a socially marginal activity, questioning

---

7   In terms of offending, Gilmour's *Saturday Night Fever* – based on the movie of the same name – says more about gangs at the time than it does about drug use in clubs. The Faces' altercations with the Barracudas are a recurring theme, whereas drugs are primarily only mentioned a few times, and not amongst the main characters (i.e. Tony and Stephanie). Also, while *Saturday Night Fever* was based on Nik Cohn's 1975 article in *New York Magazine* entitled 'Tribal Rights of the New Saturday Night', Cohn, a Briton, later revealed in 1997 that the characters were completely fabricated, not based on his fieldwork as previously believed.

8   For instance, 2004 MTF data indicates that between 1996-2004, more than 50% of 12th graders mentioned lifetime use of any illicit drug.

both 'escapist' and 'subcultural' explanations of drug use (Cloward & Ohlin 1961; Merton 1938, 1957). Rather, researchers have suggested the use of particular drugs amongst youth – particularly marijuana – may be 'normalized' (Parker, Measham & Aldrige 1995; Parker, Aldridge & Measham 1998; Parker, Williams & Aldridge 2002). By this they refer to how marijuana has moved from the periphery towards the center of youth culture, and should not necessarily be considered a 'deviant' activity for several reasons: availability, acceptability, the number of users, and supportive cultural references. For such reasons, other research has suggested that the use of ecstasy within club environments may come to be viewed as 'normalized' (Measham, Parker & Aldridge 2001; Sanders this volume). The concept of normalization has a number of implications. For instance, many punters who recreationally use of 'hard' (Schedule I/Class A) drugs at raves and clubs appear, in the main, to live relatively 'normal' lives, suggesting that their drug usage does not consume them. This picture is in sharp contrast to previous depictions of 'hard' drug users (see Agar 1991; Bourgois 1995; Hammersley et al. 1999; Measham, Parker & Aldridge 2001; Preble & Casey 1969; Thornton 1995). Moreover, if the use of certain drugs is normalized amongst young people, and these young people lead relatively conventional lives, then current drug policies effectively criminalize millions of young people who appear otherwise law-abiding. Finally, and perhaps more profoundly, if the use of certain illegal drug use is so widespread to be considered 'normalized' amongst certain populations of young people, then such behaviors are surely a public health concern, not just a criminal justice one. Widespread youthful drug use associated with raves and clubs has, nonetheless, has generated a considerable response from both agencies.

Clubbing, the Law and Public Health

Youthful drug use associated with raves and clubs has initiated both criminal justice and public health reactions, some at state-wide levels. For instance, in the UK, the Criminal Justice and Public Order Act of 1994 was partially aimed at 'underground' raves held on public property. Specifically, the Act made it illegal for more than ten people to congregate on such land while listening to music "wholly or predominantly characterized by the emission of a succession of repetitive beats" that might cause distress to the local community.[9] While this law, in part, signaled a decline in such outdoor parties in the UK, it also helped facilitate the commoditization of raving into clubbing (see Measham, Parker & Aldridge 2001; cf. Reynolds 1997). No longer did British youth need to seek out their favorite DJs playing in clandestine areas by following a series of dodgy directions. Youth nowadays in many cities in the UK are spoiled for choice in terms of which specific 'type' of club they wish to attend, and research has indicated that illicit dance drugs are readily available within such settings (cf. Measham, Parker & Aldridge 2001; Sanders this volume). The 'moral

---

9   See Sections 63 and 64 of the Criminal Justice and Public Order Act of 1994. Information available at http://www.urban75.org/legal/cja.html.

panic' in the UK generated by the mass media's agonizing over young people's use of ecstasy and other dance drugs in 'bizarre' outdoor settings was answered by legislation banning such activity.[10] The party, however, simply moved indoors into regulated and somewhat controlled environments (Sanders this volume). Today, the UK has a massive night-time economy, part of which surrounds illicit drug distribution and consumption in clubs (cf. Hammersley at al. 1999; Hobbs et al. 2003). Other laws in the UK, such as the Public Entertainment Licenses Drug Act of 1997 and, more recently, Section One of the Antisocial Behavior Act of 2003, have attempted to curb the use of drugs within clubs and other venues where illicit drug use may be common by holding owners, managers and promoters responsible and criminally liable.

So what is to be done about young people using drugs in clubs? Any criminal justice initiative would have to brace itself for a serious undertaking. The 'war' on using drugs in clubs in the UK, for instance, appears to be left up to the club's owners, managers, and security (cf. Morris 1998), as the police appear to have neither the desire nor manpower to do much about it (Measham, Parker & Aldridge 2001). In the US, the Illicit Drug Anti-Proliferation Act of 2003 incorporated much of the previous legislation drawn up in the RAVE act of 2002. The new and approved Act extended the scope of the applicability of a section of the Controlled Substance Act referred to as 'crack house' laws – mirroring the UK example. Essentially, this Act paves the way for criminal and civil prosecution to owners and managers who fail to prevent drug-related offences in their venues. Despite all best efforts and intentions of promoters, owners, organizers, managers, and security, holding a completely drug-free rave or club night would seem incredibly difficult (Hobbs et al. 2003). As discussed earlier, the use of certain drugs partially define raves and clubs. In the US, does the new Act mean that if someone pops an ecstasy pill, the whole place is prone to shut down and the owners and individuals in charge of the night liable to prosecution? A blowback of such laws could be that they push the parties further 'underground.' This, in turn, may raise some public health concerns, such as the overall structural safety of non-conventional rave or club venues (e.g. abandoned, condemned buildings), and their poor sanitary conditions, lack of water, and lack of proper ventilation. Moreover, such measures would increase the difficulty of intervention development with 'club kids' who use club drugs. How do you attempt do help a population difficult to find?

Indeed, public health initiatives in relation to clubs and club drugs have their work cut out for them. Harm reduction associated with drug use within club and rave settings has taken several forms. The Internet has greatly facilitated public health initiatives aimed at raves and clubs by offering young people a wide-variety of websites where they can download information pertaining to safer clubbing, such

---

10 Many parallels can be drawn between UK and Australia in terms of negative media attention raves received and subsequent measures to bring such parties under control through government policies. In Australia, such measures culminated in the 1990s as 'Codes of Practice' (see Gibson and Pagan 2001; Luckman 2000).

as the short and long term effects of various drugs and how to maintain proper body temperature. A central crux of such information is to allow club drug users and club attendees a more educated background concerning the behaviors they are about to engage in. In the US, the national organization *DanceSafe*, which is predominately staffed and managed by young people who enjoy raving and/or clubbing, has been particularly visible in the promotion of safety in relation to these activities. For instance, their website defines 'risk assessment' in lay terms, and offers information pertaining to the calculated risks of using various drugs (see also Newcombe and Woods 2002). *DanceSafe* and other websites devoted to raving and/or clubbing also act as informal links between harm reduction agencies, club/rave organizers, promoters and managers, and young people, fostering working relationships. In the UK, agencies such as the Dance Drugs Alliance, government publications (Webster, Goodman & Whalley 2002), and sound advice from academics (Measham, Parker & Aldridge 2001) has helped promote safer clubbing on a national level.

One controversial attempt at harm reduction employed by various organizations at or near raves and/or clubs is through pill-testing, whereby individuals can have their 'ecstasy' tablets and other 'club drugs' checked for content. An incentive for such testing was to allow the user to make an informed decision on what they were about to ingest. Moreover, such tests were aimed at detecting substances that may be fatal to the individual if ingested. Despite best intentions, pill-testing has been suggested as being defective at several levels. For instance, during investigations many of the on-site testing kits were found to be flawed, unable to differentiate between different types of drugs (Winstock, Wolf & Ramsey 2005). Winstock, Wolf & Ramsey (2005) further argued that pill-testing has more to do with quality control than harm reduction, and that the thought of testing the purity of other hard drugs such as cocaine and heroin – drugs much more likely to be adulterated by the time they reached the streets – would be unfathomable. No doubt, the thought of people lining up to test their coke, crack and smack may seem ridiculous.

The generation of young people who grew up as raving emerged will eventually witness the fate of clubbing. Will nightclubs eventually become heavily policed, drug-free zones? Perhaps nightclubs will become licensed dens of decriminalized drug consumption? Maybe nothing will change. Criminal justice agendas and public health initiatives need to work in tandem in order to successfully reduce harm amongst club attendees and club drug users. Comprehensive and accurate data about young people, clubbing and club drug use is needed in order to facilitate such a relationship.

Conclusion

This introductory chapter has served to discus the importance of sociological and public health examinations of young people, drugs and clubs. Youthful drug use has generally increased in recent years, and raves and clubs are areas where the use of particular drugs can be almost guaranteed. Research from various countries generally suggests that young people who use drugs and attend raves and clubs are by and large law abiding. Drug use does not consume their lives, but is rather a contemporary and occasional component of their recreational behaviors. Research that delves beyond statistical presentations of club drug users is much needed in order to demystify stereotypes and correctly gauge the accuracy of perspectives on youthful drug use and the policies that such perspectives generate.

Photograph courtesy of Simon Brockbank.

Chapter 2

Reluctant Reflexivity, Implicit Insider Knowledge and the Development of Club Studies[1]

Fiona Measham and Karenza Moore

Drawing on our combined experience of twenty five years both researching dance clubs and personal clubbing experiences, this chapter considers the establishment and expansion of the field of dance club and dance drug research from its inception amongst young researchers attending 'acid house' parties and 'raves' in the early 1990s British underground to its gradual academic recognition across the 'decade of dance' and beyond. In the first part of the manuscript, we outline the contributions of early 'rave research' and explore the development of the field of dance club and dance drug studies in the 1990s through the relationship between the academic, public health, and criminal justice agendas and the politics of funding. Next, our entwined academic and personal biographies are considered in relation to obtaining partial 'insider' status in our own dance club research. Here, we suggest that studies on dance clubs and dance drugs have been built on a valuable body of implicit insider knowledge, leading us to conclude that this knowledge and the operationalization of reflexivity in such studies needs more explicit and open consideration.

Early Rave Research and the Time-Lag of Academic Recognition

If the American stepfather of ecstasy is Alexander Shulgin, a Dow Chemicals chemist who rediscovered and synthesised ecstasy in 1965 (Shulgin & Shulgin 1991), and the British stepfather of ecstasy was Nicholas Saunders, a writer, researcher and hippy entrepreneur (Saunders 1993, 1995, 1997), then the global stepfather of 'rave research' must be Russell Newcombe. A drugs researcher and self-proclaimed 'psychonaut' (Newcombe & Johnson 1999) based in Liverpool, Newcombe established the Rave Research Bureau (later 3D) when the acid house and rave scene first emerged, and from 1989 onwards he conducted the first academic research on British raves (e.g. Newcombe 1991, 1992a, 1992b). Drawing on his social psychology background,

1   Thanks to Jonathan Chippindall, Paul Hodkinson, David Moore, Russell Newcombe and Eddie Scouller for comments. This chapter draws on a conference paper presented by Fiona Measham at the American Society of Criminology annual meeting in Toronto 2005.

Newcombe designed a rave research methodology that emphasised the importance of systematic *in situ* observations in raves. Such methods challenged preconceptions of what might be assumed to occur within raves at a time of sensationalist tabloid coverage (see Redhead 1993). Newcombe's academic (e.g. Parker, Bakx & Newcombe 1988) and policy orientated (e.g. Newcombe 1987) work with heroin users in Merseyside in the 1980s was further developed at the Rave Research Bureau. Along with a small band of colleagues, Newcombe conducted rave research that included: the collection of data on the demographic composition of those attending raves and dance events; the systematic observation of thousands of ravers, drug paraphernalia, the acquisition and use of dance drugs, drug-related attitudes and behaviors, drinking, dancing, and overt signs of aggression or violence; and conversations with customers and staff across the course of the fieldwork night and across the different spaces within clubs, such as bars, dance floors, chill out rooms, toilets, car parks and so forth (e.g. Newcombe 1994a). This early rave research contained echoes of the longstanding British sociological tradition of observing ordinary people at leisure (Mass Observation 1987). Moreover, this rave research fed directly into the emergent public health initiatives of the early 1990s by applying the harm reduction policies developed by Newcombe and others in the UK in the 1980s in relation to problematic use of opiates to the field of recreational dance drug usage. Action research in the true sense, the Rave Research Bureau's findings informed drug services, such as the innovative dance drug advice leaflets of the Lifeline[2] drugs agency (see also Gilman 1992; Pearson et al. 1992; Henderson 1993a, 1993b, 1993c) and the collaboration between Newcombe, Lifeline and Manchester City Council to produce the pioneering harm reduction guidelines for dance clubs known as *Safer Dancing* (Newcombe 1994b), a forerunner to the later *Safer Clubbing* advice of the British government (Webster, Goodman & Whalley 2002).

Undoubtedly, the early 1990s rave research was piecemeal, small scale and under funded. The available funding came from a diverse range of sources, which included voluntary organisations, drug services and dance magazines such as *Mixmag* (1994). Criticism of Newcombe and colleagues' early rave research followed partially because it advocated outreach workers operating within dance clubs and also because of concerns about the source of funding (e.g. McDermott, Matthews & Bennett 1992). Indeed, in a bid to defend reputations, secure forthcoming license renewals, and somewhat protect themselves from police opposition, a key source of funding for some of these observational studies of individual dance clubs in England was club management, promoters and leisure companies. Nonetheless, Newcombe and colleagues' rave research was motivated by a genuine commitment to explore what was considered to be an exciting emergent cultural phenomenon, yet to be fully recognised by mainstream academia.

---

2   Lifeline, established in 1971 and based in Manchester, is one of the oldest non statutory and non residential drugs agencies in the UK. For further information see www.lifeline.org. uk.

The difficulties of funding research on the burgeoning dance culture of the early and mid 1990s reflected academia's failure to recognize the emergence of a significant cultural phenomenon. Moreover, sensationalist media coverage (e.g. Murji 1998) and legislative and policing initiatives (e.g. Hemment 1998) appeared to leave academic funding bodies nervous of such a potentially controversial subject. The sensitive nature of funding academic research into dance clubs and dance drugs in the 1990s is evident in the funding history for the *Dancing on Drugs* study (Measham, Aldridge & Parker 2001), the first large scale academic study of dance drugs in the UK, whose club-based fieldwork drew upon the earlier *in situ* work of both the Rave Research Bureau and Measham's MA and PhD research in pubs and clubs. Various funding bodies, including government departments, turned down the original proposal in the mid 1990s. Funding was finally agreed for the study on the understanding that the word 'ecstasy' would be removed from the project title and that the researchers would not discuss the study in the media until it was completed. By the time funding was secured for the *Dancing on Drugs* study, the dance scene had matured and diversified into commercially lucrative 'superclubs' and smaller, often highly specialised, dance music club nights. This diversification occurred alongside the repression and criminalisation of aspects of the scene through a variety of pieces of legislation passed or reinstated that effectively criminalised unlicensed open air dance events (Hemment 1998; Shapiro 1999; Measham 2004a). Most clubbers, and with them most club researchers,[3] shifted their focus from outdoor and unlicensed dance events to indoor legal and licensed dance clubs.

Emotionality, Reflexivity and Degrees of Immersion

From the early 1990s onwards, studies of dance club and dance drug culture by younger researchers and doctoral students started to emerge (e.g. Rietveld, 1991; Redhead 1993; Thornton 1995; Forsyth 1995, 1996a, 1996b; Wright 1998; Malbon 1998, 1999; Hill 2002; Moore 2003a, 2003b, 2005). Bennett (2002, 2003) has noted the prevalence, particularly at doctoral level, of 'insider studies', whereby the researcher starts from an initial position of subjective proximity to respondents and a specific youth/cultural form. This happened in the in the UK in the early 1990s, when small scale academic studies on dance clubs and dance drugs were student-led, resulting in research that tapped into aspects of pre-existing, if implicit, insider knowledge. These young researchers felt a close 'connection' to the subject area, and decided not to wait until academia's interest in this phenomenon caught up with their own.

Bennett (2002) notes that despite the growing prevalence of insider studies, little reflexive analyses of these initial insider starting points have emerged. Conversely, critiques of insider research have suggested that identities in our contemporary late modern/post-structural world cut across a variety of different groupings (e.g.

---

3   With some exceptions, such as the work of Rietveld (1998).

Bennett 1999; Denscombe 2001; Muggleton 1997), and as such, are dominated by unstable and individualised cultural trajectories that render notions of insider research unworkable. In addition, particular elements of identity may fluctuate depending on audience and setting, which make the notion of being an absolute or total insider (or total outsider) problematic (Song & Parker 1995 p.243). Indeed, contemporary socio-cultural identities and forms of association are characterized by fluidity and individualisation (Miles 2000). The fluidity of contemporary identities may mean that researchers cannot claim absolute proximity to research participants, if they ever could.

Despite these reservations, Hodkinson (2005 p.134), in his study on Goth[4] youth, notes that researchers may be more or less 'proximal' to research participants "in those situations where a set of respondents are strongly and consciously united by the overall importance to all of them of a particular distinctive characteristic or set of characteristics", such as socio-economic class, ethnicity, gender, sexual orientation, or characteristics which are wholly or partially elective, such as being a Goth. Indeed, evidence demonstrates that "many young people continue to focus significant proportions of their identities upon discernable groupings that are united by often strongly held attachments towards relatively distinctive tastes, values, and/ or activities" (Hodkinson 2005 p.135; see also Khan-Harris 2004; Moore 2004; Thornton 1995). Like other youth cultural groups, clubbers are a committed and partially bounded group (e.g. Moore 2003a, 2003b). Regarding insider status in terms of the culture the researcher is, at times, 'part' of, Hodkinson calls for a cautious and reflexive consideration of the role of being an insider in a *non-absolute* sense. He traced his journey from being an insider in the Goth 'world' to becoming an insider researcher (albeit a cautious and reflexive one), noting that occupying such a role is liable to have important implications for issues of interpretation and understanding, and for the practical negotiation of the research process, including access to the field and the undertaking of interviews (Hodkinson 2005).

As Hodkinson (2002, 2005) highlights, partial insider status has theoretical and practical implications for the research process. Partial insider status also has deeply personal, emotional and even physical ramifications for both the research process and the researcher in question (e.g. Lyng 1998; Fehintola 2000). One recent consideration of degrees of involvement in the research field is discussed by Piacentini (2005) with regards to her ethnographic work on Russian prisons. She argues that "by getting inside the setting I was getting inside the emotions of my respondents and hence I was now writing myself into the story" (2005 p.204).[5]

---

4 In the UK, Goths emerged in the early 1980s out of punk, glam rock and new romantic, and are associated with "dark", "macabre" and "sinister" music, along with "black hair and clothes and distinctive styles of make-up for both genders" (Hodkinson 2002:4).

5 This echoes an in-depth study of Bradford drug users by a photo-journalist who took heroin, developed a heroin dependency and started selling heroin and crack over the course of six years, alongside his continuing research for his book and documentary. He notes in his book that "I was writing from within the text, I was part of the picture" (Fehintola 2000:xi).

Through writing herself and her emotions into her research story, Piacentini (2005) was better able to reflect on the processes of immersion – compulsive, chaotic and then restrained – she experienced during her journey from being a passionate lover of Russian literature, to feeling culturally disorientated from the demands of her research, to finally feeling able "to 'give in' to the research environment rather than operating against it" (2005 p.206). In turn, Letherby (2000) writes on the emotional and professional dangers of using personal experience (in her case of being an involuntary childless woman) as a springboard for research and as a resource throughout the research process. She considers how these dangers "can contribute to greater academic insight (both substantive and methodological) rather than just being obstacles to avoid and overcome" (2000 p.91). Letherby (2000) contends that whilst emotions (those of both the researcher and the research participants) have to be carefully 'managed' throughout the research process, a 'fuller' picture of the research subject may be achieved if such emotional involvement is critically and reflexively analysed. The physical dangers of ethnographic immersion were more literal for researchers such as Calvey (2000) and Lyng (1998). Lyng discussed his own involvement in 'edgework' with a group of adults participating in high risk activities such as skydiving whilst under the influence of drugs, noting that "many important empirical and theoretical problems taken up in the social sciences can be thoroughly and honestly studied only by placing oneself in situations that may compromise safety and security" (1998 p.222). The physical consequences of such risk taking became brutally evident for Lyng when his motorbike crashed going round a bend at 120mph after consuming alcohol and cannabis, resulting in serious injury.

The broader relationship between the researcher and the researched has been the subject of lively debate in the social sciences (e.g. Denzin 1997; Hobbs & May 1993) and feminist research (e.g. Harding 1987; Oakley 1981; Maynard & Purvis 1994) for two decades, from the 1960s women's liberation movement slogan 'the personal is political', through to the theorizing of the relationship between ontology, epistemology and praxis (Stanley 1990; Stanley & Wise 1993). For example, autoethnographic approaches[6] create a research space in which researchers' personal experiences can be considered (Ellis & Bochner 2003). Autoethnography enables researchers to reflect on the social and cultural aspects of their personal experiences, and on the interconnectedness of their own experiences and those of their research participants. Autoethnography ranges from work in which researchers focus primarily on their own experiences, through the telling of evocative personal narratives, for example, to work in which researchers' personal experiences are primarily and explicitly used as a tool for illuminating the culture under study (Ellis & Bochner 2003 p.211). This has been graphically illustrated in the field of drugs by Maher's (2002) "explicit and self-conscious" combination of ethnography and autobiography in her account of

---

6   See Ellis and Bochner 2003 (pp.209-215) for a fuller definition of what autoethnography involves. The British Sociological Association's journal Auto/biography is also a useful starting point for such approaches.

past research experiences (including a needle stick injury when conducting research with HIV+ women) in order to challenge "the scientific fantasy of the detached, distant and dispassionate observer vigilant lest she 'contaminate' her 'field' " (2002 p.313). For researchers in the field of club studies, autoethnographic approaches may open up possibilities for deeper and 'fuller' reflection on the role of partial insider status in the research process. The vulnerability researchers may experience through writing explicitly on their personal and emotional involvement in the subject (Behar 1996) can become "a source of growth and understanding" (Ellis & Bochner 2003 p.231). Consequently, the passion that many clubland researchers feel for their subject area, a passion that produces professional and personal risks and rewards, may be more openly considered than at present.

To date, researcher reflexivity within the dance club and dance drug field is relatively unexplored, with 1990s research on young people's recreational dance drug use tending to have been concentrated on the rationality rather than the emotionality of drug use (see e.g. Measham 2004b for a critique). We suggest that the history of club research from its inception in England over fifteen years ago is built upon a body of implicit insider knowledge where the implications of researcher proximity (or distance) to the research subject in terms of research design, research relations and so forth, as well as broader theoretical, methodological and epistemological considerations, have yet to be fully explored. Club studies have developed within the dominant "academic mode of production" (Stanley 1990 p.4) which distances the "knower" from the "known" to produce "hygienic research" (Stanley and Wise 1993 p.161). Furthermore, in the field of drug and alcohol studies, whilst methodological debate has moved away from notions of positivist, objective, neutral and value-free research,[7] reflexivity in general and insider knowledge in particular remain implicitly rather than explicitly utilized in the field. Ethnographic and qualitative studies of dance clubs and dance drugs have yet to develop a substantial body of literature that explores the role of insider knowledge. Indeed, as Bennett noted (2002), one of the very few club studies where the researcher acknowledges her own consumption of ecstasy – a self proclaimed Canadian 'outsider' on the British rave scene (Thornton 1995) – did not elaborate on the implications of this consumption for the study. For other researchers of dance drugs (e.g. Henderson 1993b; Forsyth 1995; Moore 1995; Hammersley et al. 2002), in some otherwise excellent pieces, no consideration of the reflexive relationship between the researcher and dance drugs is offered. In such cases, the research process is discussed neither in relation to participation in nor abstention from consumption.

The degrees of immersion in clubland, the complexities of insider/outsider identities, and the legal, ethical, emotional and physical demands – dangers even – of research work on illegal and/or illegitimate activities (Ferrell & Hamm 1998) are topics that have yet to be considered in relation to the growing global body of dance club and dance drug research. Thus, a consideration of emotionality, immersion and

---

7   For example, reflected in special editions of Addiction Research and Theory (2001) and the International Journal of Drug Policy (2002-3).

insider status may help to elucidate researcher/research subject relations in clubland. Such reflexive accounts of the emotionality of involvement in clubland can consider the ways in which biographical and personal events can shape the forms that insider knowledge and researcher-clubber experiences may take. Consider, for instance, the crossover between the authors' personal lives and our academic ones in relation to clubbing.

For Measham, the notion of being at least a partial insider researcher in clubland has some resonance. She has been attending (pre-rave) night clubs since the age of 13 and working in such environments from the age of 15. For her, clubs were a social space where she felt familiar and at ease. However, Measham did not explicitly identify as a 'raver' when she started conducting research with Newcombe and the Rave Research Bureau and, thus, would not claim absolute insider researcher status as the starting point for her involvement in the early rave research. The layers of immersion in club culture developed for Measham across the 1990s along parallel lines to her participation in dance club research. In particular, she visited a wide variety of dance clubs, and, due to a strong and continuing attraction to jungle/drum and bass, she regularly attended clubs playing that specific sub-genre of dance music that developed out of the early rave scene in the UK.[8] However, whilst in general terms Measham might be considered to be at least a partial insider in clubland, the growing diversity and sub-genres of dance that have developed have meant that she might also be considered an outsider to many sub-genres of dance and to the musical, stylistic, socio-demographic, behavioral and pharmacological distinctions of their clubs. The individual clubs were chosen for the *Dancing on Drugs* research, for example, because their dance events included a wide range of distinct musical/ style sub-genres of dance on different nights of the week. Consequently, individual members of the research team had a greater or lesser proximity to each club on each club night that, to some extent, will have affected each researcher's overall relationship to the research subject and to the clubbers being interviewed each evening. Indeed, few if any researchers could make claims to insider status across the whole contemporary club scene. The point is that both insider and outsider identification is partial, flexible, negotiated, with a range of positive and negative implications for the research process. Moreover, objectivity and neutrality in clubland is illusory, not least because clubbers form views about the researchers' presence: as social researchers we are operating within, will influence and are influenced by the social world within which we operate. As Stanley and Wise (1993 p.161) have noted,

---

8   Jungle developed out of and split off from the hardcore rave scene in late 1992 and is considered by many as the first black British dance music, growing out of urban centres in London and the Midlands. With concerns about violence and musical direction within jungle after 'darkcore' (Reynolds 1997, 1998), drum and bass developed. Jungle/drum and bass remains a popular, distinct genre of dance music in the UK with its own music magazines, websites and international following particularly in north Europe, South America and Canada. The music draws on ragga, dub reggae, dance hall and hip hop traditions, and is characterised by syncopated beats of around 160 beats per minute, shifting subsonic irregular dub-style basslines, vocal samples and live MCs (see James 1997; Metcalfe 1997).

"because the basis of all research is a relationship, this necessarily involves the presence of the researcher *as a person.*" Furthermore, if we assume that we cannot escape the social world in order to study it and that the purpose of attempting to be reflexive is to "elucidate the possible ways in which the orientations, values and interests of researchers are shaped by their socio-historical locations" (Hammersley & Atkinson 1995 p.16), then it would seem that all researchers are already using varying degrees of partial insider through to outsider knowledge. This goes beyond Howard Becker's oft-quoted point: "...the question is not whether we should take sides, since we inevitably will, but rather whose side are we on?" (1971 p.123; see also Becker 1967). For clubland researchers who are also clubbers, 'taking sides' means confronting and exploring the conflicting emotions that arise from combining academic and clubbing identities, and interacting with 'research subjects' on both a personal and professional level. This blurring of the personal and the professional is characterised by Kane (1998) as 'productive turmoil' (p.140), suggesting that emotionality in research relationships can be harnessed to better reflect on an individual's research field and their role as a researcher.

For Moore, a passion and emotional attachment to clubland grew out of the 'freedom' it represented to her from the destructive practices of a long-term eating disorder (Moore 1998). Discovering clubbing in the first year of her sociology degree meant that learning to 'do sociology' and 'being a clubber' went hand in hand. Moore's move from fan to "fan-researcher" (Bennett 2003 p.186) was often 'messy', with certain aspects of her identity, identifications and social practices coming to the fore at times when other aspects may be downplayed (during exam or holiday periods, for example). Interestingly, Moore's club research remains a 'spare time' pursuit despite it being her main sociological passion – an indication of the ways in which concerns about acceptability, respectability and funding operate for those in the earlier stages of academic careers.

For both of us, the degrees of insider knowledge and the limitations of 'front of house' experience, access and observation led to paid employment in pubs and clubs. We both worked as bar staff[9] and as dancers (for Measham in a Greek club; for Moore in a British club). Although Henderson (1997) identified a notable extra social mobility and fluidity for female customers within 1990s British raves

---

9   As a female-dominated occupation in male-dominated leisure space, the British 'barmaid' is typical of low paid, casual and ununionised female labour, a sexualised work role with complex power dynamics between female barstaff and male customers with elements of sexual labour within barwork (regarding tipping, uniforms, relations with customers and so on) and resistance to sexual harassment at work (such as through the use of humour and banter) which echoes the dynamics of other forms of sex work (eg. T. Sanders, 2004, 2005). The position of the researcher as both insider – an experienced barworker with many years' previous experience – and yet outsider – as a graduate student working in low paid casual employment primarily for research purposes – was part of the reflexive nature of Measham's Masters research (Measham 1988). This ongoing interest in women's role in traditionally male-dominated leisure space and the differences between the gendering of pubs and the gendering of clubs led from the pub to the club as the site of study.

and dance clubs, our paid employment within clubs added to our social mobility in both 'front of house' and 'back of house' settings, which increased our access across the research space with staff as well as customers. The advantages of this 'double immersion' in clubland through both paid employment and club attendance have also been significant features of the club studies conducted by Calvey (2000), Winlow (2001), Silverstone (this volume) and Sanders (this volume) who obtained jobs as door/security staff in clubs. The specific employment status we obtained as female barstaff and dancers was based on gender, age and physical appearance/ attributes, as was the employment of Calvey, Winlow and Sanders as male door staff. Additionally, Moore currently works as a club promoter. However, given that the vast majority of club promoters are male, Moore occupies a somewhat ambivalent position in gender terms that throws up further questions regarding the role of insider knowledge in club research. Is the possibility of gaining and using such knowledge structured by enduring gender divisions on the dance floor as well as in academia?

As noted earlier, few if any researchers can make claims to absolute insider status given the diversification and globalization of dance club culture in the twenty first century. Exchanges between our work – including attending 'each other's' genre-specific favored club nights and exploring our observations and experiences as partial outsiders to each other's club space – have served to highlight differences in the degrees of immersion possible in club research. Such degrees of immersion are partially dependent on the extent to which an individual researcher identifies with and commits to a particular dance music sub-genre or 'scene'. For Measham, a longstanding love of soul, ska, dance hall, dub reggae and two-tone, led to a passion for jungle/drum and bass – a black British sub-genre of dance which draws on these traditions. For Moore, her initial generalized love of dance music, which 15 years ago remained relatively coherent as acid house and rave, developed into a love of trance music and her involvement in the establishment and promotion of a monthly trance night in Manchester.[10] Thus, despite both of us having lived and worked in Manchester for years, we have quite different and separated experiences of the city's night-time economy as a result of different musical preferences, legal and illicit drug repertoires, family responsibilities, peer networks and so forth. For us, working and clubbing together has highlighted our claims that insider knowledge can only ever be partial, non absolute and non static, and hence that such 'knowledge' should be used both cautiously and reflexively.

In relation to music rather than dance clubs or dance drugs, Bennett (2003) talks about the possibility of using insider knowledge "as means of conducting a reflexive ethnography in which both the researcher and his/her respondents work through the processes via which music is transformed into a means of symbolically negotiating

---

10 Trance music, comprising of often uplifting lyrics and/or synths driven by a 4/4 beat, germinated from early rave, techno and house music, and incorporates classical music influences. It is perhaps best associated with 'superclubs', such as *Cream*, *Gatecrasher* and *Godskitchen* in the UK. Trance is now an international music scene particularly popular in the US, UK, India, Israel and numerous Eastern European countries.

the everyday" (2003 p.196). This suggests that insider knowledge is a tool or resource to be used in the bid to be reflexive about researcher/researched field relations, data collection, analysis and so forth, but is a tool that can only be fully utilized within and through interactions with research participants. On the front page of *Ecstasy and the Rise of the Chemical Generation,* Hammersely, Khan & Ditton (2002) write that "drug users are no longer a mad, bad or immoral minority. Using drugs is normal for the chemical generation, and the drug that defines them is ecstasy". Yet, for researchers who may be considered to be partial insiders within clubland, such assertions ring hollow. Being personally, emotionally and socially involved in clubland and associated dance drug use still needs to be 'managed' in terms of professional identity. This means that club researchers, whilst open about their researcher role, may feel the need to downplay or even hide their consumer role in dance clubs, particularly if that consumption also includes club drugs. Consequently, issues of reflexivity and insider knowledge in club research remain obscured by a façade of respectability, with only the bravest of researchers able to produce the sorts of fuller accounts of researcher/researched relations advocated by Bennett. These conundrums may be particularly significant for female club researchers given enduring moral discourses surrounding women's pursuit of pleasure (Ettorre 1992; Pini 2001), particularly in the public sphere.[11]

For the time being, in the field of dance club and dance drug studies, the professional boundaries between users and researchers, practitioners and teachers remain firm. Yet, our political, social, occupational and emotional relationships with the research subject deeply influence the research process. As social researchers we are a part of the social world we investigate and as drug researchers we are a part of the world of psychoactive drugs. We are also (almost) all drug users, whether of legal or illicit drugs, acquired over the counter, at the bar, under the table, procured from doctors, 'dealers' or friends. However, the relevance of this and its value to our work as researchers has yet to be fully explored. Nearly twenty years ago in her outline of three key features of feminist research, Harding (1987 p. 9) argued that reflexivity should be seen as "the new subject matter of inquiry", as a resource rather than a methodological problem:

> The beliefs and behaviours of the researcher are part of the empirical evidence for (or against) the claims advanced in the results of research. This evidence too must be open to critical scrutiny no less than what is traditionally defined as relevant evidence. Introducing this 'subjective' element into the analysis in fact increases the objectivity of the research and decreases the 'objectivism' which hides this kind of evidence from the public.

---

11 In the recent debate surrounding 'binge' drinking in the UK, concerns have been expressed particularly about young women's increased alcohol consumption and associated implications for health and safety. Professor Roger Williams, Director of the Institute of Hepatology at University College, London, is quoted as saying that "the most tragic ones are not the down-and-outs, the older ones, or the social heavy drinkers... it's the young girls who are binge drinking" (Bentham and Temko 2005 p. 2).

Clear ethical, political and practical reasons exist for the 'reluctant reflexivity' we have identified in the field of club studies. As May (1998) has pointed out, opportunities for academic musings on reflexivity can be limited in funded research projects. Furthermore, given the comments we made above about the gradual development of club studies as a legitimate, recognized and publicly funded academic subject, these have made further constraints upon the possibilities for reflexive consideration of the role of insider knowledge in this field. Can a researcher risk using and explicitly reflecting on 'insider knowledge' if it is also 'guilty knowledge' (Polsky 1967)? Grob, when interviewed about his research on ecstasy (see Grob 1998, 2000), noted in relation to repeated questioning about his own use or non use of ecstasy that drug researchers are "damned if they have taken drugs and damned if they haven't."

Have you yourself ever taken ecstasy?
Grob: My response to that sort of question is usually along the lines of 'I'm damned if I have and I'm damned if I haven't'. If I have, then my perspective would be discounted due to my own personal use bias, and if I haven't, it would be discounted because I would not truly understand the full range of experience the drug can induce.
So does that mean you're not answering the question?
Grob: [Chuckles] Exactly. (Avni 2002)

Grob's response accurately captures the dilemma drug researchers face in relation to insider status. If researchers admit to having used illegal drugs, research subjects, funding bodies or the wider academic community may feel threatened, intimidated, lose respect for that individual or see them as biased in favor of drugs. Indeed, even for club researchers to admit club attendance in other than a research capacity can result in allegations of 'potential bias' in club research.[12] Yet does such 'potential bias' due to the researcher's personal experience and involvement necessarily undermine the quality of drugs research? As Rhodes and Moore (2001 p.286) suggest in relation to ethnography, drugs research is a highly personalized undertaking, where "ethnography requires the creation and maintenance of rapport and friendship to go beyond the superficial to the private and intimate." This dilemma is more pertinent given the added ethical responsibilities involved in researching young people under 18. The 'damned if you do, damned if you don't' climate results in drug researchers walking a tightrope that signifies the understandable but unfortunate 'reluctant reflexivity' faced amongst researchers of dance clubs and dance drugs.

---

12 The reporting of Measham's longstanding clubbing history in the acknowledgements of *Dancing on Drugs* (Measham et al. 2001) prompted an academic reviewer to advise "careful reading" of the book due to "her potential bias" (Wibberley 2003 pp.207-8). "The acknowledgement section notes the involvement of the lead author in 'clubbing' from an early age; and therefore her potential bias is identified. However, given this is very much an academic text, I would have expected a less 'passioned' approach to discussion" (Wibberley 2003 p.207).

Discussion

What is the relationship between club researchers and clubbing, between dance drug researchers and dance drugs? The last fifteen years or so have seen club studies develop from small scale, piecemeal and under funded rave research by a small group of enthusiasts in England into an established and vibrant cross cultural multidisciplinary, multi method academic subject as evident in this collection. A key feature of the development of club studies has been its underpinning by doctoral and early stage researchers with varying degrees of immersion in a wide variety of clubbing cultures across the world. We are now starting to see the welcome emergence of a critical evaluation of the role of implicit insider knowledge in the research process in relation to the sociology of youth, although not yet in relation to the study of dance clubs and dance drugs.

The development of club research, its direction and its funding have reflected the tensions between, on the one hand, the consumption of leisure and its corporate exploitation in 'superclubs', café bars and dance bars, and on the other hand, the criminal justice-driven 'law and order' agenda of Western societies in their responses to dance club and dance drug culture. Here, clubbers were the first youth/cultural group to be both criminalized and 'globalized' in tandem. The story of club studies is also the story of dance club culture itself, from the underground and unlicensed raves of the late 1980s and early 1990s to global recognition and establishment (e.g. Blackman 2004). Our academic biographies have developed alongside the personal biographies of our clubbing experience, the direction of which has been shaped by a pre-existing partial insider knowledge of some aspects of clubland and at least partial identification with clubbers set against this backdrop of the globalisation of both club culture and club studies. Our concerns with understanding and illuminating the possible implications of insider knowledge (including data collection, analysis and interpretation) and what is presumed to count as 'knowledge' are built into our research design for an ongoing study of recreational ketamine use which explicitly compares interviewees' accounts and our interpretation of these perspectives, dependent on the declared subject position of the interviewer (as insider or outsider) to the research subject.

A 'commitment to clubbing' (Moore 2004) and identifications with clubbers shapes the work of the (partial) insider researcher in ways that need to be considered through more reflexive accounts of the entire research process. The personal, emotional and social connections that many club researchers have with clubland often formed the driving force behind their rationale for fieldwork, subsequent analysis and as Calvey (2000) has noted in relation to his covert participant observation of Manchester pub/club doorstaff, even after the study has ended. These connections play out in choices related to research sites and participants and even to the individual drugs that research projects focus on. For instance, when we started working together, Moore became increasingly reflexive about the reasons why alcohol and cocaine, as drugs which she *personally* dislikes, were notably absent from her work, despite indications of the growing symbolic and actual presence of both substances in contemporary leisure-pleasure landscapes (e.g. Measham 2004c, in press; Measham & Brain 2005; Parker, Williams & Aldrige 2002). For Measham, the death of a close friend after consuming psychedelic mushrooms that had been purchased legally in the UK in 2004 has affected both the line of questioning she has pursued in subsequent interviews with users of psychedelic drugs and also the content of her teaching.[13] Furthermore, the widespread, partial and often inaccurate media coverage of both her friend's death and subsequent inquest provided an added poignancy to the debate surrounding the criminalization of 'fresh' psychedelic mushrooms a year later in the UK, and the claims and counter claims about the potential harm of mushrooms, with the inquest falling within weeks of the passage of the 2005 Drugs Act.[14]

Illuminating an exploration of the emotional relationship between researcher and research subject highlights the absence of such reflection within the field of dance club and dance drug research. Without an academic environment allowing openness about a researcher's immersion in clubland, the reflexivity necessary to improve and extend our investigations is unlikely to become a staple of club research. In the absence of such an open environment, the emotionality as well as the rationality of dance club attendance and dance drug use is unlikely to be explored, given that accounts of emotional connections require a degree of reflexive thinking about researchers' relationships to their topic of inquiry.

'Club studies' have matured alongside dance clubs since the early days of acid house, rave and Russell Newcombe's groundbreaking work. Yet without a reflexive consideration of the social, emotional and intellectual location of the researcher and its implications for the research process, club research risks doing an injustice to the millions of people for whom clubs and clubbing have become an integral part of their leisure time and possibly their identity (Malbon 1998). If the last 15 years have seen the burgeoning of a global dance club scene, alongside a diversification in music genres, events, venues, drugs and club devotees, then perhaps in the next 15 years we will see a diversification and maturation of dance club and dance drug research, confident enough to pursue a more reflexive, more open and ultimately more fruitful research agenda, incorporating a multiplicity of approaches and focuses.

---

13   The topic of psychedelic mushrooms was not included in the curriculum of Measham's undergraduate Drugs, Crime and Society course for the academic year 2004/5, necessitated by the recent bereavement and the realisation that, for that academic year, it was unlikely that she could deliver a complete and coherent lecture on the subject.

14   2005 Drugs Act available online at http://www.drugs.gov.uk/NationalStrategy/DrugsAct2005.

Chapter 3

New York City Club Kids: A Contextual Understanding of Club Drug Use[1]

Dina Perrone

Ya know, like, all my friends, ya know, have jobs and go to school, and come from good families, and ya know, we're all good friends, and, ya know, when I would go out and people would ask me what you do, and I would say, 'Ya know, I'm a registered nurse'. And they would look at me like, 'What are you doing here, and you're doing drugs?' And why not? I'm a normal human being, ya know, I work all week, I wanna go out and have a good time over the weekend, so be it, ya know? And I would say exactly that. Ya know, that's right, I could work, live on my own, and maintain a lifestyle, and go out and party, then who's better than me? That's what I used to say. – Betty[2]

Most studies conducted in the US on club drug use, including ecstasy (MDMA, E), crystal methamphetamine (crystal, crystal meth, tina), ketamine (K, Special K) and GHB (G), have focused on the epidemiology of their use (e.g. Fendrich et al. 2003; Johnston et al. 2005; NSDUH 2005; Pulse Check 2004; Yacoubian et al. 2003; c.f. Kelly this volume). These findings generally indicate that the highest prevalence of use occurs among whites from suburban areas between the ages of 17 and 25. Furthermore, they, as well as other studies of club drug users, show that club drug use predominantly occurs within dance club settings, where individuals use one or a variety of club drugs at intervals throughout the night, along with licit substances, such as tobacco and alcohol (Fendrich et al. 2003; Forsyth 1996; Hammersley et al. 1999; Hansen, Maycock & Lower 2001; Johnston et al. 2005; Kelly this volume; Lankenau & Clatts 2005; Martins, Mazzotti & Chilcoat 2005; Measham 2004a;

---

1   The author was supported as a predoctoral fellow in the Behavioral Sciences Training in Drug Abuse Research program sponsored by Medical and Health Research Association of New York City, Inc. (MHRA) and the National Development and Research Institutes (NDRI) with funding from the National Institute on Drug Abuse (5T32 DA07233). Points of view, opinions, and conclusions in this chapter do not necessarily represent the official position of the U.S. Government, Medical and Health Research Association of New York City, Inc. or National Development and Research Institutes.

2   Names of venues and people have been changed to ensure the confidentiality and safety of the participants.

NSDUH 2005; Parker & Williams 2003; Pulse Check 2004; Sanders this volume; Ter Bogt et al. 2002; van de Wijngaart et al. 1999; Yacoubian et al. 2003).

The media's coverage of club drug users has provided images and some context to the numbers presented in those epidemiological data. They have presented photos of club drug users as 'ravers' wearing sun-visors and baggy clothes, sucking on lollipops or pacifiers, and carrying glowsticks at all-night parties or raves. For example, Home Box Office (HBO) (2002) repeatedly aired "Small Town Ecstasy", a documentary of a divorced father's excessive use of ecstasy while raving with his children. The media has also provided *numerous* images of club drug use as destructive and harmful (see Mitchell 2001). The Public Broadcasting System's (PBS) (2001) weekly television series "In the Mix" aired an episode titled "Ecstasy", which included interviews of teens in rehabilitation or prison as a result of their ecstasy use. Furthermore, GHB has been portrayed as a facilitator of 'date' rape (see Jenkins 1999), and *Newsweek* gave crystal methamphetamine 'America's Most Dangerous Drug' award (Jefferson 2005). Partially in response to the negative attention given to the harmful effects of clubs drugs, the government has implemented punitive public policies to eradicate club drug use (Jenkins 1999). For instance, the Food and Drug Administration has only recently added the club drugs ketamine and GHB (1999 and 2000, respectively) to the schedule of controlled substances, and the Federal Sentencing Commission increased the penalties for ecstasy possession in 2001 (see also AP 2001; DEA 2002).

While depictions of club drugs are somewhat accurate to the extent that they can be harmful and destructive, and some users fit the image of the raver, such depictions are not representative of all club drug users. The patterns, settings, rituals and triggers of harm associated with club drug use are complex. This chapter attempts to elucidate this complexity by offering interpretative accounts of club drug use among relatively affluent young people. Data are based on in-depth interviews and participant observations of a sample of club drug users that frequented New York City dance clubs. Data collection occurred between March 2004 and June 2005 at a variety of clubs and venues along the East Coast of the US.

In the first section of this chapter, norms regarding club drug using behaviors (Beck & Rosenbaum 1994; Flom et al. 2001; Latkin, Forman & Knowlton 2002; Measham, Parker & Aldridge 2001; Redhead 1993; Shewan, Dalgarno & Reith 2000; van der Rijt, d'Haenens & van Straten 2003; Warner, Room & Adlaf 1999) and the carnivalesque nature of the club drug-using experience (Baudrillard 1995; Malbon 1999; Presdee 2000; Veblen 1899) are examined. While club drug use predominantly occurred in club settings, club drug use also penetrated other aspects of the sample's lives, both inside and outside of the club settings, shaping their identity (Hebdige 1979), affecting relationships with others (Cavacuiti 2004; Kandel & Davies 1990; Latkin, Forman & Knowlton 2002; Yamaguchi & Kandel 1997) and playing a significant role in weight loss and control (Crank et al. 1999; Hammersley, Khan & Ditton 2002; Henderson 1993a; Joe Laidler 2005; Measham, Parker & Aldridge 2001). These topics are discussed in the following section. Next, how the sample obtained information regarding their drug usage is explained. In particular, this section discusses the generation of 'folk knowledge' and importance of 'experience' to club drug users in their attempt to avoid negative outcomes of club drugs, such as problems at work or emergency room visits (cf. Brewer 2003; Decorte 2001a, 2001b; Cleckner 1979; Heather & Robertson 1981; Kelly this volume; Panagopoulos & Ricciardelli 2005; Southgate & Hopwood 2001). The subsequent section explores considerations related to the samples' reduction and periods of cessation from using club drugs when many life course transitions (Sampson & Laub 1993) facilitated a decrease and alteration in their club drug usage (Allaste & Lagerspetz 2002; Beck & Rosenbaum 1994; Hammersley, Khan & Ditton 2002; Hansen, Maycock & Lower 2001; Measham, Parker & Aldridge 2001; Shewan, Dalgarno & Reith 2000; Ter Bogt et al. 2002). The chapter concludes by discussing the implications of these findings.

Methods

The research commenced in March 2004 when a key informant, Mike, the first link in the sampling chain, extended an invitation to travel with him and his friends to Miami for a major electronic music event. During that one week in Miami, many club goers were befriended, who later became informants in the study. Every weekend from that point until June 2005 was spent with a variety of 'club kids'– the label George, an informant, used to describe clubbers who use club drugs. The terms "club kids" and "the sample" are used interchangeably throughout this manuscript. Over that 15-month period, participant observations and in-depth interviews, procedures approved by the university's institutional review board, were collected.

Participant observations were gathered on 45 different occasions, each lasting no less than 3 hours for an approximate total of 200 hours in the field with club drug users as they 'partied' in Miami, the Jersey Shore, New Jersey, the Hamptons, Long Island and New York City. In New York City, observations were recorded in eleven different venues – ten dance clubs and one lounge. In the Hamptons, observations occurred at four dance clubs, two restaurants and one motel. Observations at a dance club along the Jersey Shore and three bars/clubs in Miami were also recorded. In Miami, participant observations also occurred at two separate hotel pools and two hotel rooms. The dance clubs, bars and lounges had a minimum age requirement of 21 years, and a cover charge (a fee for entry) that rarely was less than $15 and sometimes as much as $60. Only one bar in Miami and the lounge in New York City did not require a fee for entry, and on Friday nights some of the clubs in New York City permitted those 18 years of age or older to enter. Most of the clubs were open from 10pm until 8am, but it was often possible to locate an open club at any time throughout the weekend; 'after-hours' clubs opened at around 5am and closed around 2pm. Hotel pool parties or outdoor clubs tended to start around noon, and participants' hotel rooms were always open for partying. With such an extensive and flexible daily schedule, the club kids often danced and consumed club drugs for 24-hours. This tended to be longer during holiday weekends and vacations.

The time spent in the various locations with the club drug users provided a high level of rapport and trust with the participants. Informal conversations with club attendees occurred during observations – both in and outside of venues – as well as frequent and unscheduled telephone and e-mail communications. How the club kids concealed, prepared and consumed substances, as well as their drug experiences, were observed. An excerpt from an observational field note while in Mike, George and Ralph's hotel room exemplifies this:

> There were a bunch of empty water bottles, a Sprite, a six pack of Corona Light, and water bottles filled with G [GHB] on the table. George was sitting at the table crushing some 'tina' [crystal methamphetamine] wrapped in a 20 dollar bill with a Heinz ketchup bottle. As he crushed, he saw a problem. The 'tina' was pushing through the small pores of the bill. George explained that the problem with 'tina' was it is 'too fine'. Ralph told George he was incorrectly folding the bill, 'it has to be folded in four ways.' Ralph showed George how it was done. George said he doesn't 'have patience for this shit', and removed himself from the table. Since they were waiting for room service, Dan placed the microwave dish, holding the once liquid and now powdered K [ketamine], back in the microwave. Ralph took over George's job crushing the tina. He was glad they came-up with a new word indicate taking a dose of 'tina', which they called 'flicks'. It was necessary to distinguish it from 'bumps', which are used to speak about taking a dose of K (Fieldnote, March 6, 2004).

The participants' level of comfort as they were observed is largely attributable to the key informants who trusted me and substantiated my claims of a researcher. As many researchers of 'hidden' and 'deviant' populations have experienced (e.g. Douglas 1972; Polsky 1967), initially, many club drug users in the clubbing 'scene' felt threatened by my presence, and rumored I was a member of the Federal Bureau of Investigation (FBI). Because I was unfamiliar with the scene and Mike provided the only entrance to the lives of the club kids, most club kids felt, as Estevez explained, that it appeared like I "just landed in the scene; just showed up". Being affiliated with the FBI or the Drug Enforcement Agency (DEA) was the only fathomable explanation for my presence. Consequently, when one individual among a group of friends distrusted or disliked me, access to that group was blocked. I was ostracized, ignored, and poorly treated by that group. For example, Julia's negative feelings provoked her to throw ice during an observation. There were many instances, especially in her presence, when I felt uncomfortable and was harassed. Some prospective male participants asked for sex or nudity as payment for their involvement in the study. For example, when one male was solicited for an interview he replied he would only agree to participate if he "saw me in a thong."

Following a tradition of ethnographic research of users and dealers, various issues during the participant observations, as described above, were confronted (Adler 1993; Inciardi 1993; Jacobs 1998). For instance, drug deals were observed while hanging out with the club kids, and they also offered me drugs and asked that I temporarily 'hold' drugs for them on several occasions (both of which I refused). Luckily, I only witnessed one club kid's vomiting episode, while other reactions to drugs such as "G"ing out (an adverse effect to overusing GHB) or passing-out never occurred during participant observations. Other 'passed-out' club goers (not members of the sample) were carried by bouncers pushing through the crowd of club kids to reach double doors that lead into a brightly lit room. The most alerting and informative experience occurred when door access to my car was blocked by an unconscious man.

> There was a Latino man lying on the floor blocking my path to the car. Two uniformed officers and a plain clothed man, apparently an acquaintance of the guy on the ground, stood over him. The acquaintance indicated to the officer he only knew the passed-out guy from the 'scene' [i.e. going to clubs and parties]. The officers asked if he knew what the guy consumed this afternoon. It was 7pm. The acquaintance replied 'alcohol', adding he may also have taken some GHB. The cops suspected that GHB was the culprit. The cops repeatedly tried to wake him by pushing the muscles by his clavicle. But the guy didn't budge until they forcefully pushed on his sternum. At that point, the guy popped up for three seconds, and passed out again. The cop placed his foot under the guy's head to avoid it from hitting the concrete. The cop complained about the use of substances, explaining that the guy took a drug that was in some household cleaners. A few people exiting Planet [a club] walked by and around the commotion. One girl whispered to her friend, 'G'd out'. The EMS arrived. They checked his heart and blood pressure. Everything was basically normal, but he was unconscious. They stated that 'the GHB was frying his brain'. Since he was wheezing, they placed an oxygen mask over his air passages. They again tried to wake him using the same two methods. Pressure on the sternum worked, but the guy again passed out within three seconds. EMS complimented the cop for use of his foot as a pillow. When the ambulance arrived, the police recapped the story. They checked him again and documented the guy's name, which they obtained from his wallet... As they strapped him onto a gurney and carried him into the ambulance, the guy awoke in fright. Since he was strapped down and unable to move, he began to scream. He did not know where he was going or what was happening (Fieldnote, May 29, 2004).

These situations could have had serious ramifications on the research and on my safety. It was essential to adhere to the guidance of informants, to place the safety and interests of the participants first, and to use good judgment. Developing field relations and confronting such dilemmas in the dance club setting was a dynamic process – a source of strain, stress and learning. Most importantly, this process facilitated a comprehensive understanding of the realities and experiences of the club kids.

The role of the key informants was crucial to establishing trust and rapport, gaining access, and addressing issues in the field. The study originally commenced with one key informant, Mike, who eventually reduced his involvement in the study. Two other key informants emerged: John and Gary. Mike, John and Gary advised on which clubs to attend and which club kids should be involved in the study. Participants had to be 18 years of age or older, and they must have attended a New York City dance club at least once. Through both purposive and snowball sampling techniques, 18 participants (see Table 3.1) agreed to a formal tape-recorded interview.

The interviews lasted approximately two hours and concerned their clubbing and club drug using histories and experiences, and the methods they employed to address and reduce harm associated with their club drug use. Each interviewee signed an informed consent form and was compensated with a $20 gift card to a department store. Upon completion of the interview, participants remained connected to the project through phone conversations and both planned and impromptu meetings during observations. All interviews were transcribed verbatim and managed using Atlas.ti a qualitative software package. To best reflect the thoughts of the participants, all interview excerpts provided in this chapter are exact words of the respondents, including use of argot, dialects and hesitations. Many club kids such as Estevez, who did not agree to an interview, continued to play a significant role in the research project. While not included in Table 3.1, their comments from phone conversations and observations are also included in this chapter.

The club kids ranged in age from 22-33 years (see Table 3.1). Eight of the interviewees were female, and ten were male. The majority of the sample was well-educated and affluent, reflecting the image of club drug users more generally[3] (Forsyth 1996; Hammersley, Khan & Ditton 2002; Hansen, Maycock & Lower 2001; Kelly this volume; Measham, Parker & Aldridge 2001; Ter Bogt et al. 2002; van de Wijngaart et al. 1999). While most of the club kids grew up in middle to upper-middle class families, five came from low-income and working class backgrounds. Six grew up in single-parent homes, and seven still resided with their parent(s). Currently, all but one of the participants were either employed or enrolled in post-graduate programs. As can be seen in Table 3.1, the majority of the club kids were in positions of relative economic power, being well-connected both socially and financially. This relative affluence was reflected in the value they placed on expensive clothing brands, body augmentations, and extensive travel histories. For instance, the club kids – all of whom would consider New York City clubs their homes – discussed traveling to clubs in Las Vegas and Miami, as well as clubs in European cities such as London and Amsterdam. Moreover, the club kids favored expensive, designer clothing, such as Diesel, Seven for All Man Kind, Coach, Lacoste, Armani, French Connection, Gucci and Louis Vuitton. Many of the club kids also spent a generous amount of time on fitness and body appearance, and some had breast implant surgery, went to tanning salons and used steroids to enhance their physique. As Ralph indicated, 'looking good' was important in the 'club scene.'

---

3   Because most research of club drug users have focused on rave or dance club populations, they may have missed other populations of drug users (i.e. street users) (cf. Novoa et al. 2005). Recent studies have shown that club drug use is increasingly prevalent among other populations (e.g. Fendrich et al. 2003; Krebs & Steffey 2005; Martins, Mazzotti & Chilcoat 2005; Maxwell & Spence 2005; Novoa et al. 2005; Ompad et al. 2005), and among those outside of dance club culture (e.g. Community Epidemiology Group (CEWG) 2003; Fendrich et al. 2003; Krebs & Steffey 2005; Lankenau & Clatts 2005; Maxwell & Spence 2005; Novoa et al. 2005; Ompad et al. 2005).

Table 3.1 Club Kids' Characteristics

Name	Age	Highest Degree	Occupation	Housing	Family
Angelina	26	BA	Pharmaceutical Sales	With Mom	Single-Parent
Ariel	25	BS	Investment Banker	On Own	Dual-Parent
Betty	33	Associates Deg.	Registered Nurse	On Own	Single-Parent
David	30	PhD neuroscience	Post-Doc Fellow	On Own	Dual-Parent
Gary	28	HS	Computer Graphic Designer	On Own	Single-Parent
George	22	HS	Data Analyst	With Dad	Single-Parent
Isaac	34	HS Drop-out	Club Light Guy	On Own	Single-Parent
Jack	29	MD	Chief Resident Hospital	With Partner	Dual-Parent
John	30	MBA	Owns Investment Bank	On Own	Dual-Parent
Lucille	25	BA	Clothing Chain District Manager	On Own	Dual-Parent
Mary	25	BA pursuing MA	Special Ed Teacher	With Parents	Dual-Parent
Michelle	28	MS	Occupational Therapist	With Partner	Dual-Parent
Mike	26	BA	Paralegal	With Parents	Dual-Parent
Monica	28	MA	Mattress Co. Marketing Rep.	With Parents	Dual-Parent
Ralph	25	BA	Graphic Designer	With Parents	Dual Parent
Sam	27	HS Drop-out	PT-Messenger	With Mom	Single-Parent
Tina	22	Finishing BA	Student	On Own	Dual-Parent
Tyler	28	MD	Surgical Resident	With Partner	Dual-Parent

The majority of like the New York house club scene is based on looking good, goin' to the gym, gettin' in shape, bein' fit, ya know? Gettin' dolled up, fuckin' showin' off and what not.

The average age the club kids started consuming drugs, excluding marijuana and alcohol, was 19 years (see Table 3.2). Five of the club kids, Ralph, Mike, George, Mary and John, started using when they were in high school. With the exception of Betty, the other club kids started using drugs in their early 20s, mostly while in college. The majority of the sample has been using at least one type of club drug for about ten years. One final note, while many similarities among the club kids existed, they were truly a heterogeneous group. Each individual club kid had preferred styles of dress, drugs of choice and music, which in many cases differed from their friends and other club goers (c.f. Malbon 1999; Redhead 1997; Ter Bogt & Engels 2005; Thornton 1995).

Table 3.2 Age of Onset

Name	Age (Years)	Age of Onset (Years) (Excluding marijuana & alcohol)	First Drug Used (Excluding marijuana & alcohol)
Angelina	26	20	Ecstasy
Ariel	25	19	Ecstasy
Betty	33	25	Ecstasy
David	30	19	LSD
Gary	28	24	Ecstasy
George	22	15	Cocaine
Isaac	34	Not available	Not available
Jack	29	19	LSD
John	30	15	LSD
Lucille	25	19	Ecstasy
Mary	25	17	Ketamine
Michelle	28	18	LSD
Mike	26	16	LSD
Monica	28	21	Ecstasy
Ralph	25	16	LSD
Sam	27	Not available	Not available
Tina	22	20	Ketamine
Tyler	28	23	LSD

Club Drugs, Group Norms and Carnival

Research indicates that people initiate drug use with friends who show them how to use the drug, where to use the drug, and overall conditions that favor drug using behaviors (Becker 1963; Grund 1993; Zinberg 1984; cf. Akers 1985; Sutherland & Cressey 1966). To begin, group norms regarding acceptable drugs and drug use behaviors shaped and regulated the club kids' club drug using patterns (Beck & Rosenbaum 1994; Flom et al. 2001; Latkin, Forman & Knowlton 2002; Measham, Parker & Aldridge 2001; Redhead 1993; Shewan, Dalgarno & Reith 2000; van der Rijt, d'Haenens & van Straten 2003; Warner, Room & Adlaf 1999). The club kids distinguished and categorized certain drugs and drug behaviors as acceptable, while disliking and avoiding others, and many individual club kids consumed substances accordingly. For instance, Sam was the only club kid to try heroin (he smoked it once). The others disapproved of heroin as well as crack (Beck & Rosenbaum 1994; Forsyth 1996; Hammersley, Khan & Ditton 2002; Hansen, Maycock & Lower 2001; Hunt & Evans 2003; Joe Laidler 2005; Measham, Parker & Aldridge 2001; Ter Bogt et al. 2002; van de Wijngaart et al. 1999). Tyler, for instance, explained that these drugs were more dangerous than the drugs he and his friends consumed, such as marijuana, ketamine, LSD and ecstasy.

> There's really nothing that we do that's gonna fuck you up for like or send you to the hospital, ya know? No one's doin' heroin, no one's gonna overdose and die, no one's doin' crack.

David also considered heroin dangerous and highly addictive:

> So yeah, drugs are, like, that are very addictive too- those are bad, those are bad- like heroin.

Marijuana, which many smoked throughout the week, was considered the least harmful of all drugs. Many did not consider it a drug and disagreed with its current legislation. Tyler, for instance, thought marijuana "doesn't count as a drug as far as I'm concerned." David agreed and elaborated:

> Why is it that you're allowed to drink alcohol and get completely wasted out of your mind, but you're not allowed to smoke a fuckin' joint? I mean isn't that Chewbacca [ridiculous; irrational]? Doesn't that make no sense at all? Aren't you completely of, like, incapable of functioning on alcohol compared to weed? So why should one be legal and the other illegal?

Club kids also tended to frown upon excessive use of drugs (Southgate & Hopwood 2001). Ralph, for instance, would not associate with some drug users in the clubbing scene. When discussing heavy methamphetamine users, Ralph commented:

That, that I never witnessed or experienced in my life- like that's, that's out of control, that's fuckin' drug addicts straight-up meth. I've never experienced, like me or any of my friends…we wouldn't hang out with people like that…But I've met a couple of people who have shown traits or specific, ya know, or specific weird behaviors that you've seen in that movie [*Spun*] that I've met them, hung out with them for ten minutes, and said, 'Yo, this fuckin' guy's a wack job, I'm out', ya know, 'I don't even wanna be sittin' next to this fuckin' guy.'

Angelina, Mary and Lucille also separated themselves from those who used drugs excessively:

> Mary: But we don't get sloppy either. We're not like those people that sit and do three day binges.
> Angelina: Yeah, we won't go on binges.
> Lucille: Like, just like a recreational thing.

As the last excerpt indicates, the club kids tried to limit their club drug consumption to weekends for recreational purposes, which, for them, was no different from any other recreational activity (Allaste & Lagerspetz 2002; Hammersley, Khan & Ditton 2002; Hansen, Maycock & Lower 2001; Joe Laidler 2005; Parker & Williams 2003; Ter Bogt et al. 2002). Mary, for instance, said that using club drugs on the weekend was akin to a game of baseball – something done for 'fun'.

> That's what I do on the weekend, like some people go play baseball, and no- I like to do drugs, you know what I mean?…. Like I have a lot of friends that don't go out that sit around and drink and go to local bars every weekend and they call us the party goers. You know what I mean, like, it's what you enjoy.

Only a few of the club kids mentioned the occasional use of club drugs during the week in order to facilitate an effective workday (see Decorte 2000; Joe Laidler 2005; Waldorf, Reinarman & Murphy 1991). For instance, George usually refrained from drug use throughout his workweek, but has consumed crystal methamphetamine and GHB on Mondays after a long weekend.

> I'll party straight through till I have to go to work Monday morning. And then once I get to work I usually bring jus- I usually bring a little crystal with me to work, a little G with me to work, and I'll-I'll do a little bit, not to get high, but just to give me enough energy, a boost to stay awake, and not be miserable and grouchy, and edgy, and paranoid, ya know?

Likewise, Angelina and a friend in college consumed cocaine every night for two months to complete all the necessary term papers so the friend could graduate.

> Angelina: There was a two month period of time when me and a friend did it [cocaine] like every fucking night for like two months.
> Lucille: I remember you coming into the Plant like, 'We just wrote a paper, and we did this and we did that.'

Angelina: This girl, like one of my best friends, two years younger than me, needed to graduate college, and was not doing well and I slept at her house for an entire semester. She got me coke and I did all of her papers for her.

The pressures of individual responsibility and achievement the club kids faced during their work or school week provoked their desire for places to release, engage in excess, transgress, and, as Michelle said, "go nuts" on weekend nights. As such, the venues the club kids chose to spend their leisure time became spaces for excess and transgression where themed-style outfits and the consumption of multiple substances helped acquaint them with their "other-selves" (Measham 2004a). Often, venues were transformed from a dance club, restaurant, hotel pool area, or even a political forum into a carnival where the attendees entered a world outside of their everyday social norms (Presdee 2000). Presdee (2000, p. 61) further explained that these places have become essential since the rise in consumption and commercialization have caused a "less and less bearable" daily life that is rid of "deeper content" (see also Baudrillard 1995; Malbon 1999; Melechi 1993; Rietveld 1993; Thornton 1995). Club kids sought to escape the drama of their work-week, leave that 'self' at home, and enter a reality that was perceived to be free of rules and regulations. These venues legitimized participants' behavior that would otherwise be considered outside of the norm (Presdee 2000). Club Heart's sadomasochist-themed party provided an ideal example:

> Inside a box off the dance floor were two women. One was dressed as a nurse in a white plastic dress, while the other was wearing an all black patient outfit...The nurse was probing the patient with a light-up mechanism. With each touch, the patient would robotically move her body, and the nurse would laugh like Vincent Price...One guy wearing leather pants with a collar around his neck, handcuffed to two girls both wearing leather-like boy shorts, fishnets, boots, and a leather-like bra walked passed the box (Fieldnote, April 23, 2005).

Commodity culture has caused individual identities to be determined by wasteful consumption (e.g. Baudrillard 1995; Veblen 1899). For instance, Baudrillard (1995) argued that when a culture enters a state of excessive consumption and commercialism, that culture becomes flat, depthless and hyper-real. In such instances, people amplify the value of consumerism, and the concepts of truth and identity become blurred or non-existent. Individuals then become defined by what they consume, own, and buy. To achieve status in such a consumerist and commoditized society, individuals must engage in conspicuous and excessive consumption practices (Baudrillard 1995; Hebdige 1979; Hayward 2004; Presdee 2000; Veblen 1899). Veblen (1899) explained that for consumers to be judged as members of the superior class, the consumer must expend "superfluities". As Presdee (2000, p. 61) noted, "there is an increasing need for daily excitement and a blissful state of non-responsibility consumption." The dance club allowed the club kids to enter a fantasy world based on excess and consumption, free from restrictions where they can concentrate on 'fun.' Such settings are optimal for "non-responsibility consumption." Dance clubs' long corridors, hidden stairways, elaborate light displays, and attractive "eye-catching" interior allowed the club kids to enter a carnivalesque reality where they forgot about their daily concerns (Malbon 1999; Measham 2004a; Presdee 2000; Redhead 1993; Thornton 1995). George's comments illustrated this:

> I just enjoy [clubbing], ya know whatta mean?...I always say that the point of drugs and the point of partying is-is you leave all your drama and your bullshit in your daily life at home, ya know? Check that shit at the door, come in and enjoy yourself. That's what I do every time I go out. I don't carry my drama out wit me....I'm out here gettin' fucked up, I don't give a fuck what's goin' on', ya know whatta mean? I'll deal with that when I'm sober and I'm back home and it's Monday or Tuesday and I have to deal wit it.

The clubs kids' entrance into this fantastical reality was further enhanced by their use of drugs (Forsyth 1996; Hansen, Maycock & Lower 2001; Malbon 1999; Measham, Parker & Aldridge 2001; Parks & Kennedy 2004; Ter Bogt et al. 2002; van de Wijngaart et al. 1999). Several of the club kids explained that the music and the setting could not be separated from the drugs' properties.

> While at Club Wax, Gary complained that he was sober. He said, 'Without G, you can't even hear the music, and with G the music is incredible. You just feel incredible. It's a feeling you never want to go away' (Fieldnote, April 25, 2004).

Angelina offered a similar response:

> What I feel like music and drugs go hand and hand because when I was in junior high school and I smoked all that pot, I would have to listen to hip-hop. It was like hip-hop and smoking [marijuana] all the time. And then you would go into the city and it was like ecstasy, K, and house music. You know...it's like peanut butter and jelly... Why are you going to listen to music if you're not mangled [high on drugs]?

The club kids described how the use of drugs allowed them to connect to the music and enhance their clubbing experience (Beck & Rosenbaum 1994; Hammersley, Khan & Ditton 2002; Hansen, Maycock & Lower 2001; Hinchliff 2001; Ter Bogt et al. 2002; van de Wijngaart et al. 1999). Tyler explained:

> You are connected in ways that you were never connected when you were sober, with the music, with your friends that are standing around you, with everything. It feels like the entire fuckin' universe is moving to that one goddamn rhythm from the song.

Ralph expressed how the use of ketamine inside a club enhanced the carnival experience, as it made him feel as though he was in a 'video game':

> Well, with K in the club- it's like, the K fucks you up because of the lights and everything like that- that's what has the most effect when you're on K, 'cause the lights and the music and everything, you feel like, you're like literally in your own like, you're in a video game- everything's just fuckin' fucked up, everything's just weird and abnormal...

For the club kids, dance clubs offered "complete sensory experiences – ones often intensified by the use of alcohol and/or drugs" (Thornton 1995, p. 57). The club themes, the shows performed at the venues, and the drugs provided a hedonistic environment where the club kids effectively consumed 'fun'. Furthermore, the precision and monotony of the rhythm of electronic music, especially when played at a high volume (which was often done at these venues) was considered 'hypnotizing' (Rietveld 1993; Ter Bogt et al. 2002; Thornton 1995). As Thornton (1995, p. 60) explained, "the constant pulse of the bass blocks thoughts, affects emotions and enters the body". This atmosphere was the ideal setting for those seeking to 'escape' and enter "never-never-land" (Reighley 2000, p. 30; cf. Hammersley, Khan & Ditton 2002; Hansen, Maycock & Lower 2001; Hinchliff 2001; Malbon 1999; Measham, Parker & Aldridge 2001; Redhead 1993; Thornton 1995). The music, the drugs, the lights, the shows, and the beautiful people pinched each of the sensory mechanisms of the body. To the club kids, dance clubs were the ultimate hedonistic environment promoting the culture of excess and conspicuous, wasteful consumption for a weekend of recreation (Hayward 2004; Measham 2004a; Parker & Williams 2003; Presdee 2000; Stanley 1997).

Club Drugs, Body Consciousness and Relationships

Studies indicate that drug use tends to pervade various aspects of users' lives. For instance, certain club drugs, such as GHB, crystal methamphetamine and MDMA have been commonly used for their weight managing properties (Crank et al. 1999; Hammersley, Khan & Ditton 2002; Henderson 1993a; Joe Laidler 2005; Measham, Parker & Aldridge 2001). GHB metabolizes fat, and both MDMA and crystal methamphetamine are appetite suppressants. For many club kids, as with those in the UK, dancing all night on drugs was a form of exercise (see Crank et al. 1999; Measham, Parker & Aldridge 2001). Many female club kids perceived using drugs and clubbing as an effective method of weight loss. For instance, while relaxing at a hotel pool in South Beach, Miami, four women discussed the benefits of ecstasy and crystal methamphetamine consumption on weight loss:

> The girls explained their new 'South Beach diet'. They basically consume drugs and refrain from eating. Occasionally they'll eat some fruit and have some drinks (Fieldnote, March 5, 2004).

Mary also discussed weight loss in relation to using crystal methamphetamine:

> I was doing crystal. I was doing everything…When people we're like, 'What made you lose so much weight?' I'm like, 'This great diet, diet called crystal. Best diet ever in the world'.

In contrast to the women, the men tended to dislike the appetite suppressant effects of drugs, as they were more concerned with building muscle mass. Ralph, for instance, explained the importance of ordering protein shakes from club bartenders:

> Specifically, guys like me or my friends, we go out, we work out in the gym 4, 5 days a week, okay. When you're up for 24 hours straight, you can't eat solid food, it's impossible…So in order to make sure your body has the calories, the carbohydrates, and the protein it needs to function normally, you try to drink, drink shakes …So instead of your body running off nothing but the drugs as fuel, it runs off the protein and the carb- the calories that you're putting into it through a shake.

Because eating was perceived to be impossible while under the influence of these substances, George forced himself to eat throughout the drug-using episode to maintain his physique.

> Even when I party I eat. A lotta people don't eat for days. I eat. I eat whatever I could get my hands on, I eat. I don't care if it's cookies, cake, donuts. I just eat it.

Clearly, drug use and weight maintenance had an antagonistic relationship with the men in the sample and a positive relationship with the women. Ralph explained it best:

> Most girls, they go out and they party. They say, 'Okay, ya know what? I'm not gonna eat for a day and a half, so that's gonna be good, 'cause it's gonna help me lose weight', so ya know. But with guys, it's the exact opposite. We wanna make sure we don't lose weight, and keep on whatever we have.

Studies have shown that recreational activities and drug use behaviors are linked to romantic partners and peers (Cavacuiti 2004; Kandel & Davies 1990; Latkin, Forman & Knowlton 2002; Yamaguchi & Kandel 1997). Peers exert great influence over an individual's recreational activity and their use of drugs (Felson & Clarke 1998; Kandel & Davies 1990; Warr 2002). Many of the club kids discussed the importance of dating and marrying someone who was a member of the clubbing and drug using scene. For instance, one couple, who met at DJ Barbuck's weekly parties at Club Plant in New York City, chose to have their wedding ceremony at DJ Barbuck's pool party in Miami. This was one example of the importance clubbing and drug using were in the lives of the sample. Mary, Lucille and Angelina also discussed dating and drug use:

> Mary: Half the time I try to date people who don't do drugs, and it's bad because I look like–I think they're scared of me –
> *Dina: Could you be with someone who didn't do drugs?*
> Mary: I've tried it, it doesn't really work.
> Lucille: I think if they still went out [clubbing].
> Angelina: No, because number one, we wouldn't find them….because where are we gonna find this person-unless, we met them in like the supermarket?

Part of the difficulty with dating someone outside of the scene who does not use drugs, as Mary indicated, was that partners tended to be frightened of their drug habits. Young men were less likely to date someone who, like them, used drugs and attended clubs. The men in the sample tended to adhere to a 'double standard', in which men are rewarded for sexual promiscuity and sexual activity, yet women engaging in those same behaviors are derogated (see Hinchliff 2001; O'Sullivan 1995; Oliver & Sedikides 1992; Parks & Scheidt 2000; Sack, Keller & Hinkle 1981). George's comments explicitly demonstrated this:

> Ya know what? Any girls that I meet I'm not gonna even gonna give two shits about if I meet'em in a club, ya know whatta mean? I, I tried dating people who-who I met in the-in the- in the scene. It never works out, ya know whatta mean?...They're just, just not something ya wanna ...If I wanna fuckin' settle down, I'll go look for a girl in like... I'll go to like a drinking crowd party, ya know whatta mean? ...Not like an afterhours, grimy fuckin' drug party. It's just, yo, it's not gonna happen. ...Not that it can't but, I'm not gonna give it the benefit of the doubt.

Ralph, on the other hand, was more optimistic:

> *Dina: So, would you meet your wife in a club?*
> Ralph: I'm gonna say yes. I'm open to it. It's possible because just like me, I'm gonna say I'm a good person. I know I am, and I know there's other people similar in background and ya know, in wholesome and goodness to me. So I'm gonna say it's possible, but everybody you meet in a place like that you gotta keep, um, at arm's length for a long time until you actually find out the real- the real person that they really are 'cause I'm gonna say 7 out of 10 that are shady individuals you don't want nothin' to do with.

Once they found that person to settle down with, many hoped to continue clubbing and using drugs. Monica, for instance, expressed this:

> Ya know, I would like to think, ya know, the babysitter's here, and I get a night out with my husband and we can have a fun night; not over doing it.

Lucille and Angelina would also continue to use some club drugs once they have children.

> *Dina: Will you stop completely?*
> Lucille: Eventually. You know, I think that when I'm in my 30s, if I'm still like going out every once in awhile, and if it's [drug] around I would do it. I don't think I'd go looking for it, the way like you do now. But let's say you were like, if we're like at a party... you're 33 years old and maybe you have a 1 year old baby at home with the babysitter, and...somebody was like, 'Oh, I have larry' [cocaine]...You're gonna do it. I don't think it's gonna be like more, like such a habit when you're older. I think it will like stop, but if it's in front of you- I think you would do it for fun.
> Angelina: I don't think when I'm 30, like 35 I'd drop a bomb [ecstasy]. I'd probably do a little larry.

Club Drugs, Folklore and Experience

Drug research indicates that drug knowledge and drug use familiarity shape the effects of the drug – both positive and negative – and create the drug user's experience (e.g. Becker 1963; Brewer 2003; Decorte 2001a, 2001b; Grund 1993; Jansen 2001; Kelly this volume; Panagopoulos & Ricciardelli 2005; Riley & Hayward 2004; Sherlock & Conner 1999; Southgate & Hopwood 2001; Zinberg 1984). Drug knowledge gained from books, articles, Internet sites, trial and error practices, and experience is also known as user 'folklore' (Becker 1963). Among drug users, folklore has served as a reference guide to control the effects, maximize the experience, and address negative reactions to the drugs (Becker 1963; Brewer 2003; Decorte 2001a, 2001b; Cleckner 1979; Grund 1993; Heather & Robertson 1981; Kelly this volume; Panagopoulos & Ricciardelli 2005; Southgate & Hopwood 2001; Zinberg 1984). Devising methods for controlled use has been possible through the access of a large source of information, especially from the Internet (see also Jenkins 1999; Kelly this volume; Levy et al. 2005; Southgate & Hopwood 2001). For instance, Jenkins (1999) explained that simply typing the name of a particular drug into an Internet search engine provides a plethora of information, from medical studies to personal advice. The dance culture, in particular, has several advocates of harm reduction, such as the US based *DanceSafe*, the Netherlands based *Safe House Campaign*, and the *Ottawans Actively Teaching Safety (OATS)* organization in Canada, which promote safe drug use, primarily by administering information.

Using folklore, available information and drug experience, the club kids negotiated harm prior, during and after drug use events. With the exception of two club kids, the sample successfully avoided doctor and emergency room visits, and all but one of the club kids avoided arrest related to their use of club drugs. Many club kids discussed the importance of the Internet in reducing harms associated with their drug use. Monica, for instance, said she obtained information about club drugs "off the Internet." Similarly, George said, "You can find plenty of information on it on the Internet." The club kids also actively sought information on club drugs by conducting research and reading published books.

At Barroom, Estevez discussed a few studies he conducted in college on GHB ...stating GHB puts your body in 'REM sleep', so your muscles can rebuild themselves...He claimed that it is a myth that GHB is an amino acid and that it 'causes the heart to stop'. Rather, when mixed with alcohol, your body and mind enters REM sleep in an 'unpredictable manner'. 'People can fall asleep at the wheel or while they are walking'. This is why it is dangerous. He explained that this is exacerbated when 'GHB is taken in cap form [pouring GHB into a water or soda bottle cap. A cap is one dose of GHB]'...[since] the person is unaware of how close he/she is to the last stage of REM sleep...[which is when] you are completely asleep. When the person consumes too much GHB, he/she is in a 'dead sleep'...He continued explaining that 'E doesn't kill anyone either'. Rather, 'dehydration kills people'. He also discussed 'moral panics', and how 'Americans and the news media exaggerate everything'. According to him, 'the public is very stupid' (Fieldnote, May 31, 2004).

Like Estevez, many club kids largely distrusted the media's depiction and doctors' knowledge of the drugs, and disagreed with drug legislation (c.f. Coomber, Morris & Dunn 2000). Furthermore, most believed that the published information regarding the effects of club drugs was exaggerated, missing or incorrect, as it was contrary to the users' experiences with the substances (see Jenkins 1999; Kuhn, Swartzwelder & Wilson 1998). For them, such information was read cautiously. For instance, throughout the research project, Gary repeatedly phoned in search of a book or website that had unbiased findings on the effects of drugs, and consistently searched the Internet for new books. Gary's comprehension of, and disagreement with, the readily available information regarding GHB provoked him to argue with doctors after he awoke in the hospital from consuming excessive amounts of the drug. The below field note contextualizes this account.

> Gary was at the pool party in Miami when he ran-out of GHB. He began to ask around, and bought a bottle for $30. When he never experienced the effects, he realized it was a fake and left the party. He met Jesse at a restaurant who sold Gary some GHB, of which he quickly ingested a 'few swigs [sips]' at the restaurant. He decided to meet his cousin at a strip club, left, and 'jumped in a cab'. He started to 'feel funny' in the cab, and asked the driver to stop the car, as he didn't want the driver to think he was 'vulnerable and take advantage' of him. When he got out of the car he 'stumbled around' until a cop car stopped him. The officers handcuffed him and took him to the station. He recalled sitting at the station, and believed he 'must have passed out'. He awoke in a hospital bed, while the doctors were trying to put a catheter in his penis. He began to 'freak out'... The doctors were standing over him trying to explain that everything was going to be 'okay'. Gary told them that all he did was GHB. The doctors responded, 'That stuff could kill you!' Gary argued that GHB cannot kill you, and that the doctors have been 'misinformed'. He insisted they 'review the research' on the drug. He further exclaimed that he was 'fine' and was 'able to go home'. The doctors told him that he wasn't well and had to stay. He made a deal with the doctors that if he could walk to the end of the hallway, he could leave. He got off the bed, walked down the hallway, and left the hospital (Phone Conversation, April 2, 2005).

Experience gained through trial and error was another common technique the club kids employed to address harmful club drug effects. For example, Ralph and his friends learned both the dangerous and appropriate ways to counteract negative reactions to GHB or "G"ing-out:

> Like, the first time, like if somebody we know was 'G'ing out, somebody was like, 'Yeah, give him a bump [single snorted dose] of meth'. So I was like, 'Alright, I guess that makes sense, he's about to go to sleep, give him a fuckin' bump of something that'll get him up'. We tried it. It didn't do nothing, but make the fuckin' kid twitch while he was sleepin'. So I was like, 'Yo, it doesn't work.', like, ya know what I'm sayin'? People have like these, and everybody keeps bein' like, 'Yo, give him a bump of meth'. 'Yo, don't give him shit, just let him go to sleep and that's it. He'll be alright.' So I mean it's just something that you learn.

Experiences, such as Ralph's, in conjunction with the knowledge they obtained regarding the supposed effects of the drugs allowed the club kids to understand the appropriate dosage and methods to heighten the positive, and reduce the negative, effects of drugs. Essentially, the club kids were able to become fairly 'scientific', acting as doctors or pharmacists, and medicating themselves and their friends in an attempt to regulate and heighten the drug effects. Many users prescribed themselves and each other various substances depending on how they were feeling. Jack explained:

> Yeah, we tried to like not drop [take ecstasy] till we got inside the club, so better we can maximize our ecstasy time…We were all really scientific about it…We tried to take it at the right moments, that way we'd start rolling [experiencing the high from ecstasy] as soon as the DJ was gonna start spinning…We'd smoke joints [marijuana] and do bumps [single snorted dose] of K once the E started dying down…We called it giving ourselves turbo boosters—it makes you feel the E more.

In a similar fashion, many club kids engaged in a form of self-medication to ease the 'coming down' process (e.g. Hammersley, Khan & Ditton 2002; Hinchliff 2001; Joe Laidler 2005; Levy et al. 2005; Measham, Parker & Aldridge 2001). For example, many club kids, like John, smoked marijuana to relax and induce sleep after using ecstasy and cocaine.

> Um, one night I remember droppin' a pill [ecstasy], remember doin' a lotta coke, I remember doin' K to wake myself up, and smokin' pot to put myself to sleep.

Acting as doctors or pharmacists also tended to become essential when counteracting negative reactions to drugs. For example, upon returning from a night out of clubbing, Angelina and Mary swiftly addressed Lucille's cocaine induced panic attack:

> Angelina: You [to Lucille] only get panic attacks when you do like uppers, like coke and crystal…it makes them like very antsy…you just actually gotta wait it out, ya know? Talk them through it and just like –
> Mary: Offer them another drug. 'How about this?'
> Angelina: Yeah, yeah like that's what you have to do. I went to my house I got Vicodin [an opiate] and came here right away 'cause I heard it in her voice, that she was just like not gonna go to sleep she was…so upset, thinking about everything, and I was just like, 'You need to go to sleep', and there's – you're not gonna fall asleep on your own, 'cause you're that coked up. So I came here and brought her Vikes [Vicodin]
> Mary: It let her sleep.

Like Angelina, some club kids used prescription medication to go to sleep after a night of using drugs that impair the user's ability to sleep, such as ecstasy, crystal methamphetamine and/or cocaine. For example, Ralph found it necessary to have Central Nervous System (CNS) depressants such as Xanex (alprazolam) or Valium (diazepam) to counteract the lengthy effects of crystal methamphetamine (see Sanders et al. 2005).

> That's what sucks about it [crystal methamphetamine]. With this shit if you don't have something to knock you out when you, when you don't wanna be high, you get fucked, you just sit there and stare at the ceilings, like literally you stare at the ceilings, you can't go to sleep. This is what sucks about it. So we counteract that with prescription medications, such as Xanax or Valium...without those you'd be miserable...For instance, this past weekend I was doin' it [crystal methamphetamine], I was hangin' out like all night Saturday night, Sunday whatever, fine. Sunday night I took half a Xanax and I went to sleep at around 11 o'clock, my last bump [single snorted dose of crystal methamphetamine] was at 6, went to sleep at 11 o'clock woke up at 6 in the morning, slept like a good 7 hours, went to work, no problem. So you see the necessity?

Even on a much smaller, arguably less harmful scale, friends shared folklore to reduce the negative effects of snorting crystal methamphetamine.

> As the guys were getting ready to leave the hotel room, they started to discuss their nostril problems from 'sniffing tina' [crystal methamphetamine]....Todd complained about the growth he had inside his nose. Ralph suggested putting Neosporin on it. He went into the bedroom to get some. Mike suggested saline, and George agreed with that method. Mike said, 'You should clean your nose before you go to sleep because you don't want that shit lying in your nose.' Mike added that he almost 'choked once from inhaling water' when trying to clean-out his nose. Ralph brought Todd the Neosporin and Todd applied it to the inside of his nose (Fieldnote, March 5, 2004).

In many instances, friends tended to become experts in dealing with bad incidents related to club drug use, and were very important throughout the drug using experience (e.g. Hansen, Maycock & Lower 2001; Lenton & Davidson 1999; Shewan, Dalgarno & Reith 2000). Betty described the important role friends played in monitoring each other's behavior:

> If anybody is not feeling good, or somebody does get sick and like throw-up like I have, then we help each other. We don't just sit there and leave, ya know? 'Okay, you go, go throw-up in the corner there, I'm goin' to the dance floor now'. Ya know, we help each other.

Ralph pointed out an "unwritten code" amongst his friends:

> We have a crew- like our crew's pretty tight, we don't really hang out with stragglers. When we go out to a club, we hang out with who we go out with and that's pretty much it...We consider ourselves like a family, a family. We're about, like if you see somebody you know, you go tell...his boy, 'Yo, Mikey', you know what I'm sayin'? 'Your boy over there's a fuckin' mess. Go take care of him', and it's his responsibility to go take care of his boy. Ya know, it's kind of like the unwritten code of like friends, ya know what I'm sayin'? Especially in that scene and the kind of shit that we do, ya know?

In addition to addressing harms associated with use, friends shared information regarding what to expect when consuming drugs (see also Becker 1963; Cleckner 1979; Grund 1993; Kuhn, Swartzwelder & Wilson 1998; Sherlock & Conner 1999; Shewan, Dalgarno & Reith 2000; Zinberg 1984). Occasionally, when club drug users had ideas about what to expect from the club drugs, they turned potentially perceived negative effects into positive ones (Becker 1963; Kuhn, Swartzwelder & Wilson 1998; Sherlock & Conner 1999; Shewan, Dalgarno & Reith 2000; Zinberg 1984). For example, Tyler described the undesirable ketamine 'drip' (when ketamine is snorted, it turns to liquid and 'drips' down the throat) as an acceptable, welcomed and enjoyable effect:

> *Dina: What about immediate side effects? Like the drip?*
> Tyler: That's not a side effect, that's part of the process. Dude, if you do it for more than like 2 or 3 times you learn to like the drip. That's how you know you've got it up your nose far enough that it's gonna kick in. And you just have to live with the taste. Even the taste can start out as foul like lickin' a urinal cake, but after awhile, you get to like it.

User 'folklore' and friendship groups were an essential ingredient for a positive drug using experience and preventing and minimizing harm. Ultimately, drug knowledge, drug experience and friendship networks facilitated enjoyable drug experiences, and, more often than not, provided effective responses to harmful occurrences, changing potentially negative experiences to positive ones.

Periodic Reduction and Cessation of Club Drug Use

Throughout their club drug using careers, the club kids reported periods of excessive use, and use reduction and cessation. Similar to other studies on drug use (e.g. Biernacki 1986; Boeri 2002; Esbensen & Elliot 1994; Hamil-Luker, Land & Blau 2004; Robins, Davis & Goodwin 1974; Shukla 2003; Waldorf, Reinarman & Murphy 1991) and club drug use in particular (Allaste & Lagerspetz 2002; Beck & Rosenbaum 1994; Hammersley, Khan & Ditton 2002; Hansen, Maycock & Lower 2001; Measham, Parker & Aldridge 2001; Ter Bogt et al. 2002), many life-course factors influenced their drug using behaviors. Life-course perspectives suggest that as people age, their increasing bonds to conventional society reduce their likelihood of engaging in illegal and illicit behaviors, including drug use (Benson 2002; Erickson & Cheung 1999; Esbensen & Elliot 1994; Moffit 1993; Sampson & Laub 1993; Thornberry 1987). Specifically, new family responsibilities (e.g. having a child) and new employment responsibilities act as 'transitions' in individual lives that could cause a 'turning point' where the individual refrains from illegal behaviors. Having meaningful social investments in family, work and/or school act as informal social control mechanisms that buffer involvement in illegal and illicit behaviors (Hirschi 1969; Gottfredson & Hirschi 1990; cf. Erickson & Cheung 1999; Murphy & Rosenbaum 1997; Sampson & Laub 1993; Waldorf, Reinarman & Murphy 1991).

Because individuals fear the risk of harming those social bonds and investments, they refrain from such behaviors.

The club kids experienced various transitions throughout their lives that caused them to reduce their use of drugs (see also Biernacki 1986; Decorte 2000; Esbensen & Elliot 1994; Hamil-Luker, Land & Blau 2004; Shukla 1993; Waldorf, Reinarman & Murphy 1991). As the club kids grew older, they took on more responsibilities and experienced their body's decline in durability. Consequently, many chose to cease, greatly limit or alter their drug use patterns to complete daily (e.g. school or occupational) tasks (Allaste & Lagerspetz 2002; Beck & Rosenbaum 1994; Hammersley, Khan & Ditton 2002; Hansen, Maycock & Lower 2001; Measham, Parker & Aldridge 2001; Shewan, Dalgarno & Reith 2000; Ter Bogt et al. 2002). For example, during Jack's third year of medical school and as a resident, he had fewer opportunities for leisure. His previous frequent use of ecstasy and ketamine (every weekend for two years) was forced to end, and his consumption of drugs was limited to special occasions. Jack explained:

> Yeah, we probably averaged E every week for almost two years... when I started third year, I was really behind the rest of my classmates... when I got into like small groups and I never knew the answers to any of the questions, I was like, 'Fuck, I should spend more time hitting the books', ya know? So I felt guilty going out after that, and I spent more time reading. ...I mean if there's a good night that I'm not on call and I'm not broke, I'll go. I probably won't do E anymore – well, I'll do one hit for sure, if I have a full day off of work the next day.

Jack included finances and personal responsibilities as factors to consider when deciding to use drugs and go to clubs (cf. Hansen, Maycock & Lower 2001; Levy et al. 2005). Betty also reduced her substance use when she faced financial strains, increased responsibility, and started a new job as a registered nurse.

> When I started living on my own and had bills to pay and couldn't afford to go out as much as I used to. ... I did get my [nursing] license and I started working...fulltime, in a job that I had to work every other weekend [this] stopped me from going out as much as used to. Because that's very big, ya know? As a nurse, you have to work weekends, every other weekend.

Additionally, the club kids' aging bodies and increased responsibilities impeded their ability to handle the day-after effects of using club drugs and partying all night (cf. Verheyden, Maidment & Curran 2003). For instance, Angelina, Mary and Lucille simply required their strength to work throughout the week.

> Angelina: Yo, you know what it is? It's the day after it's like...you're possessed by the devil.
> Mary: You can't go to sleep, it's like you need Xanaxes, like you need something to put you to sleep.
> Angelina: You can't eat for like a couple days after.
> Mary: Yeah, you got to re-teach yourself how to eat...

Angelina: I just think that physically you can't do it any longer.
Mary: I can't.
Lucille: You can't.
Angelina: It takes a toll on you. You have more responsibilities in your life. I used to be able to feel like shit on Monday and not really have that much on my plate to worry about. Now, I can't. If I know I'm going to feel like shit on Monday, I can't risk it.

David also attributed his reduction in the use of ecstasy to the effects of the following day.

Honestly, one of the reasons why I think we stopped going and getting fucked at all those clubs was because E ...MDMA, gets to you... basically you do E and the next day you wake up feeling like absolute shit, at least I do sometimes. And um, basically you feel depressed and you uh, you feel really thirsty and your whole muscular system might feel fucked up, kind of like you're about to get fucked or something like that...so I think that's part of the reason...

The 'following day' was cited as a main reason why many stopped using ecstasy regularly and, instead, consumed GHB. Unlike the day after a night's use of ecstasy, users claimed that GHB did not leave them depressed or exhausted. In fact, subsequent to a night's rest after using GHB, they claimed to be "refreshed" and "ready" for a new day. At Barroom, Estevez described this:

Estevez said that GHB puts you in deep REM sleep. He said, "When a person awakes from REM sleep that person feels 'refreshed' and 'ready to go'. When we take short naps, we tend not to feel refreshed because we didn't get deep within REM sleep." Estevez tends not to use ecstasy anymore, or at least uses it a lot less, because he said he could not handle the two days needed for recovery. 'G', on the other hand, has no recovery time. Once you sleep, you feel 'brand new' when you awake (Fieldnote, May 31, 2004).

Ralph also contrasted the after-effects of consuming GHB to alcohol:

It's [GHB] not like alcohol where you're gonna fuckin' get hung over, throw up, if you do too much ... Let's say I was gonna go out and do it tonight, .. ya know, do like a cap of G, get a little twisted [high from GHB], and hang out with a girl, whatever...then once all is said and done, it's one o'clock in the morning, you go to sleep, you sleep fuckin' nine-ten hours like you normally would- you'd wake up the next morning like nothing ever happened. It's not like alcohol. You won't be hung over or anything like that.

Many life-course factors provoked these users to reduce, alter and ultimately control their club drug use, demonstrating the relevancy of the aging-out effect among the club kids (Esbensen & Elliot 1994; Moffit 1993; Sampson & Laub 1993; Shover 1996; Snow 1973; Winick 1962). As the sample aged, many experienced an increase in work and financial responsibilities, and discussed their bodies decreasing ability to manage going out all night and using club drugs.

Discussion

The club kids were predominantly white, well-educated and gainfully employed. Most came from middle and upper class communities, conforming to national portraits of club drug users and club attendees as revealed in epidemiological studies[4] (Johnston et al. 2005; NSDUH 2005; Pulse Check 2004; Yacoubian et al. 2003). Drug use and clubbing played a significant role in the lives of club kids. While many portrayed it as merely something they did for fun, drug use and clubbing were highly valued, significant aspects of their identities, shaping both their peer group affiliation and marriage aspirations.

The trusted relationships created within their peer groups encouraged the sample to share information on proper methods of club drug use, their general effects and how to address and avoid negative reactions (Beck & Rosenbaum 1994; Becker 1963; Grund 1993; Hammersley, Khan & Ditton 2002; Hansen, Maycock & Lower 2001; Kelly this volume; Measham, Parker & Aldridge 2001; Sherlock & Conner 1999; Southgate & Hopwood 2001; Zinberg 1984). Ultimately, these relationships fostered strong bonds and the desire to care for one another, especially while under the influence of club drugs. Many of the club kids were also socially, culturally, and financially 'embedded' within conventional society, which in many ways insulated them from harmful consequences associated with their club drug use (cf. Allaste & Lagerspetz 2002; Lenton & Davidson 1999; Murphy & Rosenbaum 1997; Panagopoulos & Ricciardelli 2005; Reinarman & Levine 1997; Ter Bogt et al. 2002). For example, several of the club kids were in the medical profession, had post-graduate careers and/or had access to various sources of information on club drugs. Throughout the club kids' life-trajectories, various factors, such as responsibilities and employment obligations, increased this 'embeddedness', which further helped regulate their club drug usage.

Many club kids disapproved of 'overusing' club drugs and refrained from excessive use (Forsyth 1996; Hammersley, Khan & Ditton 2002; Hansen, Maycock & Lower 2001; Measham, Parker & Aldridge 2001; van de Wijngaart et al. 1999). Most did not consume club drugs daily, and they occasionally reduced and/or completely ceased use without treatment. During such periods, the club kids did not physically desire club drugs. In general, these users were able to minimize the harms associated with their use of club drugs (Allaste & Lagerspetz 2002; Brewer 2003; Decorte 2000, 2001a, 2001b; Hamil-Luker, Land & Blau 2004; Panagopoulos & Ricciardelli 2005; Riley & Hayward 2004; Shewan, Dalgarno & Reith 2000; Southgate & Hopwood 2001; Ter Bogt et al. 2002). As such, addiction and dependence did not appear to be applicable to this population of users (see Davies 1992).

---

4   Recent studies have shown that club drug use is increasingly prevalent among other populations (e.g. Fendich et al. 2003; Krebs & Steffey 2005; Martins, Mazzotti & Chilcoat 2005; Maxwell & Spence 2005; Novoa et al. 2005; Ompad et al. 2005), and among those outside of dance club culture (e.g. Community Epidemiology Group (CEWG) 2003; Fendrich et al. 2003; Krebs & Steffey 2005; Lankenau & Clatts 2005; Maxwell & Spence 2005; Novoa et al. 2005; Ompad et al. 2005).

Much like users of legal and acceptable substances, the club kids occasionally viewed their use of club drugs as strategic and necessary for adjusting mood, increasing alertness and helping them focus. While plenty of research has been conducted on factors associated with addiction and dependence, few studies have sought to understand those factors that protect users from such conditions (cf. Hammersley & Reid 2002), permit controlled drug use (Grund 1993; Zinberg 1984), or shape individual desistance from club drug use (Biernacki 1986; Waldorf, Reinarman & Murphy 1991).

While the club kids sought to minimize harms associated with their use, a few reported periods of excess use and some ironies resonated within the data. For example, while Angelina said, "We don't go on binges", she also described a few months when she excessively and repeatedly consumed cocaine. Additionally, despite Gary's 'folk knowledge' on GHB, he was arrested, passed-out and awoke in a hospital as a result of overdosing on the drug. These incidents as well as staying awake for days, not being able to eat, and losing large amounts of weight in a short period of time are unhealthy behaviors that cannot be ignored. While controlled club drug use did occur, these other patterns of use and their harmful side-effects suggest that the sample tended to ignore their own advice.

The data, in part, demonstrate that media reports of club drug users as irresponsible and destructive members of society are not entirely accurate, and that, perhaps, there exists a more responsible side to club drug users than such depictions indicate. Encouraging responsible club drug use is an important public health concern. However, policing tactics of club drug users and the spaces where club drugs are used have been employed to eradicate use. Such policies could harm the social networks created by club drug users, which can ultimately hinder access to information regarding controlled and 'safe' club drug use. In addition, implementing an abstinence-only policy is limiting and impractical, and it prevents research on the positive as well as the negative effects of drug use (Leavitt 2003; Selzer 1997). Consequently, incomplete, inaccurate, and distrusted information by drug users is available, and such information rarely indicates the steps a user could take to prevent harms and engage in safe substance use (see Leavitt 2003). Harm reduction policies are additional viable strategies to addressing club drug use, which can only be effective if we: 1) understand the connections between the effects of club drugs and patterns of their use, (2) research the beneficial and harmful club drug effects, and (3) study both the triggers and protective factors of harm associated with the use of drugs. Perhaps with such information, club drug users in general can take steps to monitor, reduce and ultimately control their drug use.

Chapter 4

Conceptions of Risk in the Lives of Ecstasy-Using Youth[1]

Brian C. Kelly

As the lighting scheme shifted from staccato bursts of colors to the steady glow of blacklight, I spied Tony dancing rhythmically in the middle of the floor to the pulsing sound of house beats. I waded through the crowd of gesticulating bodies to catch up with him and see how the night had treated him to this point. Having noticed me snaking through the crowd, Tony grinned and pointed at me as I made my way over while he continued to dance. After greeting each other and exchanging the normal pleasantries, I asked him how the night was going for him. He told me that his "roll" was wearing off and he needed to take another half pill of ecstasy. "Why a half pill?", I asked, somewhat confused. He replied, "Moderation brother, moderation. I got to take care of my brain." I asked him what he meant, still somewhat confused since generally my own idea of taking care of my brain would preclude ecstasy consumption. After he paused with a stylish dance move, he explained that he wanted to achieve his "roll" – the high derived from ecstasy use – with as little ecstasy as possible because he asserted that the degree of brain damage is dependent upon quantity consumed. – Fieldnote, November 2003.

People impart different meanings upon various drugs depending upon how they understand and make sense of these drugs in their lives (cf. Agar 1985). The meanings associated with ecstasy use, for instance, vary as much as the effects of the drug. Ecstasy has been labeled as both a "hug drug" and a dangerous poison (Saunders & Doblin 1996). The way in which youth impart meaning on ecstasy shapes their understandings of its risks. Thus, to better understand the role of ecstasy amongst youth, ascertaining how they understand the risks of ecstasy use in the context of their own lives is important.

Risk is comprised of two key elements: objective determinants (i.e. the probability of a negative outcome given a certain action within a given context); and subjective determinants (i.e. the perceived or felt threat of danger given a certain action; see Luhmann 1993). Both elements are dependent upon the confluence of certain social processes and dialectically influence one another. For example, objective

1   I would like to acknowledge the National Institute on Drug Abuse for their generous support of this project (Grant # R03-DA016171). I would like to thank Peyton Mason and Marisa Ramjohn for their research assistance. Jennifer Foray, Kim Hopper, Steve Lankenau, and Dan Mauk provided helpful comments on the chapter. Lastly, I would like to thank the youth who volunteered for this study and shared their lives with me.

determinants of risk may vary across individuals depending upon biological factors, such as metabolic rate, as well as social factors, such as socioeconomic status and cultural influences. Subjective determinants of risk are grounded within a cultural framework accrued as a byproduct of experience within a given social milieu (Douglas 1992). Risk assessment is not simply a rational calculus of danger occurring in a psychological vacuum, but is dependent upon systems of belief and systems of value that shape how dangers are perceived. Thus, the perception of risk is generated through social processes influenced by cultural frameworks. Broader social, political, economic, and cultural forces have influences at local levels, forming a context that shapes both objective dangers and subjective conceptions of danger (Douglas 1992).

Within a given society, different sectors of the population have different models of understanding the same phenomena, where subtle differences may stem not only from the local inflections of culture, but from the different perspectives individuals cultivate through experiencing society from specific positions (see Berger and Luckmann 1966). These models can be loosely divided into two types: professional and folk models. "Professional models" are those which enjoy privileged status in a society; they are endowed with authority and offer official interpretations of a given practice (Agar 1985). In this instance, professionals are scientists, public health experts, and politicians. Alternatively, "folk models" arise popularly through the everyday practices of people in society (Agar 1985).

General risk data suggests that risk perception can significantly influence youth to use or not use drugs (e.g. Derzon & Lipsey 1999). However, exploring how youth who do use drugs conceive of the risks is important. The above field note provides a brief illustration of how conceptions of risk shape the patterns and practices of ecstasy use among youth. This paper describes local conceptions of risk that inform current patterns and practices of ecstasy use among youth. First, a review of the professional literature on the risks associated with ecstasy use is offered. Next, based on fieldwork data, a descriptive profile of how ecstasy-using youth conceive of risk is presented. These folk models of risk are compared with professional models. Finally the recognition of the relationship between folk and professional models is explored, which might enable health promotion efforts targeting youth.

Methods

This research employed ethnographic methods to collect data on ecstasy drug use among 'Bridge and Tunnel' youth in the New York City metropolitan area. Bridge and Tunnel is local vernacular for youth who 'hang out' or 'party' in Manhattan, but who reside in suburban neighborhoods surrounding New York City. Involved in multiple social worlds, these youth provide a window from which to examine the patterns of club drug use in both urban and suburban locales.

The prospect of data collection from a population without roots in the region of study poses numerous challenges. Manhattan has an enormous club scene, larger than most other cities in the world. A key challenge consisted of creating a social map to identify the venues in which Bridge and Tunnel youth regularly 'hang out.' On various nights of the week over a six week period, exploratory fieldwork and 'intercept' interviews were conducted with suburban youth at major points of entry in Midtown Manhattan, such as Penn Station and Grand Central Station. The commuter rail lines and suburban bus routes dropped suburban youth off at these locations. As these youth came off the trains, I approached them and asked for their consent to a quick survey. I administered a brief, structured interview, which consisted of determining their age, county of residence, preferred music genre, and the locations in which they prefer to socialize in Manhattan. In addition, I conducted informal interviews with some youth at these sites by chatting with them about why they like certain venues. I also conducted informal interviews about club drugs at environments where Bridge and Tunnel youth socialized.

The first two months of field observations, which overlapped with the intercept interview period, focused upon defining five key venues for extended participant-observation research and recruitment for an in-depth interview cohort. Ultimately, a total of 18 months were spent conducting ethnographic fieldwork at clubs and raves. This fieldwork primarily consisted of the time-honored ethnographic tradition of 'hanging out' and learning through direct observations. I listened to the music, danced, befriended a few people, got 'dissed' by others, and, most importantly, learned about the cultural context of club drug use. I partook in the experiences of club-going youth, but at the same time never became one of them or fully part of their subculture. All fieldwork resulted in descriptive documentation in fieldnotes, which were written as soon as possible after the event.

Respondents were recruited from five designated venues for inclusion into an in-depth interview cohort. This cohort consisted of youth recruited at the designated venues and did not include youth from the social mapping sample. Inclusion criteria for men and women recruited for in-depth interviews was as follows: a) aged between 18 and 25; b) reported the use of one of four club drugs within the previous year; c) lived in a suburban county outside New York accessible by public transport; and d) expressed a willingness to consent to participation. Respondents participated in one to four audio-taped interviews, which lasted between 1 and 2.5 hours, and were transcribed verbatim.[2]

The interviews consisted of open-ended questions designed to gain an 'insider's' perspective on a range of salient issues pertinent to ecstasy use (cf. Geertz 1983; Merton 1972). Amongst others, a series of topical modules included: a) initiation into club drug use; b) current practices and patterns of use; and c) conceptions of risk. Ethnographic interview techniques, such as critical incident measures, as well as analytic contrasts, were employed to gather detail-rich data with reduced recall

---

2   Informed consent was obtained from all respondents for the in-depth interviews as per the approved Institutional Review Board protocol. The study operated under a Federal Certificate of Confidentiality to ensure protection of sensitive data elicited from respondents. All names and places within this chapter are pseudonyms.

bias (Leonard & Ross 1997). Initial interviews occurred at a time and location agreed upon with the respondent, often in the suburbs. Follow-up interviews occurred at least two weeks after the first interview in order to allow respondents time to contemplate issues raised. This also allowed the investigator time to initially interpret the data, so as to direct follow-up interviews. A thematic analysis of the data was employed to ascertain the coinciding conceptions of risk among these youth. The quotations in the paper provide descriptive evidence of these thematic patterns across the interviews, and represent general sentiments expressed by many youth, not simply unique perspectives. All quotations are derived from taped in-depth interviews, except where noted.

The data for this investigation was drawn primarily from interviews with 40 Bridge and Tunnel youth hailing from New Jersey, Long Island, and the Mid-Hudson suburbs of New York City. They ranged in age from 18 to 25, with an average age of 21 years. They had an average monthly income of $1,800, with a range of $600 to $4,000 from a variety of jobs, such as part-time florist, selling drugs, and marketing analyst for a multi-national corporation. As a group, they were well educated: most were either currently enrolled in college or already completed. The cohort consisted of 28 White youth, 7 Latino youth, 3 Asian youth, and 2 youth of "mixed" race.[3]

Ecstasy was the primary club drug utilized by these youth, which supports existing prevalence data (SAMHSA 2003; Johnston et al. 2005). Each member of the cohort had used ecstasy during the course of their lives. The number of ecstasy pills consumed amongst the sample within the last year ranged from 1 to 60 with an average of 13. Ketamine had been used to a lesser degree amongst this group, though was still prevalent. Methamphetamine and GHB had been used by very few participants. These youth were also regular abusers of prescription drugs. The most common prescription drugs were Vicodin, Codeine, Xanax, Ritalin, and Adderall. Thus, a wide range of prescription drugs were abused among these club goers rather than a specific type (cf. Sanders et al. 2005). Other drugs used included marijuana, cocaine, LSD, PCP, mushrooms, and tryptamines (e.g. 5-MEO-DiPT ('foxy') & AMT). Ecstasy resonated most in the lives of these Bridge and Tunnel youth, and for this reason the focus of this chapter is on conceptions of risk related to ecstasy use.

This small study is based upon regionally specific youth, and does not make broad claims. Importantly, the sample was well-educated. These youth were uniquely primed to seek ecstasy related knowledge, as their college education provided unique resources to these youth. For example, some of these youth accessed on-line public health journals through university subscriptions – opportunities unavailable to those not enrolled in college. The pursuit of ecstasy related knowledge, as well as the ability and tendency to pursue such knowledge, may differ amongst less

---

3   These youth self-identified with a variety of racial and ethnic identifiers. For the sake of brevity, they have been subsumed under specific identifiers. For example, "Latino" included youth who identified as Latino, Hispanic, and Latin American. "White" includes youth who identified as European, white, and Caucasian.

Drugs, Clubs and Young People

affluent youth or those with fewer resources. Another limitation is that the sample was primarily white, with some Latino and Asian youth. Folk assessments of risk pertaining to ecstasy risk may differ within African-American and other ethnic minority communities (Ompad et al. 2005).

Professional Models of Risk and Ecstasy Use

One of the problems of properly identifying the professional models of risk associated with ecstasy use is the unclear nature of what exactly constitutes an ecstasy dosage. Ecstasy has generally been considered MDMA, but whether or not what is sold as ecstasy contains MDMA is ultimately uncertain. For instance, the harm reduction organization *DanceSafe* has regularly revealed the presence of adulterants in pills sold as ecstasy.[4] An analysis of 123 pills from NY tested since September 1, 1999 revealed that 54 (44%) contained only MDMA, and slightly more, 56 (45%), contained no MDMA at all. The others (11%) contained a combination of MDMA and other substances. Other substances found in 56% of the pills included methamphetamine, dextromethorphan, amitriptiline, fluoxetine, codeine, diazepam, lidocaine, and acetaminophen, among others. Nonetheless, professional models have illustrated numerous negative effects of MDMA usage, which are also generally considered to be the negative effects of ecstasy use. These include neurotoxicity, depressive disorders, hyperthermia, thoracic organ damage, serotonin syndrome, dependence, and sexual risks associated with ecstasy use. Below, each is examined in turn.

Neurotoxicity

Neurotoxicity, both acute and long-term, remains a primary concern of scientists and public health experts. In terms of MDMA use, no universal definition of what comprises neurotoxicity exists; it may comprise anything related to toxic effects on the brain from serotonin depletion briefly following MDMA consumption to long-term cognitive impairment (Baggott & Mendelson 2001). Neurotoxicity could arise in several ways, from reductions in cerebral blood flow (Chang et al. 2000), the alteration of axons in the brain due to oxidative stress (Jayathi et al. 1999; Shankaran 1999), or other serotonergic changes in the brain. Acute neurotoxic effects include memory loss and short-term cognitive impairment in the days following the use of MDMA (Parrott & Lasky 1998). Long-term neurotoxic effects of MDMA potentially include impaired memory, impulsivity, alteration of mood, and other cognitive impairments (Morgan 1998). Some animal studies suggest that neurotoxicity is dose-related, with neurotoxic effects correlating with consumption, indicating that binges of ecstasy use pose greater risk of neurotoxicity (O'Shea et al. 1998). Carlson et al. (2004) reported that consumption level appears to have an effect on the report of adverse consequences; those who consumed greater amounts of ecstasy reported

---

4   For more information on Dance Safe's pill testing program, visit to www.dancesafe. org or www.ecstasydata.org.

long-term adverse consequences higher rates. Whether some long-term effects of MDMA use surface only with aging, however, remains unclear. Prospective clinical studies on MDMA use amongst humans have not been conducted, and much remains uncertain about the neurotoxicity of MDMA. Thus, the neurotoxicity ramifications are not yet fully understood.

Depressive disorders

The potential for depressive disorders is related to neurotoxicity via the possibility of permanent alteration of the serotonin system, which helps regulate mood and psychological well-being. An acute period of depression in the days following ecstasy consumption has been well-documented, and is thought to relate to the process of restoration of the serotonin system after its disruption by the induced flooding of serotonin during the ecstasy experience (Curran & Travill 1997). However, we cannot yet determine the potential inducement of long-term depression given the inability to distinguish between pre-morbid or latent depression and ecstasy-induced depression through retrospective assessments. Further research on links between ecstasy use and depressive disorders is necessary.

Hyperthermia

MDMA may contribute to hyperthermia, when core body temperatures rise above the optimal temperature of 98.6° to anywhere from 102° to 109°. The human body cannot sustain metabolic and cardiovascular activity under hyperthermic conditions (Henry & Rella 2001). At these high temperatures, a number of negative medical outcomes – muscle breakdown, kidney and liver failure, cerebral edema, and even death – may occur. Yet, much of the cause for concern stems from the use of ecstasy under specific conditions rather than simply use of the drug (Henry 1992). The fear is that youth may use ecstasy and concurrently engage in extended periods of physical exertion through dancing in locations with high temperatures. Raves or other dance events can carry on for extended periods of time. Given the connection of ecstasy to electronic dance subcultures, hyperthermia may indeed be the most significant health challenge for such youth.

Thoracic Organ Damage

Like other amphetamine-based substances, ecstasy use raises blood pressure and heart rate and may enable complications related to tachycardia, cardiac arrhythmias, and other heart related problems (Mas et al. 1999). Though it remains unclear whether MDMA use can trigger adverse cardiac-related outcomes in otherwise healthy adults, the symptoms of high blood pressure and increased heart rate may enable negative health outcomes for those with pre-existing cardiac conditions. The effects of ecstasy on hepatic functioning also warrant further investigation. Clinical cases of liver toxicity have also been found (Henry et al. 1992). Some doctors have even expressed concern over the potential for ecstasy-induced hepatitis (Hwang et al. 2002).

Serotonin Syndrome

Serotonin syndrome is a rare complication resulting from the use of a serotonergic agent such as ecstasy (Sternbach, 1991). The use of ecstasy with MAO Inhibitors may contribute to this syndrome, manifesting in tremors, shivers, confusion, muscle spasms, and poorly regulated heart rate and blood pressure. These symptoms may lead to death (Mueller & Korey, 1998).

Dependence

A common concern with all drugs is the potential for dependence; MDMA could be no different. Though physiological dependence and physical withdrawal symptoms do not appear to occur with ecstasy use, the habitual daily use of ecstasy has been reported in some case studies of ecstasy dependence (Jansen, 1998). Thus, individuals may potentially develop psychological dependence upon ecstasy. Indeed, some ecstasy users have self-reported feelings of dependence on the drug, though the prevalence appears to be low (Solowij et al. 1992).

Sexual Risk Taking

Youth may potentially engage in risky sexual behavior under the influence of ecstasy. Studies have shown the effects of many intoxicating substances on sexual risk taking (Temple et al. 1993; Frosch et al. 1996). MDMA has been reported as a sensual rather than a sexual drug (Buffum 1986; Beck & Rosenbaum 1994). The use of MDMA has been noted to increase empathy with others, contributing to a heightened sense of intimacy, as well as a reported reduction in ability to achieve orgasm (see Topp et al. 1999). Yet, Topp et al. (1999) reported that although roughly half of their cohort of ecstasy-using youth claimed that the use of ecstasy inhibits orgasm, 70% claimed that it improved sex. Among the same population, condom use with casual partners occurred less frequently while individuals were under the influence of ecstasy (Topp et al. 1999). Clinical evaluations of MDMA use and its effect on sexuality also suggest that users report increases in sexual desire and sexual satisfaction (Zemishlany et al. 2001). Data also suggest increased impulsivity associated with the use of MDMA, which may enable riskier behaviors to occur 'in the heat of the moment' (Morgan 1998).

Folk Models of Risk and Ecstasy Use

Public health professionals have little certainty about the dangers associated with ecstasy consumption, having more theories and assumptions rather than actual proof. The scientific foundations of knowledge, no doubt, are crucial aspects of the manner in which we proceed in a variety of areas, from prevention to intervention to public policy. However, also key to the appropriate development of interventions are the folk models of risk (Agar 1985; Friedman et al. 2004). Investigating the question, "How do ecstasy using youth conceive of the risks and what do these risks mean to them?" is imperative. In contrast to the clinical basis of professional models of risk, folk models of risk are experientially based, framed in ways that youth can and do experience them (Agar 1985; Douglas 1992). Though many areas of consistency between professional and folk models exist, the youth discussed these risks as phenomenological realities rather than clinical incidents. The following are accounts of how Bridge and Tunnel youth conceived of ecstasy risks and accounted for these risks in their lives.

Dehydration/Overheating

The potential harms of dehydration and overheating were the most common concerns among ecstasy-using youth. Many spoke of these potential dangers as significantly serious, potentially mortal, and not simply akin to dehydration associated with binge drinking. They spoke specifically of the potential to 'pass out', often attributed to a combination of ecstasy consumption, overexertion, hot atmosphere, and not re-hydrating, concerns that echo those of the professionals. While conducting fieldwork at a rave during the summer of 2003, I witnessed the level of concern for these risks among youth. Midway through the evening, the venue shut off the cold water in the bathrooms, so as to prevent patrons from refilling their bottles. Later on in the evening, as I talked with some young women, we broached the subject in conversation. I mentioned that I wished I could fill my bottle at the tap in the bathroom. Immediately, one of the girls said to me,

> Oh my God, did you know that they shut the cold water off on us? That's so fucked up, isn't it? People could die.

During the next several months, I met other youth who attended the same rave. Often, when that rave came up in conversation, they mentioned the lack of accessible water and the potential for overheating. They similarly expressed concern that 'someone could have gotten hurt.' For instance, Jane said,

> Remember when they turned off the water? They're like, 'No drinking here kids. Go buy your bottle of water.' This is nuts; they shouldn't. I think they should have *more* sinks, so that we could actually drink water. Because, you know, people who don't have money they need water, because they can't go without water.

Unfortunately, this was not the only instance of unscrupulous venue owners who put dancers at risk for the sake of profit. After discussing this incident, Ed recounted an occasion when the heat was turned on during a summertime event, purportedly to increase water sales. He said:

I was at one of the clubs and they turned the heaters on in the middle of July just so people would buy more water because they were getting hotter. It was at Club Zero in 2001. They blasted the heaters in the main room. There was a good 1,000 people in there or something like that. You couldn't even stand there without 'dying.' I stood right next to it. It looks like an AC unit, but you brush up against it and it would be blazing hot. Like, there was no question about it, they put on the heaters. You can only assume the only reason they'd do that is to make you hotter so you would buy more water. The whole bar was filled with people getting water.

The practice of attempting to increase water sales by either shutting off the bathroom taps or turning up the heat is by no means standard in the club industry. However, it occurs frequently enough that several youth raised the subject without prompting. This perhaps illustrates one of a variety of ways that the ambient temperatures in these settings, when combined with ecstasy consumption, can potentially lead to overheating among youth.

Memory Loss, "Burned Brains", and Feeling "Cracked Out"

Youth spoke of 'neurotoxicity' in a variety of ways without using the clinical language of neurotoxicity. Instead, they spoke of memory loss and other impairment using expressions, such as "burning your brain" or feeling "cracked out." They addressed the possibility of both acute and long-term effects, suggesting a concern not only with present dangers, but with the potential that their use of ecstasy may 'catch up' with them in the future.

Widely held perceptions of the adverse consequences of ecstasy use were short-term impaired cognitive capacities. Many youth felt their ability to think was atypical the day following ecstasy consumption. For instance, Vicky said:

I just feel really cracked out. I just feel like I'm just useless the next day.

The impairment of feeling "cracked out" was generally of short duration, lasting for a day or two following the consumption of ecstasy. This impairment was often experienced as something more than simply a hangover, but rather as a cognitive fog as noted by Luis:

It's just messing your brain up completely. Sometimes if I go to work the next day, I can't function. You're like a zombie.

The duration of the "cracked out" feeling was short, but the qualitative nature of the impairment is significant. Youth were often able to go through their daily routines, but could not function at their usual level.

Youth were also concerned about the potential long-term neurotoxic ramifications of ecstasy use. Jane talked about the possibility of "burning" her brain through the use of ecstasy, but didn't perceive it to be a problem in her own life. She did not see a "burned brain" to be the inevitable result of ecstasy use. Others felt similarly. As noted earlier, Mike also talked about the possibility of memory loss because of the consumption of ecstasy. However, as was common among these youth, he framed his comments in a discourse of excessive consumption. Mike has been using ecstasy for six years. Though he mentioned brief cognitive problems in the days after taking ecstasy, as far as his own experiences were concerned, Mike noted, "Long-term, no, I really don't think [ecstasy] affected me in that way." More generally, the concern over a burned brain was often tempered by the perception that only excessive ecstasy use triggered damage. The dangers associated with infrequent use thus posed few concerns for these youth.

Depression

Depression is another risk widely perceived by youth who used ecstasy. Like the concern about neurotoxic effects leading to "burned brains" and feeling "cracked out", youth expressed concern both for the acute depressive episodes that followed in the wake of ecstasy consumption, as well as the potential long-term depression that could ensue following regular consumption of ecstasy. Some youth experienced a period of acute depression in the hours and days that followed the ecstasy high – a "post-E depression" as characterized by some. George said that this can last, "anywhere from a couple of hours to a couple of days." Later in the interview, George discussed his experiences with post-E depression, which highlights the unpredictable nature of this phenomenon. He noted:

> Sometimes you feel like shit the next day. Like, you get like depressed for no reason. Usually, if I take it at a party and I dance a lot, I find that afterwards, the next day, I'm just completely fine, like I can just get over it. Sometimes it has a really bad comedown though. Like, if I'm coming down after a party, if I'm going home, everything's quiet, you know, I just start thinking. And I don't even know why, I'm just depressed for no good reason and that's definitely bad.

By using ecstasy, George chances the bout of acute depression "for no good reason." The post-E depression seems to be somewhat unpredictable; not all ecstasy-using youth experienced it. Post-E depression also varied in intensity and duration. Some youth experienced this depression more frequently than George, others far less, and some not at all. For George, post-E depression, though usually not a problem remained an acceptable risk.

Some youth also concerned themselves with the risk of long-term depression. Mary, for instance, spoke of potential long-term ramifications related to depression by couching her understandings of the serotonin system. Mary expressed particular concern for those with a predisposition towards depression, a sentiment echoed by others. She said:

> Your serotonin level is definitely altered afterwards. They say it takes two weeks to get it back to its original status and even then your serotonin level will never be at the original status. You'll never get back to where you were originally. I feel that especially if you

have a lot of insecurities and you get down a lot, you know, really pessimistic, then it's not something you should be doing.

Addiction and Loss of Control

Some youth saw the potential for addiction with ecstasy, though they generally did not view it as physically addictive. Will characterized a set of actions involving ecstasy as addictive, but not the actual drug itself.

> I think maybe that whole lifestyle, it's kind of addicting. Some people, that's the only thing they can think about all day is just going to the clubs and doing drugs. It seems like a lot of people are really addicted to it. I guess maybe they're both kind of like a couple [drugs and clubs], almost like they're one thing. One really doesn't go without the other. It's kind of like you need both of them.

Will asserted that people do not get addicted to ecstasy, but rather the clubbing 'lifestyle'. Interestingly enough, Will also noted that clubs were not necessarily part of the equation of addicting experiences, as he and many of his friends initiated ecstasy use at house parties during high school, which was still a common pattern of use among his friends.

Other youth framed the risk of losing control in terms of shedding inhibitions and making impulsive decisions. As Eddie noted:

> What I would take as risky might not be dangerously obvious, for instance, persons that don't really have control. You know, a lot of people take drugs to sort of lose their inhibitions, but if they lose it totally, they could get hurt.

Adulterated Pills

Many youth felt a common risk they took when consuming ecstasy was the danger of using adulterated pills, which often contain more substances than simply MDMA (or even no MDMA at all). As Tony remarked, "It could be not what you're buying at all. Like, it's filth and you have no idea." Many youth echoed these concerns that they are being given something other than MDMA. They seemed to find this particularly disconcerting because this thwarted their efforts to cultivate knowledge about MDMA risk.

Jane related a story of a friend who thought he bought a couple of hits of ecstasy only to find out they were "speed, some sort of amphetamines" upon receiving news of his toxicology report at the hospital after an adverse event related to the drugs. Though, among this group, this was the only narrative of an acquaintance experiencing a negative outcome because of adulterated pills. Nonetheless, most youth had "heard stories" about adulterated pills. Indeed, as mentioned earlier, pill-testing programs often find drugs others than MDMA contained in tablets sold as ecstasy.

Pleasure and Danger Related to Ecstasy Use amongst Youth

The risks of ecstasy use resonated with most youth in that they perceived they were doing something with potentially harmful. Youth were often acutely aware of the dangers associated with ecstasy use because of their attempts to accumulate knowledge on the subject. For instance, Jane, when asked if there was anything bad about taking ecstasy, laughed and said:

> Uhhh, drugs are not good for you! It hurts you. It's terribly stupid…most drugs are not good for you.

Aside from the knowledge accumulated from drug education sessions in high school and health classes in college, many youth cultivated knowledge about ecstasy through a variety of sources, particularly the Internet. They used websites from health education organizations, self-developed websites, and on-line public health journals. These youth also discussed the subject of club drug use and the associated dangers within their social networks. For instance, message boards and chat rooms provided forums for discussing the harms associated with ecstasy and other club drugs. Jane elaborated of her perspective on the dangers of ecstasy:

> OK, whenever I think of it [ecstasy], I know I'm ruining my body. I'm killing my brain. I think about it, like, eventually I'm going to die anyway, so enjoy life. This is one way to enjoy it. So, take all the good stuff and keep in mind the bad stuff. Don't forget about them. Never ignore them, but know what you're doing. Always be prepared. I guess by the age of 30 there will be some retards, maybe, you know, have some side effects. I read they did research on monkeys with ecstasy and it made the monkeys have some sort of imbalance in their brains. So, OK, nothing's perfect. You have to accept that fact to enjoy something. I eat candy, you know. When you overeat, you become fat. If you eat them in normal portions, OK, so you get pimples. But nothing is good with too much, you know.

Jane spoke of keeping in mind the potential harms associated with ecstasy use. The expectation is to remember the dangers of ecstasy, "never ignore them." This knowledge enabled preparation for the use of the drug. Though the level of knowledge varied within this population, to "know what you're doing" was important among these youth, and was impressed upon others within their social networks, not for the purposes of popularity, but of health concern. Some youth likened it to 'doing your homework' before taking drugs. Despite their awareness of the dangers associated with ecstasy use, some youth valued the drug's effects. This type of payoff is part of the reason why youth take risks with ecstasy despite being aware of its potential dangers. For instance, Andrew said:

> It's the feelings of expression, the connections, and general well-being. When you take the pill, it's not the drug. E makes you open up. You're connected to everyone. I guess in a way, it's like a little bit of heaven.

Networks and the Social Nature of Risk

Social networks were a primary vehicle by which these youth gauge the likelihood of danger associated with using ecstasy (cf. Bauman and Ennett 1996; Friedman and Aral 2001; Latkin et al 2003). Youth used ecstasy, at least partly, because of their assessments of the low probability of danger, which may or may not be accurate. Vicky described this process in response to a query about why she uses ecstasy despite potentially hazardous outcomes:

> I always think about, you know, 'Wow this person did it this many times and he's still fine and he's still walking.' That's how I look at it. I know it's bad, but I know a lot of people who have done a lot and like major amounts and they're still walking today. Nothing ever happened to them, you know.

Mike discussed something similar:

> You can get in serious trouble or die, I guess, theoretically with every drug. I don't really know with ecstasy really. Long-term heavy usage eats away at your brain. It takes away from your memory and stuff like that, but that's something I really don't know the odds of.

Though most in the sample had all "heard stories," they generally did not know people who had experienced ecstasy-related negative health outcomes. The exceptions were acute episodes of short-term depression after ecstasy use, which some described as "terrible Tuesdays." These youth may have heard little of traumatic outcomes because such outcomes related to ecstasy are rare. For instance, of 19,366 autopsies conducted in NYC from 1997-2000 on decedents with "unexpected" or "suspicious" deaths, only two were directly caused by MDMA (Gill et al. 2002).

Discussion

The pervasive assumption that youth engage in dangerous behaviors because of a lack of knowledge permeates the fields of public health, from drinking to sexual behavior to drug use, which dates back to the days when youth were considered incomplete adults (Moran 2000). As Dr. Leshner, the former director of the National Institute on Drug Abuse, once remarked, club drug "users may think these substances are harmless", thus suggesting that youth accept the risks associated with club drug use because they 'do not know any better' or they 'just don't get it'.[5] This may stem, in part, from an underestimation of the capabilities of youth, but also in part to the professional treatment of risk. In certain respects, public health professionals may privilege danger when assessing risk. The nature of our jobs – to protect the public from illness – precipitates this focus on danger. Yet, discussions of risk that focus

---

5   This quote comes from Dr. Leshner's article "Club Drugs are Not 'Fun Drugs'", accessible at www.drugabuse.gov/PublishedArticles/fundrugs.html.

exclusively on danger obscure the potential for rational decision making in the face of such danger.

In practice, risk assessment proceeds with attentiveness to danger, though how seasoned that attentiveness is varies. This manuscript has attempted to illustrate that youth do not see ecstasy use as a danger-free enterprise. Public health messages that assume otherwise will not engage these youth. Youth view risk as a two-sided proposition: danger with some sort of potential payoff, such as pleasure or connectivity. These dangers are possible – not certain or perhaps not even probable – and these youth recognized them as such when they made risk assessments regarding their consumption of ecstasy. Youth conceptions of risks associated with ecstasy use often paralleled the professional models of risk associated with the drug. The young people weighed risks involving ecstasy use based upon a knowledge base cultivated about the dangers of this drug alongside the potential payoffs and practiced ecstasy use accordingly.

In a number of areas, youth expressed the same concerns as public health professionals regarding the risks of ecstasy use, though youth models were filtered down into an experiential understanding. Both the professionals and these youth have discussed depression, neurotoxicity ("burned brains"), addiction, and hyperthermia (overheating and dehydration) in relation to ecstasy use. Areas of dissonance also emerged. Other harms mentioned by professionals, such as serotonin syndrome or heart problems, did not enter the youth's discourse of risk, perhaps because such conditions are exceedingly rare, and the youth did not encounter others having experienced such problems. Since I conducted these interviews with general open-ended questions about the risks of ecstasy use rather than listing specific risks for them to identify with, it remains uncertain to what extent these youth were aware of these possible dangers or, alternatively, simply did not find them plausible dangers in their own lives.

Far from being oblivious to the potential harms, these youth were aware of the dangers of using ecstasy. This recognition of harm stemmed from a general sentiment of the importance of cultivating knowledge about ecstasy related harms. Furthermore, youth appeared to cultivate this knowledge base not for social currency, but as a necessary component for the preservation of their health. They weighed risks based upon knowledge cultivated about ecstasy alongside that of the potential payoffs, and practiced ecstasy use accordingly. Knowledge acquisition played a key role in the development of these conceptions of risk, and acquiring this knowledge was the foundational practice of risk management. As Tony noted:

> You're not supposed to be on drugs, but the smartest thing you can do while you're on drugs is research about it. Know what you should be doing. Know what you shouldn't be doing.

Research on the substances while the user is "on drugs" ultimately provided the basis for putting risk management strategies into practice. This practice was about "know(ing) what you should be doing" – translating knowledge and conceptions of risk into practice. Knowledge provided youth with the opportunity to strategize ecstasy taking, so as to manage the potential dangers.

The fundamental purpose of exploring the conceptions of risk among ecstasy using youth was to understand the informal logic surrounding such use. Youth collectively translated their concerns about risks into strategic practices aimed at minimizing these risks. They depended on a model of risk that was context dependent, and they assessed the likelihood of adverse outcomes in different ways, primarily relating potential dangers to specific features of context. Risks do not occur in a strict 'if... then' fashion for these youth, but rather as variables. Youth engaged in a variety of risk management strategies, which stemmed from the context specific manner in which they conceived of risks associated with ecstasy use. The initial case of Tony taking ecstasy in half pill increments was a vivid example of moderation put into practice. A "burned brain" from ecstasy is dose-dependent. Tony minimized his intake and subsequent risk while achieving his ecstasy high. Other risk management practices include other forms of moderation, "pre-loading" or "post-loading", and taking "breaks" – periodic interruptions in the regular pattern of ecstasy use so as to replenish one's body, or more specifically to rejuvenate the serotonin system. Thus, these conceptions of risk translated into specific patterns and practices of ecstasy use.

Conclusion

An understanding of risk based solely on professional models is incomplete at best. The incorporation of folk models of risk into our understandings of a given phenomenon enables fuller and richer explanations of why the "folk" act as they do. Folk models demonstrate how specific phenomena resonate on the ground. Only through ascertaining fuller understandings of folk models can we adequately inform health promotion efforts and public policy by eliminating the assumptions inherent in professional models. In certain respects, the models of risk put forth by ecstasy using youth contain areas of both harmony and discord with respect to the professional models of risk advanced by scientists and the federal government. For the most part, youth recognized many of the same potential dangers outlined by professionals – dangers such as neurotoxicity, hyperthermia, and depression. However, youth assessed the likelihood of these adverse outcomes in different ways and primarily related potential dangers to specific features of context. As a result of the recognition of context in risk, youth not only nurtured a sense of agency over their ecstasy use, but translated their conceptions of risk into specific strategies for the use of ecstasy.

The analyses of professional and folk models of risk have a number of implications for promoting health among ecstasy-using youth. One such area is that it allows for an attempt to understand the harmony and discontinuities between how public health professionals view ecstasy-related risks and how youth view them. We can thus explore areas for potential mediating health education interventions.

In particular, we can examine how youth models of risk shape the ways in which they practiced ecstasy use, so as to contend with that risk. Many of the ecstasy-using youth interviewed maintained an interest in harm reduction approaches to ecstasy use, even those unaware of harm reduction as a specific function. Youth engaged in a wide range of risk management practices that grew out of how they conceive of risk. Some of these practices have grown out of and been transmitted via organized harm reduction movements within the club and rave scenes, other practices are indigenously cultivated ways of strategizing about risk. Certain key risk management practices regularly encountered and routinized within club cultures include regulated water consumption, "chilling out," moderation, avoidance of alcohol, pre-loading and post-loading, social network utilization, and pill testing. Efforts should be made to enhance existing harm reduction organizations targeting ecstasy-using youth, and allow for the development of new organizations through private and public funding.

Public health professionals have a responsibility to offer healthier alternatives through secondary and tertiary prevention, so as to minimize the harms associated with ecstasy use among youth. In recognizing the nuances of risk, these youth resisted the dogmatic drug education efforts aimed at them. They were willing to listen to professionals, but wanted to engage in a dialogue about the significance of potential dangers, rather than simply be instructed that drugs can be harmful. Greater efforts must be made to direct harm reduction methods at these youth rather than solely the bombardment of messages of danger.

One final note, it remains clear that public health professionals have much to learn about the long-term harms associated with ecstasy use. Efforts to fund such clinical research should be a priority for both public and private funding sources of drug-related research. Furthermore, several public policy recommendations and enactments related to ecstasy (e.g. the RAVE act) have occurred in the last several years in the United States, despite a dearth of clinical and behavioral research on the drug. Only further clinical and social research on ecstasy will provide fuller understandings for well-informed policy.[6]

Photograph courtesy of Simon Brockbank.

Chapter 5

"Chem Friendly":
The Institutional Basis of "Club Drug"
Use in a Sample of Urban Gay Men

Adam Isaiah Green

Survey research has long indicated comparatively high rates of drug and alcohol use among sexual minorities (Bradford & Ryan 1987; Connelley et al. 1978; DeCrescenzo, Fifield & Lathan 1975; Koopman, Rosario & Rotheram-Borus 1991; McKirnan & Peterson 1989; Nardi 1982; Noell & Ochs 2001; Remafedi 1987; Stall & Wiley 1988). When homosexual feelings initially emerge amongst homosexual youth, such individuals may feel alienated from heterosexual families, churches, friendship networks, and the larger community, and, as a result, may heavily use drugs and alcohol as an anesthetic agent to buffer anxiety, depression, and social dislocation (Finnegan & McNally 1987; Hammond 1986; Kus 1985; Lewis, Robins & Saghir 1982; McKirnan & Peterson 1989). A substantial proportion of urban adult homosexual men also engage in drug use, participating in subcultures that revolve around substance use (Buchbunger et al. 2001; HNCR Group et al. 2001; Levine 1998). Drug use in this latter group has been associated with unsafe sexual practices (Baxter et al. 1997; Halkitis & Parsons 2002; Hope, McKirnan & Ostrow 1996), and, in turn, what some have called "a double epidemic" of drug addiction and HIV/ AIDS (Halkitis, Parsons & Stirratt 2001; Jacobs 2002; Reback 1997). Yet unlike their adolescent counterparts, some drug using gay men develop patterns of drug use that follow self disclosure, the formation of solid social ties to gay friendship networks and institutions, and relocation to urban gay centers (Buchbunger et al. 2001; Ditman, Eggan & Reback 1996; Donovan et al.1996; Halkitis, Parsons & Stirratt 2001; Heischober & Miller 1991; Lewis & Ross 1995; Mayer et al.1990; Ostrow 1996). Thus the antecedents of adult drug use for these men are unlikely to hinge on perceptions of social isolation or stigma from sexual identification alone, if at all. Furthermore, of those who use recreational drugs, a significant contingent report using particular kinds of drugs in particular social venues.[1] For these men,

1   For instance, Halkitis, Parsons & Stirratt 2001 found that 12.7% of subjects who frequent bars and bathhouses indicated use of methamphetamine in the prior three months. Other studies indicate rates of club drug use among urban gay men ranging from 5–30% (Anderson et al.1994; Ditman, Eggan & Reback 1996; Donovan et al. 1996; Gordon et al. 1993; Heischober & Miller 1991; Malotte, Rhodes & Woods 1996), Additionally, studies throughout

"club drugs"—like cocaine, ecstacy methamphetamine, ketamine, and GHB—are consumed in the context of gay bars, dance clubs, sex parties, and bathhouses (Halkitis & Parsons 2002; Levine 1998; Lewis & Ross 1995; Buchbunger et al. 2001). Hence, this form of drug use among "out" and socially stabilized urban gay men represents a distinct pattern of substance use requiring its own explanation.

This chapter seeks to develop an explanation of this latter form of club drug use by drawing from a larger study examining the sociological antecedents of sexual patterns in a sample of New York City heterosexual and homosexual men. To the extent that prior research correlates use of drugs like cocaine, methamphetamine, ketamine, GHB, and ecstasy with a particular gay subculture revolving around commercial, gay-identified venues, such as dance clubs, bars, and bathhouses, I focus on a segment of gay men who use these drugs and frequent these locations. Among these subcultural actors, two forms of substance use are strongly associated with the anticipation of anonymous sex, perceptions of sexual competition, and gay sociality. In the first form, "drugs for sexual performance," respondents report club drug use as a strategy to negotiate tensions that arise from sexualized interactional patterns within urban gay communities. In the second form, "drugs for community," respondents report using drugs to experience a sense of "insta-community," transforming atomized strangers into new homoerotic collectivities on a nightly basis. I argue that the basis for both patterns of drug use lie in an important dimension of the social organization of urban gay life—sexual sociality. In the context of gay bars, bathhouses, gyms, and the streets that connect them, the men in this study encounter prominent modes of social interaction that hinge on casual sex, sexual competition, and a sense of collective membership among individuals with fleeting social ties. Taken together, these institutionalized interactional practices produce patterned anxieties around sexual intimacy, sexual competence, and perceptions of group membership that require an affective "lubricant" readily produced by the use of club drugs. I argue that club drug use facilitates those interactional patterns, which might otherwise be too awkward or too intimidating to enact on a regular basis.

Method

This chapter is based on a research project that examined the life histories of 59 homosexual and 50 heterosexual urban men, between the ages of 21 and 52, with an average age of 33 years. In contrast to survey research, the primary methodological concern of this study was not to make behavioral generalizations through representative distributions of the population of gay and straight men. Rather, the goal of this qualitative approach was to contribute to the theoretical understandings of the development of the sexual career and associated behaviors. Toward this end, the respondent pools were acquired through a targeted, snowball, community-based

---

urban areas in the United States find that use of club drugs, particularly methamphetamine, has greatly increased in popularity over the last decade (Hall 1996; Lewis & Ross 1995; Mendelson & Harrison 1996).

sampling procedure with multiple starting points from a diverse range of local organizations, athletic teams, gyms, bars, churches, friendship circles, and civic associations (Biernacki & Watters 1989). These starting points produced variability in sexual practices and experiences within the sample and thereby maximized the discovery of processes relevant to the sexual career.

All respondents lived or worked in New York City for at least one year prior to their interview. Most respondents were college educated, though their occupations varied widely from actor/waiter to retail manager to physician. As a whole, respondents characterized themselves as middle class, but were raised in either working class or middle class families. The majority of respondents held a bachelor's degree, though 15 respondents held graduate degrees while 10 respondents had less than 4 years of college education. The homosexual sample (n=59) was also racially stratified: 30 subjects characterized themselves as "White," and 29 characterized themselves as "African-American" or "Caribbean."

New York City, like other major urban areas in the United States, supports a wide range of sexual communities, including extensive gay enclaves with "institutional completeness" (Fitzgerald 1986; Murray 1996). Like other large urban centers, including Los Angeles, San Francisco, Chicago, and Miami, New York serves as an important laboratory producing homosexual communities and careers uniquely distilled from the influences of dominant heterosexual norms and institutions. Hence, the life histories of men in this study are embedded in particular urban settings that will not necessarily reflect the experiences of gay men in smaller cities or in non-urban locales.

All interviews were conducted either in the researcher's office or at the home of the participant during September 2000–November 2001. Interviews typically lasted 3.5 hours, although they ranged from 1.5 to 6 hours. All interviews were tape-recorded, and later transcribed, coded, and analyzed using open and axial coding procedures (Corbin & Strauss 1998).

Drugs for Sexual Performance: Gay Men "Let Themselves Go"

One of the chief motivations for club drug use among gay men of this study was to reduce sexual inhibition and increase sexual performance. For these men, cocaine, methamphetamine, and other chemical substances promoted a sense of self-confidence, well-being, and diminished feelings of self-consciousness or awkwardness. In this altered state, users were better able to participate in the interactional patterns they encountered in the sexual institutions of urban gay enclaves.

Sam, in his early thirties, demonstrates this general point. On many weekends in the past few years, Sam has met men on the Internet or in local bars in Chelsea for casual sex. Recently, Sam enjoyed a night out at "Slip"—a gay bar situated only blocks from his apartment. There, Sam met Michael, a 28-year-old Latino. Michael was in possession of methamphetamine, and asked if Sam would like some. The two men promptly went to the bathroom where each man snorted the white powder in a stall together, and later returned to Sam's apartment. Sam reported that methamphetamine prevents him from getting distracted while having sex, and maximizes the intensity and pleasure of an encounter even if he does not feel a particular "connection" to his partner.

> I really like sex on that drug—it like makes sex incredible especially if you want to bottom . . . it loosens you up and it makes you really focus on what you're doing and not get distracted by anything else, like maybe if you had a bad day or if you feel like maybe you don't have the greatest connection to the guy your with, you can do crystal and have the best sex of your life . . . We went back to my place and had sex like three times that night. It was hot—very, very enjoyable . . . I doubt I'd see him again but when you're doing crystal you don't care about that—you're not thinking with your heart, you're thinking about the sex.

Don, too, routinely used club drugs in anticipation of casual sex. In his late thirties, Don—a college instructor—has found that drugs like cocaine and methamphetamine allow him to focus all his attention and energies on sex, canceling out the distracting "uncertainty" associated with sexual rendezvous.

> You see, when I do a bump of cocaine or Tina [methamphetamine], all I feel is the sexual energy of whomever I am with . . . It takes all the uncertainty out of the experience. It makes you feel like you're invincible, like you can do anything or be anything you want to be.

Roman, a gay masseur in his late thirties, particularly liked when the men he slept with used cocaine or methamphetamine because these drugs gave his sexual partners more staying power and added to the intensity of their sexual performance.

> Sex with guys on crystal or coke is amazing, it's just amazing. They can go for hours and hours and they are much wilder and carefree in bed. If I meet someone out at a club or online and they are doing coke or crystal I know I'm going to have a great time. And sometimes they'll ask me if I have any drugs at home—party favors—and I don't even usually do the drugs myself but I have some to offer them. Honestly, I think maybe 9 out of 10 times if the guy has done crystal I can tell right away and the sex is just amazing. They're just so into it and wild and creative that I love it . . . I love to have sex with guys on that drug.

Mitch—a self-described "leather daddy" in his late forties—also used club drugs in a strategic manner to enhance sexual performance. As an organizer of leather sex parties, Mitch stated that he was "chem friendly"—a term that means "chemical friendly." Interestingly, Mitch's preferred drug combination includes methamphetamine with either Viagra or amyl nitrate—both drugs that are well known to enhance erection and sexual pleasure. To the extent that crystal makes him much more sexually aggressive, Mitch used the drug strategically to prepare for group sex. Yet, to the extent that too much crystal will dampen his ability to sustain an erection, Mitch adds Viagra into the crystal in a formulation he calls "trail mix." Hence, Mitch has developed a self-medicating strategy to optimize his sexual performance:

> I'll do a bump or two of crystal and, yeah, I usually take like half a Viagra just before the party. They call that "trail-mix." My friend and I do all the topping. I want Viagra because I want to party. It gives me a hard-on for about two hours (and) I'm fucking guys as much as I can now . . . I fuck five, six, or seven guys in a night.

Like Mitch, Willy—a hairdresser in his early thirties—also reported strategic use of drugs to facilitate sex. For Willy, cocaine enabled him to go into a gay bar without hesitation or self doubt and to approach other men for sex.

> I can literally walk into a bar—and I've done this many times—scope it out, see who I want, walk up to them and go, "hi." And of course, now I am high out of my mind because I could never get the courage if I wasn't. And I say, "hi! What's your name? Where do you live?" And then I'll say "oh, why don't you show me your place." And they say, "OK." And literally, I'll leave—go in a bar, and be out with someone in ten minutes.

While cocaine gave Willy the "courage" to seek men out for sex, it also made him feel hypersexual. Willy described how cocaine keeps him sexually aroused in bathhouses for hours at a time. In this sense, drug use supported sexual desire and prolonged sexual sociality—but only until the drugs ran out. Then, Willy was unable to enjoy sex in these contexts, where the nature of interaction demands a fast sexual response, the ability to handle rejection, and the ability to navigate through sexual exchange with confidence and a sense of control.

> The actual having sex with guys without cumming is more pleasurable to me than cumming. Like I'd rather sit there in the bathhouse and have sex with a guy for like five to six hours as long as I have enough drugs to last me that long. You know when I cum? I cum when I just did my last bump of cocaine. Once the drugs are gone, I have to be the hell out of there, immediately! I cannot stay there another minute . . . because I know that I don't have any more drugs left. The drugs are the only thing that keep me there, keeps me wanting to stay.

While drugs enhanced Willy's sexual desire and confidence, other gay men used drugs as an anesthetic agent to numb the potential pain of intercourse, fisting, or other sexual practices that push the body to new limits. Leo, an African-American real estate agent in his late twenties, reported using cocaine or ketamine as a way to lessen the pain associated with fisting or hard anal intercourse. In the context of the bathhouse, Leo used cocaine to increase his sexual marketability, competing with other more attractive men through intensive sexual performance. It's not that Leo felt no pleasure during these interactions, but rather that the ratio of pleasure to pain was favorably transformed by strategic drug use. Having experienced first hand the link between drugs, sexual competition, and sexual pleasure, Leo observed the central role of drugs for his sexual performance.

It's a competition sexually with stretching yourself to sexual limits. I would buy it more if it weren't so connected to external drugs and alcohol . . . (In bathhouses) you go in, you're stripped completely naked, there are a series of runways that you walk along and people connect for different sexual reasons . . . But there, men compete through their looks, mint body, gorgeous face, and another way to compete with each other is, "look how far I can shove my fist up his ass" or "look how much I can get fucked" . . . But at a certain point . . . you're getting fisted and you have to do poppers or ten lines of blow to get someone's arm up your ass.

Sam, Don, Roman, Mitch, Willy, and Leo demonstrate the ways in which drugs help to facilitate performance in the context of gay social venues that revolve sexual exchange.[2] For these men, drugs like cocaine, methamphetamine, and ketamine increased sexual desire and self-confidence while decreasing self-consciousness and physical strain associated with anal intercourse or fisting. These emotional and physical effects were strategically induced by men who sought out and anticipated impersonal sexual encounters but who found such interactional patterns to be less pleasurable or difficult to negotiate without drug intake and its associated affective transformations.

Drugs for Community: Gay Men "Get to Intimacy"

The use of club drugs helped men of this sample feel more at ease with erotic repertoires revolving around impersonal sex. Club drugs also helped some men feel more at ease with collective integration within particular sexual settings. In this second pattern of drug use, men of this study used drugs to manufacture spontaneous community membership among individuals with fleeting social ties.

Ken, a Manhattan resident in his late twenties, moved from Georgia to New York at the age of 24 in search of gay community. There, Ken joyfully discovered the many gay bars, dance clubs, and bathhouses of the West Village and Chelsea. These venues served as optimal sites to satisfy his sexual desires and to develop gay

---

2   It should be noted that anonymous sexual practices are not always associated with drug use. Humphreys (1970) and Delph (1978), for instance, found that public restrooms—or "tearooms"—served as sites of anonymous homosexual sex in the absence of alcohol and drugs. Nonetheless, a number of explanations might explain this latter finding. First, club drugs were far less available and less popular during the time of Humphrey's and Delph's research. Moreover, tearoom sex often occurred during the day—before, during, or following work—and among "heterosexual" men with wives and children to whom they returned each evening. Thus, intoxication would pose much higher opportunity costs and risk of discovery. Finally, sex in public restrooms may be more highly structured to a degree that presents less ambiguity about the negotiation of sexual activity and more anonymity. Indeed, those frequenting tearooms rarely made conversation. By contrast, the same could not be said of gay men in a bar, a sex party, or even a bathhouse (Tewksbury 2002), where there exists wider latitude for sexual negotiation and decision making, and where opportunities (and challenges) for the management of self are greater.

friendships. So too, these sites provided Ken with a sense of identity as a gay man. For Ken, drugs created the physiological foundation upon which differences between people were blurred and perceptions of community built. On this point, Ken likened the gay "club scene" to a cultish "niche" where ritualized sexual practices and drug use made him feel that he was a part of something larger than himself:

> The club scene is like a cult . . . All the men dress the same, take the same drugs, and live in a "sex-fantasy" world . . . I have been looking for my niche for so long now and finally found it.

Edward, an advertisement executive in his early thirties, went dancing most weekends in a given month at "Twilight"—a large gay dance club located in Manhattan. Though his sense of self was less dependent on gay nightclubs than Ken's, Edward derived great pleasure dancing throughout the evening and into the morning at such locations. Over the years, MDMA and cocaine have become a part of his weekend ritual.

> I meet friends at Twilight and usually someone will have some stuff with them . . . like some "X" [ecstacy] or blow [cocaine]. It's all about just having fun, losing yourself to the music, gett'n sweaty, dancing and flirting and checking out guys . . . So many beautiful men and the deep house [music]. It's like a trance . . . You're transported into another world and even though you're all in your head you're kinda doing it together with all these beautiful guys.

Jim, an aspiring actor in his early twenties, also participated in the urban gay nightlife. His interpretation of interactional patterns within the sexual institutions of New York City builds upon and deepens the sentiments of Ken and Edward. While Jim was particularly enamored with the intense sexual energy that surges through gay dance clubs, he was also aware of the central role of drugs in these environments. Describing his experiences, Jim emphasized the ways in which drugs facilitated the development of intimate connections within the impersonal environments of the crowded dance club. As Jim explained, drugs become the way that hundreds of shirtless strangers on a dance floor develop a sense of "insta-community" without self-consciousness or perceptions of sexual competition. Drug use in these settings was *de rigueur*, creating a mood that allowed large crowds of atomized party participants to experience perceptions of unity and collective eroticism on any given evening.

> Drugs give you an incredible feeling of closeness—being in a room with a group of half-naked men, celebrating homosexuality, all the masculine sexual energy . . . It's all tied to drugs; they can't get to intimacy until doing K.

While Jim's social life was contained to New York City, others travel to urban centers around the country to participate in circuit parties. Circuit parties are large gay social events that occur throughout the year in various cities— hence, the "circuit." In a typical major circuit party, thousands of gay men convene at a given urban location for the weekend, and will meet, dance, socialize, and do drugs (Buchbunger et al. 2001; HNCR Group et al. 2001). The circuit party itself occurs over a 12–24 hour period, and most attendees arrive well after midnight, "partying" until the next morning or afternoon. In these contexts, drugs allow party-goers from all over the country to interact in a prolonged and highly sexualized manner. Keith, for instance—a physician in his early thirties—attends circuit parties throughout the country. In the last year alone, he participated in six circuit events, using club drugs at each party. When asked why he thought club drugs were so prevalent at circuit parties, Keith underscored the way in which drugs "connect" people.

> Drugs put everyone in the same mental space. You can bring guys together from all different backgrounds and when you party together, you connect on a different level than if you were sober . . . You don't even have to speak the same language. Like at the "Black" party last March there were these two gorgeous guys from Germany and I spent practically the whole night with them even though I could barely understand them. We didn't have to speak, it was all there in our eyes and in our bodies.

Like Keith, Evan—a heavily muscled, gay office manager in his mid thirties—and his 39-year-old boyfriend, Mark, enjoyed attending circuit parties on the east and west coasts. Generally, the couple traveled to approximately one party every month. Once there, Evan and Mark enjoyed dancing until sunrise, meeting new gay friends, and finding new partners for three-way sexual encounters later in the day. Drugs were a central part of this process. As Evan explained, drugs made friends and lovers out of strangers.

> Yeah, we usually have some cocktails, some bumps of coke, and maybe once in a while we'll do ecstasy. It just helps you to feel more relaxed, and to have a good time. Circuit parties can be great because there are a lot of really handsome, buff guys there that you might not ordinarily see at home . . . I don't have to do drugs but I like to, especially there. When you're doing drugs you just feel like everyone is your friend. And for that night, they are.

Ken, Edward, Jim, Keith, Evan, and Mark illustrate the ways in which club drugs may serve to create spontaneous community. Club drugs enable them to experience membership in large social venues among participants who might otherwise have little in common, or hold little knowledge of each other. Through drug-induced affective transformations, club drug users lose their social inhibitions and self-consciousness, and are better able to experience intimacy and sexual solidarity with new friends and lovers.

Discussion and Implications

Historically, gay bars, dance clubs, and bathhouses have served as "sexual institutions" for homosexual men who journey to urban centers in search of sexual community (Achilles 1967; Adam 1987; Fitzgerald 1986; Levine 1998; Murray 1996; Teal 1971;

Tewksbury 1996; Weinberg & Williams 1975). While "erotic oases" like public restrooms, parks, or bookstores have long provided meeting sites for anonymous homosexual encounters (Delph 1978; Humphreys 1970; Tewksbury 2002), bars, nightclubs, and bathhouses hold a special status as agents of gay socialization (Bronski 1993; D'emilio 1983; Fitzgerald 1986; Loughery 1998; Nardi 1982). These institutions operate as "launch pads" into gay life, providing safe havens for the expression of sexuality or gender transgression, a place to meet gay friends and lovers, or as a place to disseminate political and public health information or organize against anti-gay state repression. Blocked from the institutionalized rites of passage that define and organize (heterosexual) adulthood, some gay men find that commercial sexual institutions have a powerful and enduring presence in their lives well past the age when their heterosexual counterparts move out of nightlife and into sexual trajectories tied to marriage and family. Indeed, for this latter group of men, commercial sexual institutions come to replace marriage and family as a primary vehicle for anchoring social and sexual life. For some, the use of specific drugs is a central component of their pleasure while attending such institutions.

The life histories of men in this study illustrate two prominent, sometimes overlapping, forms of club drug use that reflect the social organization of a particular urban gay subculture. In the first pattern of substance use, "for sexual performance," gay men like Sam, Ron, and Leo used drugs as a strategy to increase sexual desire, sexual longevity, and self-confidence. Commercial sexual institutions are a prominent place around which urban homosociality orbits, and these men used drugs to strategically negotiate tensions that arose from impersonal sexualized interactional patterns. Under the influence of drugs, these men were better able to make the psychological transition from "stranger" to "lover." Moreover, that some respondents reported using drugs as a catalyst to sexual desire is particularly interesting to note. In other words, drug use facilitated sexual desire; chemical substances enabled men like Mitch and Willy to achieve and sustain the necessary level of sexual arousal required for satisfactory participation and performance.

The second prevalent pattern of club drug use—"for community"—enabled respondents to convene in a given location and build a sense of instant community without awkwardness or self-consciousness. Under the influence of club drugs, men like Jim, Edward, and Ken achieved a powerful, binding sense of membership and homoerotic camaraderie in large venues among strangers and casual associates. At circuit parties, gay men like Keith, Evan, and Mark used drugs in their travels on "the circuit" in cities across the country. From their perspective, drugs and alcohol made "everyone your friend," and provided the necessary transformation for prolonged sexual sociality and instantaneous collective intimacy. Thus, for these men, these drugs produced a "mobile" sexual community wherever gay men traveled and convened.

In the context of gay bars, dance clubs, sex parties, bathhouses, and the streets that connect them, urban gay men encounter prominent modes of social interaction that hinge upon an erotic-centered sociality and promote commercialized and impersonal sex, bachelorhood, sexual competition, and fleeting social ties (Adam

1987; Levine 1998; Tewksbury 1995; Warner 1997). Circuit parties extend the logic of this system, pairing drugs and casual sex in cities throughout the United States (Buchbunger et al. 2001; Mansergh et al. 2001; Mattison et al. 2001). In New York City, institutionalized features of urban gay life produce patterned anxieties around sexual performance and perceptions of membership readily alleviated by club drugs, such as cocaine, methamphetamine, and ketamine, diminish inhibitions, fuel the sexual desire of its users, heighten sexual pleasure, and, in turn, permit full participation in commercial sexual sociality. Thus, for Sam, Don, Roman, Leo, Mitch, Willy, Ken, Keith, Evan, and Mark and other gay men like them, club drug use represents a strategic adaptation to the institutional conditions in which they find themselves. In the context of commercial gay sociality, club drugs lubricate interactional patterns that might otherwise be too awkward or too alienating to enact on a regular basis.

While uncertain, it seems unlikely that the sexual interactional patterns described in this study could be sustained in the absence of mood altering substances. Would individual gay men like Willy or Sam feel as free to initiate casual sex with a stranger met in a bar, nightclub, or local gay hangout? Would sex for men like Mitch or Leo be as intense or pleasurable? Would these men have the sexual desire and fortitude to initiate sex with multiple partners in a given evening or sustain sexual arousal for hours at a time? Would men like Ken or Jim derive the same sense of "insta-community" in a dancehall in the company of hundreds of "half-naked" gay men—many of whom are strangers or fleeting associates? And could men like Evan and Mark travel the circuit throughout the United States and find new friends, new sexual partners, and "mobile community" among thousands of atomized party participants in any given weekend and in every port? At the very least, commercial homosociality of these sorts would be dampened as individual gay men stumbled in sobriety through the awkwardness that often comes with impersonal sexual exchanges. Sexual inhibitions would likely be stronger, self-confidence would likely diminish, sexual desire would likely weaken, and, in turn, sexual performance would suffer. So too, the instantaneous esprit de corps among party goers at large gay events would likely wane without the disassociating influences of drugs and the attendant "blurring of difference." In effect, devoid of "chemical" lubrication, interactional patterns that revolve around sexual sociality would be interrupted as participants wrestled with new ways of relating and forging collective membership.[3]

Chapter 6

On Ketamine: In and Out of the K hole

Stephen E. Lankenau

Ketamine, also known among recreational users as Special K, K, and Kat, has been defined as a "club drug," (ONDCP 1997) along with other manmade substances such as ecstasy, GHB, and speed, given its common association with clubs, raves, and dance settings. This chapter describes the wider context of ketamine use and associated risks – both inside and beyond the confines of club and rave environments. In particular, I provide a brief history of the development of ketamine and its emergence as a recreational drug, detail the forms of ketamine consumed and modes of administrating ketamine, describe populations of ketamine users, and explain health risks associated with ketamine use. This information is drawn from the limited literature on recreational ketamine use and findings from our previously published research (Lankenau & Clatts 2002; Lankenau & Clatts 2004; Lankenau & Clatts 2005; Lankenau & Sanders 2004; Lankenau et al. 2005) as well as an ongoing study of ketamine use among high-risk youth in three U.S. cities.

A Brief History of Ketamine

Ketamine is a pharmaceutical originally developed in the United States in 1962. Ketamine, known as CI-581 during its testing phase, became labeled as ketamine soon after Parke-Davis patented the substance in 1966, and was introduced into general clinical usage in 1970 (Hansen et al.1988). Ketamine was developed as the medical community sought an easily administered anesthetic with few side-effects. Phencyclidine (PCP), originally developed in 1959, was a prototype agent in the search for new types of anesthetics. However, PCP proved to be too long-acting, and patients complained of hallucinogenic effects following emergence from sedation, which resulted in its withdrawal from human use in 1965 (Weil & Rosen 1983). Designed to be an improved version of PCP, ketamine afforded physicians and surgeons a "safe and potent intravenously administered anesthetic of short duration which combined analgesic and sleep-producing effects without significant cardiovascular and respiratory depression" (Corssen & Domino 1966, p. 29).

Ketamine is a non-competitive N-methyl-D-aspartate (NMDA) receptor antagonist. NMDA receptors are concentrated in the cerebral cortex and the hippocampus – two regions of the brain important for higher executive functions and memory. As a NMDA receptor antagonist, ketamine interferes with the action of excitatory amino acids, such as glutamate and aspartate, which are the most prevalent neurotransmitters in the brain (Curran & Morgan 2000). Ketamine redirects the electrical impulses traveling between neurotransmitters and suppresses information entering the brain. In particular, ketamine inhibits reuptake of dopamine into cells and enhances the spontaneous release of dopamine – a neurotransmitter present in regions of the brain that regulates movement, emotion, motivation, and the feeling of pleasure. The sensory association areas of the cortex, components of the limbic system, and thalamus are directly depressed by ketamine. As a result, higher central nervous system (CNS) centers are unable to receive or process sensory information, while the functions of the limbic systems, the regulation of emotions, such as fear, anger and pleasure, are impacted (Bergman 1999). Consequently, ketamine affects a wide range of functions, including memory, emotion, language, sensation and perception (Jansen 2001), and produces a unique state of sedation that has been labeled "dissociative anesthesia" (Domino, Chodoff & Corssen 1965). During ketamine sedation, a patient's eyes remain wide open and assume a slow, spasmodic gaze (Gill & Stajic 2000). Patients become unconscious or remain partially conscious, but incapable of responding to external stimuli or verbal commands. Ketamine is also a mild respiratory depressant, causing an effect similar to opioids. However, ketamine does not depress the protective airway reflexes, including coughing, sneezing and swallowing (Bergman 1999).

Ketamine is currently used in a variety of medical settings involving human patient populations. Ketamine has been used effectively on pediatric patients via intramuscular administration (Bergman 1999; Green et al.1998). Given its analgesic properties, ketamine has been useful in post-operative treatments of particular types of patients, such as cancer patients (Fine 1999) and burn victims (Enarson, Hays & Woodroffe 1999). Recently, Reflex Sympathetic Dystrophy (RSD) – a chronic pain, neurological syndrome – has been effectively treated through ketamine induced comas (Wong 2005). Ketamine is particularly valuable for sedating patients with asthma due to the drug's minimal effects on airway reflexes (Hirota & Lambert 1996). Since the drug allows patients to maintain control of respiratory functions (Bergman 1999), medical staff can act as both surgeon and anesthetist, which differs from typical anesthesia used during an operation that requires a doctor dedicated to monitoring breathing functions. Given these properties, ketamine has been a particularly practical anesthesia in treating war injuries as evidenced in Vietnam (Li 1971), Thailand (Bion 1984), Afghanistan (Rogers 1997; Halbert 1988), as well as treating patients located in remote hospitals (Walker 1972; Ketcham 1990). Similarly, ketamine is widely used in emergency departments. Due to adverse side-effects, however, ketamine has been used less frequently in standard medical settings since it was introduced in 1970. Ketamine is more widely used as a veterinary anesthetic (Curran & Morgan 2000).

The non-medical use of ketamine extends back to the mid-1960s soon after the drug was invented. Ketamine was dispensed by underground "medicinal chemists" from Michigan to Florida as early as 1967 (Jansen 2001), and solutions of ketamine were sold on the streets in Los Angeles and San Francisco in 1971 (Siegel 1978). Ketamine's abuse potential was noted as early as 1971 (Reier 1971). Despite reports of ketamine being sold on the streets, the majority of non-medical users during the early to mid-1970s tended to be experimentalists within the medical profession or educated individuals interested in exploring different states of consciousness – a few of the more prominent persons being Timothy Leary, Marcia Moore, and John Lilly (Jansen 2001). However, by the late 1970s, the Food and Drug Administration (FDA) released a report on ketamine abuse, and the National Institutes on Drug Abuse (NIDA) published an article on "ketamine intoxication" that included profiles of sniffers and injectors (Siegel 1978). These reports signaled a shift in the population of ketamine users from older experimentalists towards younger recreational users. In the early 1980s, ketamine emerged as an important ingredient in the birth of dance culture in the United Kingdom and the United States among urban youth and young adults, where it was sometimes sold in pill form as counterfeit ecstasy (Jansen 2001). However, ketamine soon emerged as a prominent drug of choice in its own right among young ravers, DJs and musicians (Dotson, Ackerman & West 1995). Ketamine inspired the sounds and lyrics of certain songs popular within rave culture, such as "Lost in a K Hole," "Ketamine Entity," and "K- Street D-tour" (Jansen 2001). The unique dissociative properties of ketamine – out of body experiences and visual enhancements – seemed to fit or perhaps impact the larger rave culture (Reynolds 1997).

Forms and Administrations of Ketamine

Ketamine hydrochloride is originally manufactured in powder form and is imported by U.S. pharmaceutical companies from Germany – the largest source country – as well as Colombia, China and Belgium (ONDCP 2004). U.S. firms and pharmaceutical companies in Mexico process and package powder ketamine into 10 mg/ml, 50 mg/ml, and 100 mg/ml injectable doses (Jansen 2001). Ketamine reaches the illicit drug market primarily via diversions from legitimate pharmaceutical sources or through burglary of veterinary clinics (Lankenau & Clatts 2004; ONDCP 2004). Mexico has been a primary source of ketamine diverted to the United States. For instance, over 250,000 vials of ketamine were seized by the Drug Enforcement Administration (DEA) in 2002 that had been diverted from a pharmaceutical producer in Mexico and were bound for distribution throughout the U.S. (ONDCP 2004). Indeed, our own research has indicated that young people in Los Angles procure ketamine from Tijuana, a border city.

Ketamine can be synthesized illicitly in underground laboratories, and the process is detailed in postings on Internet websites (Zealot 2005). However, the synthesis process is complex, more so than speed, for instance, and law enforcement sources have not reported instances of clandestinely manufactured ketamine (Copeland & Dillon 2005; ONDCP 2004). Additionally, our research of over 200 ketamine users has revealed no one with the expertise to synthesize ketamine in an underground laboratory (Lankenau & Clatts 2002; Lankenau & Clatts 2004; Lankenau et al. 2005).

Upon reaching the illicit drug market, ketamine is sold in the original pharmaceutically packaged liquid form or is converted back into a powder (Jansen 2001; Lankenau & Clatts 2002; Lankenau & Clatts 2004). Our research has shown that liquid ketamine can be transformed into crystals using everyday household appliances: baking the liquid in a microwave or oven; heating the liquid with a hair dryer; heating the liquid on a plate atop a pot of boiling water; or simply allowing the liquid to evaporate in open air. Crystals of ketamine are ground or crushed into a fine powder that can be marketed in small plastic bags, small glass vials, glassine and paper folds, as well as pressed into capsule and pill form (Copeland & Dillon 2005; ONDCP 2004). Liquid ketamine is sold in 100 ml vials for $80 to $100, while 100 to 200 mg packages of powder sell for $20 (Lankenau & Clatts 2002; ONDCP 2004).

Prior to becoming reclassified as a Schedule III drug in the United States in 1999, few reports existed of ketamine of being adulterated with other substances (Copeland & Dillon 2005; Tori 1996). However, as the drug has become more common within the illicit drug market, reports of adulterated ketamine have surfaced. For instance, on-site pill testing at a rave in Australia revealed that high rates of pills were mixed or adulterated with other substances thought to contain only ketamine (Camilleri & Caldicott 2005). Additionally, approximately 3% of pills tested between 1996 and 2005 by *DanceSafe* – pills purportedly sold to users as ecstasy – contained ketamine.[1] Interestingly, the only pills testing positive for ketamine during this ten year period were those submitted for testing between 2000 and 2001 – a period immediately following the scheduling of ketamine in 1999.

Drug forms, such as powder or liquid, are important as they impact a user's mode of administering the drug. Since ketamine is packaged and sold in multiple forms, the drug may be administered intranasally, orally, rectally, and via injection and inhalation. Mode of administration is significant since it determines the rate at which a drug is absorbed into a user's blood stream, which impacts how quickly and how long the user feels 'high.' Injection, intranasal and inhalation modes produce faster though shorter lasting highs, whereas rectal and oral administrations produce slower and longer lasting highs (Julien 1992). Also, mode of administration is important because it impacts upon risks for the transmission of bloodborne pathogens, such as HIV and Hepatitis C (Des Jarlais et al. 2003; McMahon & Tortu 2003). Intravenous injections presents the highest risk for transmitting bloodborne pathogens (Rich et al. 1998).

Various reports suggest that sniffing ketamine is the most common mode of administrating the drug (CEWG 2005; Copeland & Dillon 2005; Curran & Morgan 2000; Jansen 2001). Among intranasal users, ketamine is consumed by placing "bumps" – small amounts of powder ketamine – on a surface, such as the back of a hand, a key, or a small spoon, and then sniffed. Alternatively, powder ketamine is divided into lines and snorted through a straw or banknote. Ketamine is administered orally by swallowing a pill or by adding liquid or powder ketamine to a drink. Ketamine is inhaled or smoked by adding powder ketamine to a tobacco

---

1   Information available at www.ecstasydata.org.

cigarette or joint of marijuana; alternatively, the cigarette or joint is dipped into liquid ketamine and smoked (Lankenau & Clatts 2005). Ketamine is administered rectally by pulling either liquid or powder ketamine into a syringe, removing the needle point, and injecting the drug solution into the rectum.

Additionally, ketamine is injected intravenously, intramuscularly, and subcutaneously – though intravenous and intramuscular modes are most typical (Lankenau & Clatts 2004; Lankenau et al. 2005). Ketamine injection is facilitated by the fact that liquid ketamine is packaged in a pharmaceutically-sealed vial with a permeable lid designed to be pierced by a needle point. Our research has shown that recreational users draw liquid ketamine into a syringe and inject it into a muscle, such as a shoulder or thigh, or inject it into a vein. Powder ketamine is prepared for injection by adding water, and then pulling the drug solution into a syringe. Whether an injector chooses to inject ketamine intramuscularly or intravenously depends on several factors, including drug form, the injection group, and the experience of the injector. Intramuscular injections are more common among users possessing liquid ketamine and among novice injectors, whereas intravenous injections are more typical among users possessing powder ketamine and among more experienced injectors (Lankenau & Clatts 2004).

Ketamine is frequently consumed in the context of a polydrug using event (Degenhardt, Darke & Dillon 2002; Lankenau & Clatts 2005; Parrott, Milani & Parmar 2001; Topp et al. 1999). During polydrug using events involving ketamine, users may combine or sequence their drug use in particular ways. Simultaneous drug use is mixing two or more substances together and administering them at the same time (Ellinwood, Eibergen & Kilbey 1976; Leri, Bruneau & Stewart 2003). Mixing ketamine and speed and then shooting the combination intravenously is an example of simultaneous drug use. In contrast, co-use is the sequential administration of two or more drugs during the course of a drug using event, a particular day, or longer periods (Ellinwood, Eibergen & Kilbey 1976; Leri, Bruneau & Stewart 2003). Smoking marijuana and later sniffing ketamine is an example of co-use. Often, ketamine users have a particular motivation for using the drug one way versus another. For instance, simultaneous administration may reflect the desire to create a particular novel effect – an effect which could not be produced by ketamine alone, or by taking the drug combination in a sequence. Similarly, co-use may be motivated by the wish to reduce the unwanted effects of ketamine or another drug by sequencing the amount of time between the first and second substance (Leri, Bruneau & Stewart 2003).

Profiles of Ketamine Users

Recent reports suggest that prevalence of ketamine use is increasing in Europe and Asia but stabilizing or declining in North America. In the United States, annual prevalence of ketamine dropped between 2002 and 2004 from 1.3 percent to .9 percent among 8th graders, from 2.1 percent to 1.3 percent among 10th graders, and

2.5 percent to 1.9 percent among 12th graders (Johnston et al. 2005). The number of emergency room drug episodes involving ketamine increased from a low of 19 in 1994 to 679 in 2001, but have since declined to 260 in 2002 (OAS 2003). The latest Community Epidemiological Working Group (CEWG) reported stable or declining use of ketamine in all regions of the United States (CEWG 2005). In contrast, while not representative of Asia as whole, reported use of ketamine in Hong Kong has increased dramatically in the past several years. The proportion of reported younger drug users using ketamine increased from .6% in 1999 to 70.4% in 2002 – a rise that has been fueled by low prices of ketamine compared to other drugs, an active club/ dance culture, and a belief that ketamine has few negative health side effects (Joe Laidler 2005). Similarly, while ketamine has long been associated with London club culture (Jansen 2001; Reynolds 1997), it has emerged as a drug with a much broader appeal within the past year. For the first time, ketamine is listed as a major drug for sale in eight of 15 English cities in a recent survey (Travis 2005).

Unlike hard drugs, such as heroin and cocaine, ketamine's legal status varies from country to country (Copeland & Dillon 2005), which may impact upon rates of use. In the United States, the DEA placed ketamine in schedule III in July 1999, making it a federal offense to possess ketamine without a license or prescription. In Canada, ketamine is not scheduled, and therefore individuals can possess the drug without a license, though sales are regulated by pharmaceutical laws. In Mexico, ketamine is scheduled as a category 3 drug under Mexico's General Health Law, which limits acquisition of ketamine to licensed veterinarians. In the United Kingdom, it is legal to possess ketamine, though the sale and distribution of the drug is prohibited without a license. However, the UK is considering making it illegal to possess ketamine amidst reports of rising rates of use among young people (Travis 2005). In Hong Kong, possessing ketamine is illegal, though penalties are typically minimal, such as probation or community service (Joe Laidler 2005).

Research conducted in the United States, England, and Australia indicates that ketamine users tend to be white, male, younger (under 30 years old), and moderately to well-educated (Clatts, Goldsamt & Huso 2005; Curran & Morgan 2000; Dillon Copeland, & Jansen 2003; Lankenau & Clatts 2005). Perhaps more than other drugs, ketamine users can be further identified by behavioral practices, lifestyles, or occupations. Ketamine users are often identified as "ravers" or young people involved in club/dance settings (Curran & Morgan 2000; Degenhardt & Topp 2003; Dillon et al. 2003; Dotson et al. 1995; Jansen 2001); gay men and men who have sex with men (MSM) (Degenhardt & Topp; 2003; Dillon Copeland, & Jansen 2003; Rusch et al. 2004); young injection drug users (IDUs) (Lankenau & Clatts 2004); or workers in the medical field (Ahmed & Petchkovsky 1980; Jansen 2001; Moore & Bostwick 1999). Of course, there are overlaps between these groups: MSM are frequently among young people attending clubs or raves; or young people who attend raves are also IDUs. These behaviors, lifestyles, or occupations typically impact upon access to ketamine and the rational for using ketamine.

Ketamine is frequently available at raves or in clubs that provide ravers and MSM the opportunity to buy and use ketamine in these settings. While ketamine produces a range of effects, some report that ketamine can enhance the experience of listening or dancing to music depending upon the dose (Jansen 2001; Joe Laidler 2005; Joe Laidler et al. this volume). Ketamine can also lower inhibitions, which may encourage sociality or sexual explorations in certain settings. Medical workers, such as doctors, veterinarians or medical staff, frequently have access to ketamine in the course of their jobs and may be familiar with its effects on patients or animals. Our research indicates that diverting large amounts of ketamine from work settings is often risky, while smaller amounts for personal use are often taken without detection.

As indicated previously, ketamine is known as a 'club drug,' suggesting that the drug is primarily consumed in club, rave, or dance settings. Although, data contextualizing the settings where ketamine is used are limited, since most research studies on ketamine are epidemiological or clinical in nature and primarily focus on groups of users and associated health behaviors (Copeland & Dillon 2005; Lua et al. 2003; Morgan, Monaghan & Curran 2004). Among IDUs, however, ketamine is typically injected in non-club or rave settings, such as private residences, along streets, and within parks (Lankenau & Clatts 2002; Lankenau & Clatts 2004; Lankenau et al. 2005). These settings reflect certain populations of ketamine injectors, which may include young homeless IDUs who do not have permanent residences to inject drugs. Many of these street-based young people, who often survive through panhandling, drug selling, sex work, or petty criminal activities, transition into injecting ketamine after initiating injection drug use with heroin, cocaine or speed (Lankenau & Clatts 2004; Lankenau et al. 2005). From a practical standpoint, injection drug use is difficult in a club setting since security personnel frequently monitor bathrooms and dance spaces. Our research has captured only a few descriptions of users injecting in a club setting:

> I was at a rave in Queens the last time I shot K [ketamine]. One of my friends showed up with a lick [vial of liquid ketamine] and some needles. We had nothing to do so we stood in the corner of the place and I did two small shots in my vein. Afterwards, we took ecstasy. I don't remember much about the whole experience – except that I probably did some dancing. It was all kind of a blur. The next day I was kind of out of it.

Additionally, injection drug use produces a rapid, profound drug experience that may not be conducive to club or social environment. In particular, ketamine injectors often report an experience that leaves them immobilized and unable to function in a social setting:

> At first, it was the same thing as when you sniff it – you start getting dizzy, feeling weightless. But I did not expect to black out – I couldn't walk. I felt like I was watching a movie about this guy's life. He goes to work, he hangs out, and he goes to parties. Then it hits me – all this stuff is my memories and I'm like inside my body. I got to learn how to use my body again. So, I get up – I see my shoulder, my arms, my fingers – they work. When I came out, the whole city looked like it was made out of cardboard.

If drugs are going to be part of a long night in a club or rave, more experienced users opt for drug titration – timing and sequencing drug use over the course of the evening to enhance moods and sensations within the club (Joe Laidler 2005). With this objective in mind, oral or intranasal administrations of ketamine may be preferred over injection. In fact, the drug form and mode of administration, such as powder sniffed intranasally, may result in a qualitatively different experience compared to another form and mode of administration, such as liquid injected intravenously, as described by this ketamine injector:

> The difference between snorting and injecting it [ketamine] are greater than I've felt with any other drug. It's almost a completely different drug. I find that when you snort it you get a rushy kind of feeling and your perception is a little bit fucked up. When you shoot it, your world is completely different. One time, I shot it in a small bathroom in somebody's basement, and within seconds the bathroom felt like the size of a football field. I couldn't find the door to get out. It was a crazy experience.

As the above quotes illustrate, ketamine produces a range of effects depending upon the dose, mode of administration, the intentions of the user, the setting, and other drugs consumed during the event. A novice ketamine user sniffing a small amount of powder ketamine after ingesting a pill of ecstasy inside a club, for instance, is likely to have a very different experience compared to an experienced ketamine user injecting a large amount of liquid ketamine intravenously before sniffing speed with a few friends in an apartment. Some of the experiences associated with ketamine use include sensations of light passing throughout the body; unique feelings of body consistency, such as feeling wooden or plastic; wildly distorted perceptions of space and time; out-of-body experiences; colorful visions; and imagined interactions with famous or fictious persons (Hansen et al. 1988; Jansen 2001; Lankenau & Clatts 2004). The most pronounced effect is what has been called a "K-hole", which is achieved through higher doses of ketamine. For some, a K-hole is a sought after state that is exciting and pleasurable, while for others, a K-hole is a frightening experience to be avoided:

> My first time injecting K was a bad experience. I couldn't see anybody. Everybody was all blobby looking. One of the other kids asked, "Is she alright?" I felt like I wasn't there. I bugged out. I started crying. And then finally, I came out of my [K] hole…I was sitting outside on the lawn and I was talking to him my boyfriend, and he came out of his hole. And I was like, "Yo - that sucked. That was really bad." And he was like, "Yeah, I know. It was wack."

Due to its unusual and unpredictable effects, as described above, for instance, some users who may be otherwise experienced drug users try injecting ketamine only once. The reasons for initiating ketamine injection include curiosity about its effects, a desire for a new or greater high, a tolerance for the drug after prolonged periods of sniffing ketamine, and viewing it as a less stigmatized and less risky form of injection drug use:

I injected it because I know K is clean - it's not like heroin, right. It comes from a lab, and it's inside a bottle. And it was a clean needle, and it's all clean. So I was like, "Fuck it, I'll do it." And it was in my muscle. Back then I was scared to do it in the vein. So I go ahead and did it in my muscle.

For most injectors, ketamine is not a drug of choice, but rather a drug that is used occasionally or is combined with other drugs for different effects (Lankenau & Sanders 2004). These individuals finding ketamine compelling and continue to explore its effects:

While I was on it, it was so deep and the forest was so dark. I couldn't see anything. It felt like I was waiting my whole life for the injection. That was the [K] hole that I was in. That's what I felt like...It was interesting. I liked it.

Health Risks Associated with Ketamine

The health risks associated with ketamine include risks for infectious disease, drug overdose, drug dependence, and cognitive impairment (Copeland & Dillon 2005; Jansen 2001; Lankenau & Clatts 2004; Morgan, Monaghan & Curran 2004). Regarding infectious diseases, since ketamine is injected intravenous and intramuscularly, using the drug in this manner poses risk for HIV and Hepatitis C transmission. Studies of young IDUs indicate that drug paraphernalia, such as vials and cookers, are frequently shared during injection of ketamine, which represents risk for infectious diseases (Lankenau & Clatts 2004; Lankenau et al. 2005). Ketamine has also been linked to high-risk sexual activity. A study of MSMs indicated that unprotected anal intercourse, a risk factor of HIV transmission, was twice as likely among MSM who used ketamine during a sexual event or two hours prior to a sexual event (Rusch et al. 2004). Among MSM, ketamine is infrequently the drug of choice, but rather used in combination with other drugs, such as methamphetamine, ecstasy, or GHB (Degenhardt & Topp 2003; cf. Green this volume).

Case reports and small studies examining the cognitive effects of recreational ketamine use indicate that ketamine may impact cognitive functioning. Jansen (1990) reports of an anesthetist who after becoming dependent on ketamine developed problems with memory, attention, and concentration, and experienced slight changes in perception during periods of abstinence from ketamine. Curran and Morgan's (2000) study of ketamine users in England found significantly higher scores on dissociation and schizotypal symptomology three days after use compared to non-ketamine using controls. The authors conclude that "ketamine appears to induce acute and severe impairments on working, episodic and semantic memory as well as dissociative effects" (Curran & Morgan 2000, p. 575). A follow-up study conducted three to four years later reported that memory impairments to semantic memory were reversible after significant reductions in ketamine use. However, episodic and perceptual distortions may persist following attenuated ketamine use (Morgan, Monaghan & Curran 2004).

Tolerance and dependence on ketamine has been reported among recreational users. For instance, Jansen (2001) asserts that ketamine is more likely to draw users into periods of dependence than any other "psychedelic" drug. Two studies of small samples of ketamine users suggest the possibility for dependence based upon reports of compulsive use and binging (Dalgarno & Shewan 1996; Siegel 1978). A psychedelic "user's guide" (Turner 1994) states that ketamine has a very high potential for psychological addiction. Like cocaine and amphetamine, ketamine causes dopamine to shoot into the brain's 'pleasure centers.' However, little evidence exists to suggest that heavy users of ketamine develop physical withdrawal symptoms, like heroin or alcohol users, if they reduce or stop using the drug (Jansen 2001).

Drug overdoses from ketamine alone are rare. In fact, a wide margin of safety exists between a large dose administered in a medical setting and a lethal dose. For instance, reports of accidental injections of 10 times the amount required for surgery with no lasting effects have emerged (Jansen 2001). However, deaths have been reported during episodes using ketamine recreationally, though typically in the context of using other drugs. For instance, a review of non-hospital, ketamine-positive cases researched by New York medical examiners between 1997 and 1999 revealed 13 deaths attributed to acute intoxication. Though, in no instances was a fatal intoxication caused solely by ketamine, but always in the context of another drug, such as an opiate, amphetamine or cocaine (Gill & Stajic 2000).

Ketamine, along with other drugs, such as Rophynol and GHB, have been designated as "date rape" drugs (DEA 2001). There have been reports that ketamine, with its dissociative properties and ability to impact short-term memory, is given to unsuspecting men or women to commit sexual assault (Kronz 2000; Negrusz & Gaensslen 2003). In our research, numerous young people reported sexual activities after either sniffing or injecting ketamine. However, none described receiving ketamine unknowingly, or being sexual assaulted after using ketamine. Moreover, actual media reports of such instances are relatively rare. These findings suggest that the threat posed by ketamine as a date rape drug may be exaggerated.

Conclusion

Ketamine is a drug with a relatively short, but complex history. Perhaps, ketamine's complicated role as both a useful anesthetic and as a drug of abuse is best revealed by reports from two emergency departments filed two years apart: one concludes that "intramuscular ketamine can be administered safely by emergency physicians" to treat pediatric cases (Green et al. 1998, p. 447), while another states that "emergency physicians need to be aware of this emerging drug of abuse" and be prepared to treat ketamine abusers when they present to emergency departments (Weiner et al. 2000, p. 450). Regarding its medical uses, ketamine has been well-researched and has proven to be an effective anesthetic when given in limited doses under controlled medical conditions. As a recreational drug, ketamine is consumed by a much broader range of users than club kids in the cities in the US, UK, Australia and elsewhere (Lankenau et al. 2005). In fact, ketamine is used by a wide cross-section of users, in a variety of forms, via different modes of administrations, in various settings, and presents particular public health risks. As such, ketamine has become another recreational drug, though not nearly as normalized or prevalent as marijuana, for instance. The movement of ketamine outside the club environs into other settings and populations of users may signal a long-term stabilization of the drug on the menu of illicit substances consumed by recreational users and pursued by law enforcement.

Chapter 7

Ecstasy Use Amongst Young Low-Income Women[1]

Zhao Helen Wu

In general, males have a higher incidence of illicit drug use, including the use of 'club drugs', such as ecstasy. Over the past several years, however, an upward swing in the incidence of methlenedioxymethamphetamine (MDMA), or ecstasy, use has been seen in both genders, rising from 2% in the general US population in the mid-90's (SAMHSA 2004a; von Sydow et al. 2002). Use increased dramatically between 1998 and 2001(Landry 2002; National Institute on Drug Abuse 2001; Rosenbaum 2002; Schwartz & Miller 1997; Sullivan 2000; Weir 2000), and leveled off between 2002 and 2003 (Johnston et al. 2003; Johnston & O'Malley 2001; SAMHSA 2005). Even more interesting is the fact that while use among males has increased slightly, female incidence has done so drastically, with one study reporting a 200% increase from 3.8% to 7.6% (von Sydow et al. 2002). In addition, more and more young people under the age of 17 have started using ecstasy (Arria et al. 2002; Gouzoulis-Mayfrank et al. 2000; Milani et al. 2004; Moeller et al. 2002; SAMHSA 2004a, 2005). Studies have shown that a large portion (20%-40%) of those users are female (Milani et al. 2004). Past the age of 17, female incidence drops to approximately the same level as male incidence, and after age 22-25, incidence drops drastically among females, as compared to males (Ho, Karimi-Tabesh & Koren 2001; Milani et al. 2004; Parrott & Lasky 1998; Pope, Jr., Ionescu-Pioggia & Pope 2001; Pumariega, Rodriguez & Kilgus 2004). Another distinct feature of ecstasy use is polysubstance abuse, with tobacco, alcohol, marijuana, cocaine, and LSD being used in conjunction with ecstasy (Ho, Karimi-Tabesh & Koren 2001; Milani et al. 2004; Schuster et al. 1998). Numerous studies have shown that the strongest connections are between

---

1   This study was funded by the National Institute of Drug Abuse (R03DA14841), with additional support from the General Clinical Research Center at the University of Texas Medical Branch (UTMB) (Protocol No. 567). The author expresses her appreciation to Ms. Areli Duran, Ms. Lindsay Maurer, and Mr. Liu Mouyong, the members from the UTMB Regional Maternal and Child Health Program, Pathology Outreach Services, and Ms. Kimberly Bufton and laboratory technicians from the Pathology Laboratory. I also thank the members of The Writing Effectiveness Group (Center for Interdisciplinary Research in Women's Health, UTMB) for their critique of the earlier versions of this manuscript. Special thanks are indebted to Ms. Alisha Goldberg for her editorial assistance with this manuscript and Stephen Rosales, MD for literature updates.

ecstasy and marijuana and/or cocaine, with 84% and 72% concurrence, respectively (Gamma et al. 2000; Gamma et al. 2001; Ho, Karimi-Tabesh & Koren 2001; von Sydow et al. 2002). In addition, the increased use of ecstasy in the population has been related to more intensive patterns of ecstasy use by individuals (Scholey et al. 2004).

Although ecstasy (or MDMA) has been extensively studied in both pharmacological and physiological arenas during the past ten years, few studies have focused on ecstasy use among women. The 'rave' culture and university populations that have exploited use of this drug have provided the majority of study subjects for research conducted thus far (Arria et al. 2002; Boyd, McCabe, & d'Arcy 2003; Gamma et al. 2000; Gamma et al. 2001; Halpern et al. 2004; Reneman et al. 2001). However, data pertaining to women in these studies has not been assembled and analyzed. In fact, most of the 'rave studies' have not focused on women at all, but rather on students, rave/club attendees, and certain at-risk subgroups, such as juvenile detainees or men who have sex with men (Arria et al. 2002; Gamma et al. 2000; Gross et al. 2002; Klitzman, Pope, Jr. & Hudson 2000; Reneman et al. 2001; Yacoubian et al. 2002). Only a few studies outside the United States have observed patterns of occasional ecstasy use (e.g. taking one or two ecstasy tablets on a typical-use occasion, with use occurring several times per month. See (Degenhardt, Barker & Topp 2003)). Although these studies provide valuable information, few epidemiological studies have targeted at-risk female populations other than students and rave/club attendees.

Women in the general population, particularly those from lower socioeconomic groups, comprise an important at-risk group that requires further study. These at-risk women have reported higher rates of illicit drug use than the general population (Comerci & Schwebel 2000). As these women exhibit low levels of literacy, they may not be aware of the adverse consequences of ecstasy use (Comerci & Schwebel 2000). Negative health outcomes related to ecstasy use can include hyperthermia, seizures, hepatotoxicity, hyponatraemia, retinal hemorrhage, psychological problems, psychiatric disorders, and even death (Parrott et al. 2001; Parrott et al. 2002; Verheyden, Henry & Curran 2003). Ecstasy's adverse consequences can be especially detrimental to young women (Topp et al. 1999). In addition to the adverse health effects for women, maternal drug use has far-reaching implications for the health and well-being of their children. For instance, ecstasy use may increase infant congenital defects (McElhatton et al. 1999), and children can suffer developmental problems resulting from inadequate care and nurturing often prevalent among drug-using mothers (Ornoy, Bar-Hamburger & Greenbaum 2001). Despite these serious risks and consequences of ecstasy use among young, low-income women, the prevalence and perceptions of ecstasy use, as well as other illicit drug use, have not been adequately explored (Gross & McCaul 1991).

Gynaecological and reproductive sequelae and their correlates also represent important risks which are pertinent to female substance users (Greenfield, Manwani & Nargiso 2003; Zemishlany, Aizenberg & Weizman 2001). Ecstasy use results in emotional changes, inducing feelings of closeness and familiarity with those around the ecstasy user (Zemishlany, Aizenberg, & Weizman 2001). Ecstasy use has also been correlated with increased feelings of sexual desire in both genders, with women users, in particular, reporting heightened sensation and greater satisfaction during intercourse (Zemishlany, Aizenberg & Weizman 2001). Additionally, many subjects report that they do not practice safe sex after using ecstasy (Klitzman, Pope, Jr. & Hudson 2000). Risky sexual behavior obviously has potential to increase incidence of sexually-transmitted infections (STIs) and unplanned pregnancies. However, the connections between ecstasy use and gynecological behaviors and sequalea have yet to be reported.

The effects of ecstasy on psychological wellbeing have been studied. General findings indicate that if mood disorders, such as anxiety, depression or hyperactivity, increased the likelihood of ecstasy use among females (Gamma et al. 2000; Halpern et al. 2004; Ho, Karimi-Tabesh & Koren 2001; Milani et al. 2004; Parrott & Lasky 1998; Singer et al. 2004; Verheyden et al. 2002). Another important finding suggests that pre-existing conditions, such as depression, may lead to a higher rate of dependence amongst females (Milani et al. 2004; Schuster et al. 1998). Other gender differences exist. For instance, while males have frequently reported feelings of aggression about 3-4 days after using ecstasy, females have reported increased depression and/or anxiety after such use (Milani et al. 2004; Verheyden et al. 2002). As such, women who used ecstasy may have elevated levels of psychological distress.

Contextualizing the social environment of ecstasy use, where peer pressure can exert an influence on youth to use substances, is very important (Andrews et al. 2002; Urberg et al. 2004). Our previous research found that a large percentage of young, low-income women reported lower levels of education, worked part-time or at a minimum wage, tended to be independent and lived on their own at a young age, and were abused physically or sexually (Wu, Berenson & Wiemann 2003). Peers are often the primary source of social support, which contributes to substance use among young adults (Andrews et al. 2002; Urberg et al. 2004). As such, peer pressure may be strongly associated with ecstasy, as well as other illicit drug use.

This manuscript attempts to answer two questions: To what extent do women who have used ecstasy exhibit elevated levels of psychological distress and to what extent do peers influence women to use ecstasy and other illicit drugs? To answer these questions, data collected from a sample of 760 low-income women from southeast Texas was utilized. Patterns of ecstasy use among these women are reported here with a particular focus on the differences, if any, between women who used ecstasy and women who used other illicit drugs with respect to risk factors, such as knowledge and perceptions of drug use, gynecological and reproductive correlates, psychological distress, and characteristics of the social environment.

Study Design and Sampling

This cross-sectional study utilized a self-administered survey, supplemented by a face-to-face interview for a subgroup of respondents who reported using ecstasy. The sample consisted of women aged 18 to 31 years old who, between December 1, 2001, and May 30, 2003, sought gynecological care from two community-based family planning clinics operated by the University of Texas Medical Branch (UTMB).

Using a protocol approved by the University's Institutional Review Board (IRB), women who were pregnant or less than 6 months postpartum, those who refused, and those unable to provide informed consent were excluded. Trained bilingual (Spanish and English) research assistants approached and recruited potentially eligible patients. Each participant consented in writing to complete the survey and to allow investigators to review her medical record. All study materials were available in English and Spanish. The subset of women (n = 50) reporting ecstasy use were invited to discuss their perceptions and experiences surrounding club drug use in face-to-face interviews.

A total of 906 women were approached for this study. There were 141 (15.6%) women who refused to participate because of time constraints. Women who refused to participate did not differ from respondents with regard to age ($P = .08$), but more black women (8.1%) refused to participate relative to white (4.3%) and Hispanic (3.2%) women ($P < .01$). Of the 765 women who agreed to participate, 31 left the clinic before they finished the survey. An additional 38 participants did not respond to questions regarding drug use and were excluded from the analyses, leaving 696 participants in the final analyses.

Measurements

Drug use measures A modified version of the Drug History Questionnaire (DHQ) by Sobell and associates (Sobell, Kwan & Sobell 1995), the Substance Abuse History Form by Huba and associates (Huba et al. 1997), and the drug instrument from the 1999 Monitoring The Future (MTF) study (Johnston & O'Malley 2001) were used to assess self-reported use of 13 illicit substances, including marijuana, ecstasy, GHB, Rohypnol, ketamine, methamphetamine, cocaine, LSD, PCP, heroin, other narcotics, barbiturates, and tranquillizers. A summary measure of the number of illicit drugs ever used was created by counting how many of the 13 drugs each respondent had ever used. Age at first use ranged from 5 to 29 years old. Respondents were asked to indicate any of 14 reasons for drug use on a multiple-choice format derived from the MTF survey (e.g., "to experiment in order to see what it is like." see Johnston & O'Malley 2001).

Drug use was classified based on the type of drug each woman reported ever using: 1) ecstasy; 2) other illicit drugs; 3) marijuana only; and 4) no drugs. As the primary focus of this study was ecstasy use, women who reported ever using ecstasy were assigned to the first group, even though they may have also reported using other types of drugs. The second drug-use group included women who used other 'hard' drugs (even once), but never used ecstasy. Women who only ever used marijuana comprised the third group. These women were classified as a separate drug-use group because marijuana may be a 'gateway drug,' predictive of future 'hard' drug use (Morral, McCaffrey & Paddock 2002). Women who reported never using any drugs comprised the last group.

Knowledge of drug use   Adapted from a Substance Abuse & Mental Health Services Administration (SAMHSA) report on club drugs (SAMHSA 2004b), respondents chose "true" or "false" for each of five general drug knowledge items. Such items included the following questions: 1) "The term 'club drugs' describes drugs that are used at night clubs and raves." (False); 2) "The effect of ecstasy lasts for about 3 to 6 hours; however, anxiety and paranoia have been reported to occur weeks after the drug is taken." (True); 3) "There are no long-term effects from using ecstasy." (False); 4) "If you were in a club or bar and someone slipped one of these club drugs into your drink without your consent, you would be able to recognize a difference in your drink immediately." (False); 5) "Low doses of ketamine can result in impaired attention, learning ability, and memory." (True). One point was given for each correct response, which were tallied to compute a total score as recommended (SAMHSA 2004b).

Perception of drug use   Using an item from the MTF survey (Johnston & O'Malley 2001), women were asked to report how much they approved of people aged 18 or older using each of the drugs either occasionally or regularly. Responses were "strongly disapprove", "don't disapprove" or "disapprove". For analytical purposes, these responses were dichotomized and scored with 'strongly disapprove' equaling one and other responses zero because stronger expressions about opinions or attitudes may be better discriminate the acceptance of deviant behaviors, such as substance use, among young individuals who are at a cognitive-developmental stage and more likely to accept a wide range of beliefs when compared to adults. For the same reason, responses of intention to use each drug within five years were dichotomized for analysis as "definitely will not use" equaling a score of one, and all other responses, which included "definitely will use," "probably will use," and "probably will not use", scored as zero.

Risky sexual behaviors and consequences   Respondents were asked to report the number of sexual partners during their lifetime, the last 12 months, and the last 30 days. Inconsistent contraceptive practices were ascertained from medical charts and whether respondents never or sometimes used condoms or birth control pills in the last 12 months. Further, we gathered information about having sex with strangers in the last 12 months, having sex under the influence of drugs or alcohol, and having sex in the last 12 months with partners who have injected drugs. Subjects received a score of one for each of the acts committed, and a score of zero for each act not committed. Scores were tallied and used as a summary measure called, "other risky sexual behaviors".

Information about subjects' STIs was obtained through medical chart abstraction approved by the University IRB. At the initial or annual medical visit (when the survey was also conducted), each subject was asked about her gynecological history, including history of abnormal Papanicolaou (Pap) smear, Chlamydia, gonorrhea, syphilis, herpes, and condyloma. Each positive history was counted as one past infection. At the same visit, biological cultures were obtained and assessed through laboratory tests for different STIs, including *N. gonorrhea*, *C. trachomatis*, and Syphilis, and through Pap smear. Positive test results for each infection were classified as current infection by that bacterium or virus. Then women with the past infection and the current infection were combined into one group as women who ever infected with STI during their lifetime. For the study, women's lifetime infection scores were then tabulated as 0=never infected and 1=ever infected.

Stress measure   Cohen's Perceived Stress Scale (PSS-10; Cohen et al. 1985) was obtained from respondents between July 1, 2002 and May 30, 2003. A total of 443 respondents completed this measurement. Comparing those who were not asked for PSS-10 (n=322) to the PSS-10 respondents (n=433), no significant differences in education ($p=0.378$) or employment ($p=0.697$) emerged using Chi-Square tests. PSS-10 respondents were younger ($p=0.010$), included more blacks and fewer Hispanics ($p<0.001$), and were less likely to be married ($p<0.001$). Thirty-six respondents did not provide complete information regarding drug use and were excluded, leaving a total 407 for the current analysis. No statistical differences in demographic characteristics emerged between those excluded (n=36) and those included in the analysis (n=407).

Using PSS-10, we asked respondents about their feelings and thoughts during the past month (Cohen et al. 1985).[2] For each item, respondents indicated how often they felt or thought a certain way on a 5-point Likert scale (never (0), almost never (1), sometimes (2), fairly often (3) and very often (4)). After the scores for the four positive items (e.g., 0=4, 1=3, 2=2, etc.) were reversed, scores for all 10 items were summed up to create a summary score of PSS_10 index, ranging from 0 to 40.

Social environment   Social environment was assessed by asking respondents the number of close friends and the number of respondents' friends who had engaged in certain substance use behaviors, such as smoking. Each of 10 items to assess the

---

2   The sample were asked the following questions, which started with, "In the last month, how often have you: been upset because of something that happened unexpectedly?; felt that you were unable to control the important things in your life?; felt nervous and "stressed"?; felt confident about your ability to handle your personal problems?; felt that things were going your way?; found that you could not cope with all the things that you had to do?; been able to control irritations in your life?; felt that you were on top of things?; been angered because of things that were outside of your control?; felt difficulties were piling up so high that you could not overcome them?"

Drugs, Clubs and Young People

amount of their substance-using friends was rated on a five-point scale from none (=0) to all (=4) (Johnston & O'Malley 2001). To assess any exposure to peer substance use, the responses were recoded as "none" vs. "any friend" in the bivariate analysis. In the final statistical models, an index of friend's substance use was created to sum up the original item scores, ranging from 0 to 40. Responses to two neighborhood items related to substance use were coded as "agree" vs. "disagree."

Statistical Analyses

Chi-square tests were used to assess group differences among types of substance use when explanatory variables were categorical. Averages are reported as mean ± standard deviation. Analysis of variance (ANOVA) was used to test for group differences in continuous variables. When the assumptions for ANOVA were not met, a Kruskal-Wallis test was used. After controlling for covariates of interest, two sets of exploratory multivariable logistic regression analyses were used to model two dichotomous outcomes: 1) ecstasy use vs. other illicit drug use; and 2) ecstasy use vs. marijuana use only. Statistically significant variables ($P < .05$) in the bivariate analyses were entered into the multivariable logistic regression analyses, which employed a forward-selection approach. The above analyses were conducted by including the summary indicator of perceived stress (PSS-10) in separate models based on preliminary analysis and the amount of data obtained using the PSS-10. Odds ratios (OR) and 95% confidence intervals (95% CI) were reported from the final models. SAS for Windows, Version 9.1, was used to conduct analyses (SAS Institute Inc. 2004).

Results

The average age of the total sample (n = 696) was 24.2 (± 3.6 years). Overall, 15.2% of women reported using ecstasy at least once during their lifetime, with 7.2% reported using it in the last 12 months. Among women 18 to 24 years old, lifetime use was 8.9% and use in the last year was 4.7%. Compared with the two other illicit drug groups (women who used any other illicit drugs and women who used only marijuana but not other illicit drugs), ecstasy users did not differ by age, marital status, education, or employment status (see Table 7.1). However, differences were observed by race/ethnicity, and more non-Hispanic whites reported using ecstasy ($P < .01$), while more non-Hispanic blacks reported marijuana use ($P < .01$).

Among women who had used ecstasy at least once, 53.0% had used the drug within 12 months prior to the survey, while 26.0% had used it within the last year, but not within the last 30 days. Moreover, 21.0% had used it within the last 30 days. Women reported using between half a pill to four pills on each occasion. Many users also reported smoking cigarettes (82.1%), drinking beer and wine (91.5%), drinking hard liquor (84.9%), smoking marijuana (87.7%), and using crack cocaine (53.8%) or LSD (34.0%) in their lifetime. Initiation of ecstasy use occurred between age 14 and 29 (mean = 19.9 years ± 2.9) (Figure 7.1). Overall, ecstasy users reported first use of cigarette, beer/wine, hard liquor, or marijuana at a younger age than the other two groups of illicit drug users. Ecstasy users, if they used crack cocaine, initiated use at the same age as the group who used other illicit drugs.

Table 7.1   Characteristics of Young Low-Income Women, by Drug-Use Status (N = 696)

Demographics	n	Drug-use status			
		Ecstasy (n = 106)	Other illicit drugs (n = 64)	Marijuana (n = 173)	None (n = 353)
Age (y)					
18–24	350	58.5	56.3	60.1	41.9
25–31	346	41.5	43.8	39.9	58.1
Race/ethnicity					
Non-Hispanic white	248	67.9	65.6	37.6	19.6
Non-Hispanic black	253	17.9	15.6	52.0	38.0
Hispanics	195	14.2	18.8	10.4	42.5
Marital status					
Currently married	214	16.0	26.7	18.2	45.1
Never married	356	61.0	58.3	64.9	45.4
Divorced/separated	92	23.0	15.0	17.0	9.5
Education					
<High school	155	19.1	11.3	19.7	27.0
High school/GED diploma	294	41.9	43.6	44.5	42.0
Some college	239	39.1	45.2	35.8	31.0
Employed > 20 hours per week					
Yes	426	74.0	71.9	74.7	51.6
No	253	26.0	28.1	25.3	48.4

Face-to-face interview responses from 41 ecstasy users (from 52 invited survey participants who reported using ecstasy during their lifetime) revealed that principal use was at a friend's home. Specifically, 93.7% reported using it at their friends' homes compared with only 48.8% reporting using it at a bar or night club and 34.2% at a rave. In addition, 37.5% reported using ecstasy at other places such as a beach and 34.2% used it in their own home.

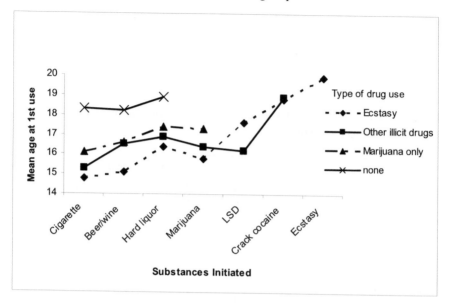

Figure 7.1 Mean Age at First Use of Substances by Type of Drug Use

Ecstasy users were more likely to report using a larger number of illicit drugs relative to the two other drug groups (see Table 7.2). They also initiated use of other illicit substances, except crack cocaine, at earlier ages. Among users of ecstasy, the three most frequently identified reasons for using the drug were to: experiment; have a good time with friends; and relax or relieve tension. The following statements are examples of the participants' reasons for Ecstasy use:

I never really knew about it [ecstasy] and then I started hearing how it could make you feel really good, improves your hearing; you could really feel the music... Before I took it, my friends had talked me into it. I was curious but it is a pill and once you take it you do not intend to stop doing it...It made me happy.

The first drug I tried was marijuana then ecstasy and then cocaine... I was with friends when I started using ecstasy. Friends chose this drug... I felt guilty after using ecstasy but being with friends, and partying, you just don't think about it.

In general, I used ecstasy with my boyfriend, friends, or a couple of friends. It just made me feel good, took everything away. I don't care about things, anything gone bad, it was OK. It would work itself out.

Table 7.2 Substance Use History in Young Low-Income Women (N = 696)

Substance Use	Ecstasy (n = 106)	Other illicit drugs (n = 64)	Marijuana only (n = 173)	None (n = 343)
Cigarette use in the last 30 days	66.4	47.6	42.2	9.1
Beer drinking in the last 30 days	68.6	53.1	45.9	23.7
Hard liquor use in the last 30 days	51.9	37.5	29.7	8.4
Marijuana in the last 12 months	65.4	42.2	41.0	0.0
Ecstasy	100.0	0.0	0.0	0.0
Marijuana	91.4	75.0	100.0	0.0
Cocaine	56.3	46.9	0.0	0.0
LSD	36.4	28.1	0.0	0.0
Barbiturates	34.0	29.5	0.0	0.0
Amphetamine	31.1	25.0	0.0	0.0
Other narcotics	30.7	23.8	0.0	0.0
Tranquillizers	23.8	11.5	0.0	0.0
PCP	17.4	17.2	0.0	0.0
Rohypnol	16.5	7.7	0.0	0.0
Heroin	5.8	9.4	0.0	0.0

No significant differences were detected with respect to knowledge of club drug use by the paired comparisons of drug use groups, except that ecstasy users were more likely to know that 'club drugs' were not limited to night clubs and raves (P = .02; see Table 7.3). Compared with the two other drug groups, fewer ecstasy users strongly disapproved of other adults using illicit drugs either occasionally or regularly (see Table 7.4). They also expressed a greater intention to use ecstasy, marijuana, and cocaine within 5 years. The following statements are examples of ecstasy users' attitude or intension for drug use.

I smoked marijuana at 15. ... I was at a New Year 's Eve party. At the time, my dad had just gone in jail. My dad used to smoke marijuana. He went to jail for drug use several times. I was told that I wasn't supposed to do drugs. But there was drug use going on in home, my mother drunk alcohol, but did not do other drugs. I kind of got mixed messages. Ok, I was at a party, I know what I do but I don't do what I am supposed to do. I was at this New Year's Eve party and drugs were goin' around. They said, "You might try it. If not, it is not a big deal." I wasn't really pressured to do them. I am not sure what to do.

Right now I have not used Ecstasy since January. I am not certain that I will use it again. … I know that I am young, that is going to be every once in a while [when I may use it]. I may use it again when I party.

Table 7.3 Percentage of Correct Responses to Knowledge Items About Drug Use Among Young Low-Income Women, by Drug-Use Status (N = 696)

	Ecstasy (n = 106) %	Other illicit drugs (n = 64) %	Marijuana (n = 173) %	None (n = 353) %
The term "club drugs" describes drugs that are used at night clubs and raves. (False)	93.2	90.3	83.3	84.4
The effect of ecstasy lasts for about 3 to 6 hours; however, anxiety and paranoia have been reported to occur weeks after the drug is taken. (True)	78.2	86.2	83.5	74.7
There are no long-term effects from using ecstasy. (False)	86.3	86.7	87.3	81.8
If you were in a club or bar and someone slipped one of these club drugs into your drink without your consent, you would be able to recognize a difference in your drink immediately. (False)	73.1	78.0	79.6	64.3
Low doses of ketamine can result in impaired attention, learning ability, and memory. (True)	91.9	93.3	90.2	82.4

Table 7.4 Women's Perceptions of Drug Use by Others and Their Own Future Use of Drugs Among Young Low-Income Women, by Drug-Use Status (N = 696)

	Drug-use status			
Perceptions	Ecstasy (n = 106) %	Other illicit drugs (n = 64) %	Marijuana (n = 173) %	None (n = 353) %
% Women who strongly disapproved of people aged 18 or older using the following drugs occasionally				
Ecstasy	32.4	80.9	81.9	86.6
Marijuana	17.3	33.3	28.6	74.7
Cocaine	61.5	84.4	93.0	86.9
% Women who strongly disapproved of people aged 18 or older using the following drugs regularly				
Ecstasy	64.7	88.7	90.8	88.9
Marijuana	31.4	53.2	52.7	80.3
Cocaine	84.3	91.8	94.6	88.3
% Women who definitely would not use the following drugs 5 years from now				
Ecstasy	57.6	95.2	94.5	97.0
Marijuana	38.4	67.2	61.8	94.4
Cocaine	81.4	98.4	97.6	96.4

Ecstasy users were more likely to have a greater number of sexual partners both in their lifetime and in the last 12 months prior to the survey, compared with other two drug groups (see Table 7.5). No significant differences were noted between groups on condom use, gynaecological and obstetric histories.

Table 7.5 Sexual, Obstetric, and Gynaecologic History of Young, Low-Income Women, by Drug Use Status (N=696)

	Ecstasy n=106	Other illicit drugs n=64	Marijuana n=173	None n=353
Sexual behavior				
# of lifetime sexual partners (median)	10	7	6	2
# of sexual partners in the last 12 months (median)	2	1	1	1
condom use in the last 12 months (%)				
Never	8.3	3.6	16.8	14.6
Sometimes	54.2	52.7	49.7	45.6
Always	37.5	43.6	33.6	39.8
Gynaecological history				
Had a sexually transmitted infection (STI) (%)	66.0	56.2	62.2	40.7
Had a positive culture result of a STI at the visit (%)	28.3	24.6	29.8	23.8
Had an abnormal Pap Smear (%)	34.9	44.3	33.1	21.7
Had a positive culture result of an abnormal Pap at the visit (%)	9.4	19.7	19.8	12.7
Obstetric history				
Age at 1st pregnancy (mean, SD)	18.1 (2.5)	18.4 (3.4)	18.1 (2.3)	19.1 (2.8)
# of pregnancies (%)				
0	42.5	28.3	32.7	26.8
1	18.9	30.0	32.1	24.1
2 or more	38.6	41.7	35.2	49.1
Had abortion at least once (%)	31.7	29.8	31.5	20.1

Higher scores on Cohen's Perceived Stress Scale (PSS) were reported by ecstasy users (21.9), as well as exclusive marijuana users (21.2) and other illicit drug users (22.0), reported higher scores on, compared to the score (18.4) by those who never used any illicit drugs ($p<0.001$) (see Table 7.6). Associations were further examined between stress levels and type of substance use.

Table 7.6 Levels of Perceived Stress among Young, Low-Income Women by Drug-Use Status (n=407)

Cohen's Perceived Stress	Drug-use status			
	Ecstasy n = 54 %	Other illicit drugs n = 36 %	Marijuana n = 90 %	None n = 227 %
In the last month, have you….				
been upset because of something that happened unexpectedly?	2.26	2.03	2.22	1.51
felt that you were unable to control the important things in your life?	2.02	1.75	1.82	1.29
felt nervous and "stressed"?	2.80	2.39	2.52	1.93
found that you could not cope with all the things that you had to do?	1.87	1.78	1.81	1.54
been angered because of things that were outside of your control?	2.02	1.83	2.08	1.60
felt difficulties were piling up so high that you could not overcome them?	2.13	1.89	1.77	1.49
Subscale	*13.09†*	*11.78*	*12.20†*	*9.31‡*
felt confident about your ability to handle your personal problems?*	1.74	1.19	1.57	1.45
felt that things were going your way?*	1.85	1.50	1.82	1.64
been able to control irritations in your life?*	1.80	1.39	1.74	1.85
felt that you were on top of things?*	1.83	1.51	1.79	1.84
Subscale	*7.22*	*5.56*	*6.88*	*6.73*
Total scale	*20.31†*	*17.22*	*19.08†*	*16.04‡*

*variables are recoded; higher scores indicate more stressful feeling.

† indicates statistical difference at α<0.05 level from ‡ in ANOVA test.

Compared to nonusers (with a PSS score of 18.4), more recent ecstasy users (with a PSS score of 24.2) and other illicit drug users (with a PSS score of 24.4) reported significantly elevated levels of stress ($p<0.001$). In addition, among those who never used any illicit drugs, those who smoked or drank had significantly elevated levels of stress when compared to those who never used any substances (with a PSS score of 16.6; $p<0.001$). Below, an 18-year old female ecstasy user said she coped with her stress by using different substances:

> I was engaged previously. When I graduate from my job corp, my fiancé was still there. I came home and I got a phone call from this woman – his new girl friend. That was my first true love. It just broke my heart. I got high... I was plastered for 4 days, I was in my best friend's house. ... I mainly smoked marijuana ...we drank. Everyone hanging out with us is over 21. That is why they call me 'baby girl'. I was the youngest of all... I am so scared since alcoholism runs in my family, both sides of my family. I am scared, I don't want to be like my mom.

More ecstasy users reported having friends who used cocaine and club drugs, brought drugs to parties, and drove while drunk or high (see Table 7.7). There were no differences between the three drug groups in terms of their social environment, which, as discussed earlier, included the presence of people selling drugs and people moving in and out in the neighborhood.

After controlling for demographics and other characteristics except stress variable (PSS-10), the first set of multivariable logistic models showed that ecstasy users were more likely than marijuana users to: (a) be non-Hispanic white (OR = 3.54; 95% CI: 1.62, 7.73) or Hispanic (OR = 6.03, 95% CI: 2.05, 17.90); (b) not strongly disapprove of other's use of ecstasy on a regular basis (OR = 3.99, 95% CI: 1.73, 9.18); (c) intend to use ecstasy five years from now (OR = 5.18, 95% CI: 1.89, 14.16); and (d) have friends using many different substances (OR = 1.23, 95% CI: 1.08, 1.41). PSS-10 was added to the second model, and the statistical significances discussed above did not change. However, the magnitude of each indicator did change slightly.

In addition, the second model indicated that women with higher levels of PSS-10 were more likely to use ecstasy (OR = 1.09, 95% CI: 1.00, 1,19).

The second set of multivariable logistic models indicated that ecstasy users were more likely than the other drug use groups to: (a) use other illicit drugs (OR = 1.58; 95% CI: 1.21, 2.05); (b) not strongly disapprove other's use of ecstasy on a regular basis (OR = 2.79, 95% CI: 1.12, 6.95); and (c) intend to use ecstasy five years from now (OR = 9.52, 95% CI: 2.38, 38.03). When PSS-10 was added to the model, no statistical significance emerged in PSS-10 between ecstasy users and other illicit drug users.

Table 7.7 Social Environment of Young, Low-Income Women by Drug-Use Status

Social environment	Drug-use status			
	Ecstasy (n = 106) %	Other illicit drugs (n = 64) %	Marijuana (n = 173) %	None (n = 353) %
Has at least two close friends	85.8	78.1	71.5	75.6
Contacts friends at least 3 times/week	80.0	79.7	77.1	66.4
Invites friends to home more than 3 times/month	60.0	59.4	40.7	36.9
Has friends who				
Smoke marijuana or hashish	93.4	67.2	86.7	28.3
Use "crack" cocaine	21.9	11.1	9.3	4.0
Take cocaine powder	55.0	31.2	13.4	3.9
Take club drugs including ecstasy, ketamine, etc.	80.2	36.5	32.7	9.4
Bring drugs to parties	77.1	47.6	43.9	11.7
Get drunk at least once a week	87.4	79.7	72.1	48.6
Get bored at parties when no alcohol is served	76.4	70.3	57.9	36.7
Cut work a lot to drink or get high	30.2	21.9	16.8	6.0
Drive a car while drunk or high	87.7	64.1	57.1	26.8
Have ever had an arrest in their lifetime	79.2	73.4	70.2	39.3
Lives in a neighborhood where				
A lot of drug selling goes on in the neighborhood	42.6	34.4	42.9	52.0
People move in and out of the neighborhood often	31.4	39.1	35.2	50.3

Conclusions

In this study, the rate (7.2%) of ecstasy use in the last 12 months among young, low-income women is slightly higher than the rate (5.6%) reported for women of the same age in national surveys (e.g. SAMHSA 2001; SAMHSA 2003a). Results confirm the findings of other studies that young, low-income women are at high risk of substance use and, in particular, of trying newer emerging drugs such as ecstasy (Jayakody, Danziger & Pollack 2000). Consistent with reports from previous population-based studies, these women reported occasional use of ecstasy, but were usually poly drug users (Degenhardt, Barker & Topp 2003; Gross & McCaul 1991). However, compared with women who used other illicit drugs (LSD, PCP, crack cocaine, etc.), but not ecstasy, women who used ecstasy differed from expectations in that they tended to use even more illicit drugs besides ecstasy.

The locations where these young, low-income women used ecstasy differed from other studies reporting that ecstasy use occurs primarily at clubs, rave parties, or other dance-related scenes (Gross et al. 2002; Pedersen & Skrondal 1999; SAMHSA 2003). However, this investigation found that almost all ecstasy users in our sample reported using the drug at a friend's home, which is consistent with a previous report from Australia (Degenhardt, Barker & Topp 2003). Ecstasy using habits were consistent with the financial status of these young women, who did not have much discretionary money to attend raves or clubs. This suggests that previous research, which focused on students or rave/party attendees, may have missed a substantial proportion of ecstasy users.

With respect to stages of drug use, this study reported a slightly different progressive sequence of drug use – cigarettes, beer and wine, marijuana, hard liquor, other illicit drugs except ecstasy, and finally ecstasy (Pedersen & Skrondal 1999). Marijuana use was initiated at an earlier age than hard liquor use, suggesting that, for these women, it may have been easier to obtain marijuana than certain types of alcohol (Morral, McCaffrey & Paddock 2002; SAMHSA 2004a). As ecstasy has only recently gained popularity within the US over the last 10 years, it may be the case that ecstasy initiation might occur later than that of other illicit drugs that have been around much longer, such as crack cocaine or LSD (Landry 2002; Rosenbaum 2002). Most importantly, ecstasy users were seen to use almost all substances (including tobacco and alcohol) earlier than their peers in the other drug use groups. The very early initiation of ecstasy and other substances may indicate that these women tend to be risk-takers or pleasure-seekers (De Micheli & Formigoni 2002) or that they have experienced other problems at an early age, precipitating self-medication through substance use (Najavits, Weiss & Shaw 1997).

Regarding risk factors surrounding ecstasy use, many young women in this study who used ecstasy reported favorable attitudes towards other people's use and intention to use illicit drugs in the future. Compared with marijuana and other illicit drug users, fewer ecstasy users reported that they strongly opposed other people's use of ecstasy, marijuana, and cocaine, and they more often reported their intention to use these drugs within five years. This subgroup of young women may be at high risk to continue their drug use or try new drugs as they appear on the market.

The ecstasy group reported having more sexual partners than the other two drug use groups. Since one major psychopharmacological property of ecstasy is heightened acute tactile sensitivity, women who use it may be more likely to engage in sex, which could lead to seeking more sexual partners (Liechti & Vollenweider 2000; Parrott 2001). However, among our sample of ecstasy users, having more sexual partners was not associated with increased gynecological or obstetric problems, as compared to the other two drug use groups. In addition, compared to nonusers, more ecstasy users self-reported having an STI in the past. This is consistent with previous literature that drug users, even without injection drug use, could result in higher risks of STIs through their engagement in risky sexual behaviors (Gyarmathy et al. 2002; Neaigus et al. 2001; Strathdee & Sherman 2003). Ecstasy users and those who never used any drug did not differ in the incidence of current positive results for abnormal Pap smear or other STIs. Possibly, because the study sample was obtained from gynecological clinics, other risk factors for STIs, such as higher rates of infections among sexual partners, may be found (LaMontagne, Fine, & Marrazzo 2004; Lee, Jennings, & Ellen 2004).

Ecstasy users in this study reported higher stress levels. Since their stressful feelings or thoughts at the time of ecstasy use were not measured, the direction of this relationship – whether women used ecstasy to alleviate their stress or, alternatively, experienced stress as a result of ecstasy use – cannot be determined. Previous research has shown that women with prior psychological/psychiatric symptoms or conditions were more likely to use ecstasy (Gamma et al. 2000; Halpern et al. 2004; Ho, Karimi-Tabesh & Koren 2001; Milani et al. 2004; Parrott & Lasky 1998; Singer et al. 2004; Verheyden et al. 2002). Studies have also demonstrated that after ecstasy use, women reported increased psychiatric symptoms or conditions (Milani et al. 2004; Verheyden et al. 2002). Overall, this investigation revealed a strong connection between negative psychological symptoms or conditions and ecstasy use. Young, low-income women felt more stress during their daily living and used more ecstasy compared to the general population. Further studies are recommended to investigate the directionality of the relationship between ecstasy use and stress, and to contextualize the stressful living situations that may impact women's lives, including illicit drug use.

Consistent with previous health studies of illicit drug use (Andrews et al. 2002; Urberg et al. 2004), peer association plays an important role in substance use in young people. The cross-sectional study design of this study indicated that young, low-income ecstasy users reported having more friends who used more licit and illicit drugs. This may reflect a tendency to choose a social network or environment that fosters their habit or includes others with similar interests (Clatts et al. 2003; Miller & Neaigus 2001).

The current study does have some methodological limitations. First, the data are self-reported, subject to recall bias and socially desirable response tendencies. Moreover, because ecstasy is an illicit drug and the study was conducted in a medical setting, women may have underreported their use. Second, this is a cross-sectional study and the causal relationships between the risk factors of interest and ecstasy use cannot be determined. Third, this study used a convenience sample whose findings may not be generalized to other populations with similar characteristics in different settings. Fourth, data on perceived stress were obtained from only part of the sample. Women who did not answer the stress questions were younger, more likely to be black and single. These characteristics are significantly correlated with higher levels of stress (Boardman et al. 2001; Cerbone & Larison 2000; Turner & Avison 2003). Thus, our study may underestimate levels of stress among these women. Future studies are needed to clarify such relationships.

Despite these limitations, this study has described the characteristics of young, low-income female ecstasy users. In general, these women perceived themselves using illicit drugs in the future, were at higher risk of continuing to use these drugs, and indicated higher levels of stress than respondents who used marijuana only or those who used other illicit drugs. These results suggest that future interventions may be more cost-effective if designed to target this high-risk subgroup of young women. In addition, if young women who started using substances at very young ages have already tried a variety of illicit drugs, the next step may be for them to try newer, popular drugs available on the market. Future longitudinal studies are necessary to identify trends of new drug use among young, low-income women.[3]

---

3   Reprinted from *Addictive Behaviors*, vol. 31, no. 4, by Z. Helen Wu et al., 'Patterns and perceptions of ecstasy use among young, low-income women', pp. 676-685, Copyright 2005, with permission from Elsevier.

Chapter 8

The Emergence of Clubs and Drugs in Hong Kong[1]

Karen Joe Laidler, Geoffrey Hunt, Kathleen MacKenzie
and Kristin Evans

Over the last twenty years, the dance scene has gradually emerged and developed into a global phenomenon. This phenomenon is expressive and indicative of a distinctive youth culture. Across the world, from Europe to the Americas to Australia, observers have noted the hip and trendy lifestyle in dress, music and setting of the contemporary dance scene (Hunt & Evans 2002). This globalizing dance scene has also been inextricably connected to the use of illicit drugs. As many researchers in Australia, Canada, England, Scotland and the Netherlands have noted (Adlaf & Smart 1997; Forsyth 1996; Lenton, Boys & Norcross 1997; Measham, Aldridge & Parker 2001; Pedersen & Skrondal 1999; Pini 2001; Redhead 1997; Thornton 1995; Wijngaart et al. 1998), psychoactive drugs like ecstasy, amphetamines, cocaine and marijuana have become an integral part of the dance scene for many participants. Ecstasy has been, perhaps, the most widely recognized drug associated with the scene, as users report its ability to stimulate a euphoric and empathetic state, and at the same time "prolong trance dancing" (Beck & Rosenbaum 1994 p. 54). According to observers, this interplay between ecstasy, dance and the environment of the event has made this form of leisure so attractive and popular among youth. As McRobbie (1994, p. 168) noted, "the atmosphere is one of unity, of dissolving difference in the peace and harmony haze of the drug Ecstasy."

Despite this increasing globalization of the dance and drug scene, most observers would agree that knowledge of the phenomenon remains far from complete, with many countries trying to keep pace with the changing patterns of illicit drug use and the context in which these drugs are used. For example, in Scotland, ecstasy users are reportedly taking five or more tablets in a single session and combining it with sleeping pills like Temazepam (Reynolds 1998). In England, researchers have noted the shift away from ecstasy toward increasing use of cocaine and cannabis (Williams & Parker 2001). The combination of these two drugs "creates a sensory

1 Collection of data for this chapter was made possible by supplementary funding from the National Institute on Drug Abuse (DA14317-S1), administered by Moira O'Brien. We would also like to thank Dr. Steve Gust from the International Office of NIDA for assisting us with our international research.

intensification without euphoria, tinged with nerve jangling paranoia", which fits with the mood of post-rave music sub-genres (Reynolds 1998 p. 85). Measham (2004c) has also recently observed that the decline in ecstasy use in the UK must also be understood in the context of the growth of alcohol binging, spurred on in part by legislative and enforcement changes.

In addition, while raves and large scale warehouse parties were once the premiere sites for the dance drug experience, reports from different locales suggest that a transition to a 'post rave' culture has emerged (Measham & Moore this volume; Reynolds 1997, 1999; Silverstone this volume). This transition reflects a diversification both in the types of music appearing in dance venues and the emergence of new cocktails of drugs being consumed (i.e. the effects of particular combinations of drugs being conducive to particular moods of music). This transition is also reflected in an increasing diversification of venues for dancing and drug use. For example, in the UK, where the rave scene first flourished in the late 1980s, raves were primarily large-scale events that were held in abandoned warehouses and open fields (Collin & Godfrey 1998). As the scene developed, the music and the type of venues began to diversify and grow. In the UK context, the term 'venue' covers a wide range of different places including: "large warehouses, premises traditionally recognized as night-clubs, and pubs or bars, especially those which feature music and a dance floor" (Morris 1998 p. 2). This expansion and diversification resulted in an extremely lucrative industry estimated as worth in excess of $2.7bn in 1993 (Thornton 1995 p. 15; see also Hobbs 2000).

Despite the globalization of the dance drug scene, our understanding of the phenomenon has principally been informed by the experiences and developments in the UK, Europe, Australia and North America. This is not surprising, as the rave scene first emerged in these countries. In the UK, sociological and epidemiological studies on raves, clubs and drugs appeared in the early to middle 1990s and, as such, have documented the shifts in drug patterns and locale (McRobbie 1994; Redhead 1993; Thornton 1995)[2] Our understanding of dance drug scenes in other cultures has been relatively limited, but from available studies on other locales, it appears that the settings may be different and varied, reflecting the interaction of global club cultures with more specific local factors. For example, Saldanha (2002) has shown that the primary settings for youth dance culture in Bangalore, India emerged in pubs rather than the large scale events held in abandoned warehouses and open fields, as happened in the UK (Collin & Godfrey 1998). These venues provide entertainment during the afternoon instead of the evening to accommodate lifestyle and restraints on middle class female youth. Such local characteristics suggest that, while global homogenization of dance cultures and drugs is a growing trend, these imported global universals are shaped and transformed by the local context and culture (Bennett & Peterson 2004). As Howes (1996) has noted, the process of globalization occurs alongside the process of "hybridization or "creolization" by which imported objects

---

2   See Hunt & Evans (2002) for a discussion of the separation between sociological and epidemiological studies.

and cultures "become imbued with alternative meanings" (1996 p. 5) and take on features adapted from the local culture. Such local adaptations are important features that need to be examined in their own right in order to understand the "articulation between global and local" (Howes 1996 p. 6) and see how these global features become played out in different ways in different social settings and cultures.

Hong Kong has witnessed the emergence of a dance drug scene and, within a relatively short period of time, shifted into a "post rave" period similar to that described in other locales around the world with a diversification in the patterns of drug use and venues in which to use them. In the following sections, we describe the emergence of the dance drug scene in Hong Kong. In doing so, we look at the ways in which drug use features in the dance music scene, the meaning of drug use in these settings and the reasons for the rapid development of the dance drug scene in Hong Kong. We begin with an overview of the drug use trends over the past ten years.

Hong Kong Drug Trends

Hong Kong has a long colonial history with opiates. From the 1800s through to the 1940s, opium dominated, but eventually heroin became the primary drug on the local market, and its use remains associated with lower class adult males (Joe Laidler, Hodson & Traver 2000). Although highly stigmatized, heroin users are generally perceived as relatively non-threatening in the community. Given the sedating narcotic effects of heroin, these users infrequently engage in drug related violence (cf. Goldstein 2004). Drug use trends among young people, however, have changed rapidly in recent years with the growth of a distinctive dance scene.

The Hong Kong government's Central Registry of Drug Abuse database (CRDA) has been one source for documenting the changes in drug use patterns. The CRDA has documented, since 1972, those users who come to the attention of agencies like law enforcement, hospitals and clinics, social welfare agencies and treatment centers. The CRDA has been viewed as a relatively reliable indicator of heroin use, and has been able to capture the general increase in psychoactive drug use. Table 8.1 summarizes CRDA data on rates of drug use in Hong Kong among interviewed drug users.

Table 8.1 Most Common Drugs Abused in Hong Kong by Age Group

	1995	1996	1997	1998	1999	2000	2001	2002	2003	2004
	%	%	%	%	%	%	%	%	%	%
Under 21										
Heroin	72.5	66.6	64.3	58.4	49.1	21.5	13.3	10.7	7.7	5.3
MDMA	-	@	1.7	2.0	13.1	56.2	53.0	37.1	34.1	37.4
Ice	1.5	7.6	14.4	17.3	17.3	11.0	10.8	8.1	6.5	6.7
Cocaine	@	@	@	@	0.3	0.3	0.4	0.6	0.5	0.9
Cannabis	20.2	21.0	21.8	26.6	30.2	21.2	17.4	25.9	28.4	25.4
Ketamine	-	-	@	-	0.6	36.9	59.8	70.4	62.5	69.4
# of Persons w/Type of Drug Reported	3,581	3,363	2,887	2,551	2,219	3,467	3,210	2,494	1,758	2,062
% polydrug use	12.8	13.4	15.8	15.5	21.1	41.4	45.7	43.1	43.7	47.6
Over 21										
Heroin	93.0	90.8	91.4	91.7	91.8	88.3	85.0	86.0	84.4	81.0
MDMA	-	@	0.1	0.1	0.4	3.0	4.4	3.3	2.6	3.6
Ice	0.7	1.8	3.8	3.8	4.9	4.5	4.6	3.0	3.6	4.0
Cocaine	@	@	@	@	0.1	0.2	0.3	0.2	0.4	0.6
Cannabis	4.8	5.8	5.1	5.5	4.8	5.4	5.1	4.8	4.3	4.6
Ketamine	-	-	-	-	0.1	2.5	6.3	6.9	6.4	8.9
# of Persons w/Type of Drug Reported	14,425	15,265	13,609	13,195	12,984	12,957	13,122	13,438	12,079	12,358
% polydrug use	5.0	6.5	10.0	9.9	11.6	12.6	13.6	15.2	17.7	20.0

@ For data confidentiality, figures in these columns are suppressed. Multiple answers are possible, therefore, totals do not equal 100%. Source: CRDA, 2000-2005.

As this table documents, heroin consumption today among young persons under the age of 21 has declined with the number of reported young users falling from 73% in 1995 to 5% by 2004. At the same time, Hong Kong has experienced a significant increase in psychoactive drug use, following trends reported in other countries (e.g. Johnston and O'Malley 2004; Chivite-Matthews et al. 2005; EMCDDA 2004; NDSHS 2001; SAMHSA 2003a). According to the CRDA, reported psychoactive drug use (non-opiates as defined by the Hong Kong government) among those under 21 years of age rose from 34% in 1995 to 98% by 2004 (data not shown). Much of this rise is attributable to stimulant and synthetic drug use. While less than two percent of reported young users were consuming the methamphetamine 'ice' in 1995, its use among young people grew gradually to 17% in 1998, but by 2004 had tapered off to 7%. A more significant change occurred towards the end of the 1990s with the rise in ecstasy use. In 1994, no documented cases of ecstasy use existed, but this pattern changed and gradually rose so that by 2000, the percentage of reported young persons using ecstasy increased to 56%, but slowly declined to 37% by the end of 2004. So although Hong Kong experienced a significant rise in ecstasy use, its popularity among local youth has begun to taper off. This latest decrease, however, has occurred while ketamine has become the most reported drug used among youth. The percentage of ketamine consumers has risen rapidly in the last few years with only a few cases reported in 1999 to 69% in 2004. Cannabis use among reported young persons has grown slightly over the past ten years. Importantly, reported poly-drug use amongst young people also increased from 13% in 1995 to 48% in 2004. Given these drug consumption trends, with a shift in preference among young persons from heroin to psychoactive drugs and poly-drug use, we turn to look at the local context in which youth consume and engage with the dance drug scene.

Research Methods

The data for this discussion are principally drawn from the Hong Kong portion of a National Institute of Drug Abuse-funded comparative and cross-national study of the social setting of club drug use in Hong Kong, San Francisco and Rotterdam. The main focus of this research has been to examine the dialectical process of the global and local in the dance and drug scene. In this article, however, we predominately explore the local expression and practices of Hong Kong's dance drug scene.

The data from this study are based on in-depth interviews with 100 persons who had used ecstasy and/or other drugs at least three times in their lives and had frequented a dance venue within the last six months. The interviews were conducted over an 18 month period, from April 2003 through October 2004. In the first part of the interview, respondents answered a series of socio-demographic questions from a quantitative schedule. For the rest of the interview, a semi-structured guide was used to collect primarily open-ended qualitative data on the respondents' backgrounds, their current lives, their drug and alcohol use, and their involvement in the dance scene. Quantitative data on drug use were collected at the beginning of the drug use section, utilizing frequency and quantity measures based on the National Household Survey on Drug Abuse (NHSDA, now called the National Survey on Drug Use and Health) and Monitoring the Future (Johnston, O'Malley & Bachman 2001; SAMHSA 2001). This combined approach of a qualitative and close-ended questionnaire provided an opportunity to focus on respondents' personal histories, initiation, motivations and problems with alcohol and drugs, involvement in drug sales, and experiences in different dance venues. The interview schedule was translated into Chinese, which was cross-verified and pilot tested before use. The recorded interviews were then translated back into English and verified twice by the transcriber and the interviewer to ensure accurate translation for analysis.

Six local Chinese interviewers – five females and one male – were involved in conducting the interviews. All but one of them had a master's degree in the social sciences. Three of the interviewers had extensive experience in conducting in-depth interviews with drug users in Hong Kong, having worked with one of the author's drug related research projects in Hong Kong, and had developed contacts and networks with various types of users (Joe Laidler, Day & Hodson 2001; Joe Laidler, Hodson & Day 2004; Joe Laidler, Hodson & Traver 2000). One of the interviewers had extensive contacts with user groups given her prior experience as a youth social worker. The interviewers seldom had difficulties in establishing rapport and trust with respondents due to their backgrounds and knowledge of the scene. Given the 'hidden' nature of illicit drug use and the fact that this was an exploratory study, we adopted a convenience sampling strategy, beginning with contacts with users from former research studies (37%), and from there, chain referrals from respondents (46%). The remaining 17% of the respondents were recruited from other sources, including outreaching social workers and a drug counseling outpatient clinic. The interviews lasted an average of two hours, with a range of between 75 minutes to five hours. The interviews were conducted in a variety of settings ranging from the respondent's or their peer's home to public parks, coffee shops, fast food outlets, bars, quiet lounges, and at a university office. Most of the interviews were conducted in Cantonese, the local Chinese dialect, although ten were conducted in English, as that was the native language of those respondents. We provided an honorarium of approximately US$40 in recognition of the respondent's participation and time.

Several steps were taken to address validity and reliability issues. Given the interviewers' familiarity with the scene and with some of the respondents, the respondents were probably less likely to exaggerate or minimize their experiences. During the course of the interview, the interviewer rephrased questions at different times to detect inconsistencies and to ensure truthfulness. At the end of each interview, the interviewer was required to make judgments about the veracity of responses. This involved the interviewer assessing the general truthfulness of the respondent and the extent to which inconsistencies existed. This assessment is based principally on the interviewer's own knowledge and understanding of the scene and the community, which increased over time as they accumulated broader knowledge of the scene. The interviewers also periodically conducted field observations to further cross-check respondents' veracity and to provide a more comprehensive portrait of different venues.

Characteristics of the Sample

Table 8.2 provides the basic socio-demographic traits of our sample. Of the 100 respondents, two thirds of them were male and one-third of them were female. This proportion of 1:3 females to males is similar to that of the CRDA data. That is, female users of ecstasy and ketamine account for about one-third of the total youth who reported using those drugs over the last few years (CRDA 2005; Joe Laidler, Hodson & Day 2004). Respondents ranged from 14 to 31 years of age with a median age of 21 and a mean age of 22 years. The interviewed females were slightly older than their male counterparts. The majority of respondents were Hong Kong Chinese (85%), while the remaining were from mainland China (7%) or other ethnic or national backgrounds (8%). The majority of them were born in Hong Kong (79%), 17% were born in mainland China and the remaining 4% were born in another country.

Nearly three-fourths of the respondents came from lower class or working class families. This characteristic was also reflected in the majority of the employed respondents who worked in the service industry or in trade occupations; one-third were employed in trade jobs or at the lower end of the service industry. The most common occupations were hair stylists, cosmetologists, sales clerks, decorators, telemarketers, servers at restaurants and discos, and those working in the construction industry. One third of the respondents were unemployed at the time of the interview, some of whom were students. Those working in professional positions were employed as accountants, bankers, flight attendants, business owners or managers, teachers, and journalists. Only 30% of them earned the equivalent of more than $1,000 per month. Forty percent of them received "pocket money" from their families every month, and for more than one-fourth of them, that was their only source of income. About 10% of them supplemented their income through various illegal activities, such as selling or delivering pirated videodiscs and selling drugs.

Sixty-eight percent lived in a household that was headed by a family member, including 42% who lived with both parents and another 26% who lived with only one of their parents. Seven respondents lived on their own, 11 resided with their spouse or partner, and three lived with roommates. The remainder lived with other family members.

Hong Kong's education differs from the US, with compulsory schooling lasting until Form 3 or about 11th grade (15-16 years of age). Slightly over 60% had not advanced beyond Form 3. However, it should be noted that one-third of the respondents were currently attending school, and among these, 16% were attending a secondary or technical school.

Drugs, Clubs and Young People

Table 8.2 Socio-Demographic Characteristics

	Males N=66	Females N=34
Median Age	20	21.5
Years of School Completed:		
Less than 11	36%	29%
11 Years (High School Equivalent)	24%	35%
12-13 Years	21%	15%
14-15 Years	11%	12%
16 Years or more (University Graduate/Higher Degree)	8%	9%
Income Sources:*		
From Employment	73%	65%
Median Income from Employment	HK 7200	HK 8000
From Family	39%	41%
Median Income from Family	HK 2000	HK 2500
Household Composition		
Lives with Both Parents	48%	29%
Lives with Mother Only	24%	18%
Lives with Father Only	3%	6%
Lives on his/her Own	6%	9%
Lives with Spouse or Boyfriend/Girlfriend	8%	18%
Lives with Other	11%	20%

*Income sources do not add up to 100% as some respondents have multiple sources.

Patterns and Reasons for Drug Use

As has been found elsewhere, the respondents in this study appear to be drug experienced and their use is, at least initially, connected to the dance scene (Measham, Aldridge & Parker 2001; Perrone this volume). Importantly, since the goal of the project was to interview club drug users who attend dance events, our sample will, by definition, have high rates of club drug use. As Table 8.3 indicates, nearly all of the respondents had used marijuana at some time, typically at around 16 years of age (median). Approximately three-quarters of them reported use of marijuana in the last year.

The majority of respondents had also used ecstasy and ketamine, typically at the age of 17 or 18 for males and females respectively (median age). While slightly more males had tried ecstasy and ketamine, proportionately the gender differences were not consistent (although they were relatively small) for use in the past month and year. By contrast, the proportion of females who tried ice or other methamphetamines was higher than their male counterparts (50% compared to 23%

respectively). Importantly, the attraction to methamphetamines among females is partly related to the perceived appetite suppressant (and therefore weight reducing) qualities of the drug (Joe Laidler, Hodson & Day 2004; Perrone this volume). Moreover, methamphetamines are typically used in private settings, since users do not consider them to be conducive to public settings like discos or parties, as their use entails a relatively quiet environment in which to prepare the necessary equipment for smoking (Joe Laidler, Hodson & Traver 2000). Females also had higher rates of using cocaine and 5 Jai (Erimin/nimetazepam, a benzodiazepine), which is sometimes used to temper the high from ketamine. Clearly, marijuana, ecstasy and ketamine are the primary drugs of choice among this sample, but the data suggests that the majority of the respondents were occasional users rather than frequent or heavy users.

Table 8.3 Drug Use by Gender

	Drugs Used Lifetime		Median Age First Used		Drugs Used Last Month		Drugs Used Last Year	
	Males N=66	Females N=34	Males N=66	Females N=34	Males N=66	Females N=34	Males N=66	Females N=34
Ecstasy	94%	85%	17	18	33%	38%	73%	74%
Ketamine	88%	82%	17	17.5	45%	43%	67%	74%
Methamphetamine	23%	50%	17	16	6%	9%	11%	18%
5 Jai/Give me Five	44%	59%	18	18	8%	26%	30%	41%
Cocaine	27%	41%	20	20.5	5%	3%	15%	32%
Cough Mixture	18%	9%	16	16	5%	0%	6%	0%
Marijuana	89%	94%	16	16	38%	47%	70%	79%

The rise in the popularity of ecstasy and ketamine is linked to a number of factors. First, users perceived ecstasy and ketamine to have few immediate side effects and no long-term consequences, even with the knowledge that such drugs are not pure. They did not perceive these drugs as being addictive. Moreover, most respondents believed that they were able to control and regulate their use, and produce the desired effects without negative health or social consequences (see Kelly this volume; Perrone this volume). Among the desired effects, users reported that ecstasy allowed them to express their emotions and to feel connected to others, "you can express your deepest sentiments and feelings at the time. After that experience, my view in seeing the world changed" (HK28). Ecstasy's hallucinogenic effects, often described as "illusions", were perceived as a positive attribute of the drug.

> I couldn't control my hands. And I had an illusion. I felt like I had been in another world, but I could still identify others' voices. I felt like I was riding on a roller coaster, it was very exciting.

Ecstasy also allowed users to be uninhibited, to be more open and free without the restraints they normally feel in everyday life. One respondent described it this way:

> Dancing is kind of like drinking. Getting high on ecstasy is also like drinking. You don't think so much. I'm a very shy person and don't dance much, and I wasn't very good at it... but after drinking or taking ecstasy, I don't care about these things anymore. And... I would talk more to friends and even strangers.

Ketamine, like ecstasy, has become associated with Hong Kong's dance drug scene. Ketamine is easy to use in dance settings as users can snort part of a packet either in the bathroom, private VIP rooms, or sometimes in the open. Some users preferred to dissolve it into their drinks, usually beer or Diamond Black, an alcopop.[3] Users' initial motivations to use ketamine were related to peer influence and curiosity, but also to the desire to shift and elevate the ecstasy high (Joe Laidler 2004). The above respondent, who clearly likes the sociability produced by ecstasy, described why he likes to experience the out of body experience of ketamine:

> With ketamine, I was just numb. It seems like you've jumped outside of your body and look back at yourself. You see yourself sitting there. Like... in a state of meditation where Zen in Buddhism says "Dhyaana" [a state of bliss]. There are monks in Tibet saying these kinds of things. They explain that "Dhyaana" was just like taking a drug, when one reaches that state...One would be [blissful] but it would be short. Yet the [bliss] that Dhyaan brings about should be very stable and calm. When one reaches Dhyaan, one could compare it with taking drugs. Both are very happy states.

The increase in ecstasy and ketamine also lies in their association with a distinctive and trendy social scene. The characteristics of this youthful 'hip' culture contrast greatly with that of heroin (Joe Laidler, Hodson & Traver 2000). Heroin use is culturally defined as part of the older generation (30s and over) and users are seen as having 'hit the end of the road' when they shift to heroin (Joe Laidler 2004). Drugs like ecstasy and ketamine are not associated with the negative identity or stigma of heroin users (cf. Perrone this volume; Sanders this volume).

Importantly, ecstasy and ketamine are relatively inexpensive, making it affordable across social classes to be part of this trendy hip youth culture. The average retail price of ecstasy per tablet has declined from US$32 in 1997 to US$10 in 2004, while

---

3   Alcopops are sweet tasting alcoholic beverages primarily marketed towards young consumers.

the average retail price of ketamine per gram similarly dropped from US$23 in 2000 to US$19. The drop in prices has been accompanied by a decline in the quality of these drugs, as reported by our respondents.One of the most salient links to the increase in ecstasy and ketamine's popularity is the emergence and proliferation of venues for dancing. From our past studies and our respondents' reports in this study, ecstasy clearly appeared in Hong Kong in the early 1990s and was mainly found in the occasional organized rave parties frequented by the expatriate population who brought in small quantities from abroad. By the mid 1990s, there appeared to be a slow rise in the number of local residents frequenting rave events.

> It started in 1995 or 1996, there were some local promoters who employed some UK DJs to hold some private parties in some small places. About 150 to 200 people. It was very happy because they used ecstasy. The noise people were making were very good. As more people went, the organizers started to look for bigger venues for these parties. At Barcity,[4] the maximum was about 800 to 1,000 people. The people were trendy.. listening to the in-est songs, wearing the in-est clothes, and taking ecstasy. At that time, very few people knew about it or had access to it, so you would feel especially in. Naturally when the noise got louder, more people would want to know what was happening. So the quality of the people declined. Especially in Hong Kong, a trend spreads fast, and the police started paying more attention to it. So, only in a short time, 1997, 98, 99... in 2000, some parties had 6,000 people and there were some regular parties with 2,000 people. In a short time, so many knew about it. I mean, it's fast, in a few years...compared with overseas, clubs and parties are part of their lifestyles. It's similar to our singing karaoke. But the Hong Kong scene didn't give opportunities for the investors of these kinds of events. There weren't opportunities or space to organize these events.

The limited success of organized rave parties was related to the density of living and lack of space in Hong Kong, the increased policing of these events, and the government's enactment of legislation mandating organizers and promoters to meet stringent health and safety requirements (Joe Laidler 2004). Many of our respondents partly attributed the decline to increased police surveillance.

> The change was that it got more annoying to go to raves due to the cops and eventually not a lot of people organized them. If you can't go to parties, people will find other things to do.

The popularity of these organized party events began to diminish by 1998 as many Hong Kong entrepreneurs recognized the potential profits of converting existing karaoke bars and restaurants into permanent venues for dancing and clubbing. From 1998 onward, the dance party scene began to take hold and established itself in different venues, which attracted a wider audience (Joe Laidler, Hodson & Traver 2000).

The differences between organized rave parties and the developing club scene during the latter part of the 1990s can be understood in terms of the music and people

---

4   All the names of venues have been changed.

who attended these two types of scenes. While the music at raves was typically from abroad and without lyrics, more permanent local venues tended to include local Cantonese pop music. Raves were also recognized as sites with a high degree of anonymity, thereby allowing participants to be bolder and freer than in discos and clubs where space was more constrained and the risk of knowing or being under the scrutiny of others was greater.

> They are certainly different. The disco is a place for social communication though it's true that a rave party can also be a place for communication. Yet you are talking to some strangers in the rave party. There are two halls inside the rave party. One is for music and one is for people to sit down after dancing for a long time to rest from being tired. There would be strangers sitting next to you talking to you… The relations among people become closer in a rave party. However, if one goes to a disco, he or she is going out with others. It's a place for social communication with some familiar people. It's not so good to take your drugs inside the disco. You might meet them the next time. At rave parties, you might see the same person the next time, but they won't remember you. There are so many people in the rave, and we won't exchange numbers and keep in contact. Yet you might keep in touch with someone you know in the disco. Also, the music inside discos doesn't always match with the drugs taken.

The proliferation of more permanent discos and clubs has resulted in a range of dance venues catering to different types of participants and experiences. At one end are large clubs that can accommodate at least 400 attendees. More than one-half of the respondents had frequented one of these establishments. Such clubs tended to charge relatively high entrance fees ranging from about US$35 to US$65, and drinks are expensive when compared to smaller discos. These large dance venues have strict security controls, trying to ensure that minors do not gain entry. Participants were fully cognizant of the differences between large clubs. For example, Club Space has been characterized as being a very trendy, upscale, clean and spacious venue with Western style music and expensive décor. VIP rooms are available to rent and typically groups of friends pool their money to share the expense of about US$150. The patrons of this club are described as young, mature and professional. Club 6 is also a very popular venue, but tended to attract more 'gangster like' patrons. As one respondent noted, "Club 6 is more like where the thugs go, and the music is more general, and the people there don't have as much class".

> Obviously those who go to Club Space don't look like gangsters. Only one or two out of 10… seem to be triad members. But in Club 6, you can see that more than half of them look like triad members. That's the biggest difference. Also in Club Space, visitors come in groups of two or three. That makes it easier to meet new friends. You feel relatively safe to hang around there. At Club 6, there are fights quite often.

Aside from these large clubs, the number of discos, clubs and lounges catering to working class youth as well as the affluent has increased. Unlike the larger clubs, smaller clubs were more likely to be short lived, often closing and re-opening months later with a different name and a modified style. Respondents who attended the more upscale clubs expressed a social and class distance from those who attended working class discos.

> In those shabby discos, the lighting is dim and I don't want to go there. I've been to that popular one before, it was very small and crowded. I don't want to go there again.

> I go to that upmarket club because of the friends, and I don't want to go to any that are too mixed. It's a bit mean to say but we also consider the class of people who go to a particular place. We don't want to see "them" in a high-class club.

The consumption of drugs, especially ecstasy and cocaine, was more commonly associated with venues attracting more affluent patrons than discos catering to working class youth. These latter types of venues were more likely to have a regular established clientele with a strong attachment to the club. Part of this affinity may be related to the respondents' connections to triad members,[5] which meant that they often gained free entrance. These connections also allowed underage patrons to gain entry, which is difficult at upscale clubs.

Clearly the dance scene in Hong Kong provides a range of venues for party goers to choose from. For those with limited resources, local clubs allowed their clientele to gain entry for little money or, in some cases, even for free. For the more affluent club goers, expensive and upscale clubs existed. In these larger venues people could hide in anonymity and a different sense of liberation existed in experiencing the music, the people and the drugs.

Conclusion

We return to our initial queries about whether Hong Kong's recent experiences reflect the changes in the global dance drug scene. One concern has been on the extent and nature of dance drugs. Official government data (CRDA) indicate that overall, the number of reported young persons under the age of 21 using drugs in Hong Kong has been on the decline since 1995, falling from 3,581 in 1995 to 2,062 in 2004. This decline, however, bears scrutiny. When we examine the nature of this change, it becomes clear that the decline has largely been in relation to heroin consumption, a drug which has historically been associated with working class males and 'hard core' addiction. By the start of the new millennium, official data documented another significant change with over 50% of reported young users indicating use of ecstasy and within one year, about 60% of them reported using ketamine. In Hong Kong, these drugs of the new millennium have been associated with the emergence of a distinctive dance drug youth culture. Importantly, whether the CRDA data reflect an overall decline in the number of youths using drugs or whether the 'hidden' population of contemporary drug users has increased is unclear (Joe Laidler, Day

---

5   See Joe Laidler (2004) for a further discussion on the connection between triads in organized crime and drugs sales.

& Hodson 2001). As noted earlier, the nature and settings for using ecstasy and ketamine differ greatly from that of heroin, with psychoactive users perhaps being at less risk of encounters with reporting agencies (e.g. law enforcement, social workers).

Our interviews with psychoactive drug users suggest that young users are drug experienced and tend to use multiple drugs in ways similar to that reported in other countries. As young persons elsewhere, many Hong Kong psychoactive drug users are introduced to ecstasy in dance party settings, and continue to use with the belief that ecstasy facilitates an emotional and liberating state not normally experienced in their everyday life (cf. Hayward 2004; Presdee 2000). After their initial experiences, many sought to alter their ecstasy high with ketamine, using it as a 'top-up' after several hours of dancing on ecstasy. As found in this study and our others (Joe Laidler, Hodson & Day 2004), ketamine, also very much embedded in the dance drug scene, shifts the ecstasy high from an emotional "head shaking" experience to an out of body, free floating one. This expansion in the repetoire of drugs – of mixing and matching and extending with alcohol - enjoyed in the dance drug scene is similar to reports from other locales (see Lankenau and Clatts 2005; Measham 2004c). Also, users in Hong Kong generally perceived their use of ecstasy and ketamine as controlled and unproblematic based on the belief that these drugs are not addictive and do not result in long term negative health consequences (cf. Kelly this volume; Perrone this volume).

Another significant issue related to the dance drug scene has been the shift identified by a number of researchers from organized events to a situation which has been defined as a "post rave" culture. This shift can be seen in the Hong Kong case. In fact, as we have indicated, one of the most important reasons for the flourishing dance drug scene in Hong Kong is due to the proliferation of venues where young people can dance and use drugs. The rise and popularity of organized events, as some of the respondents in this study suggested, was relatively short lived in Hong Kong, attracting particular types and groups of young persons. Government controls and law enforcement pressures on promoters also made it difficult for organized events to continue. A number of entrepreneurs in the entertainment industry, many with links to local organized crime, seized the opportunity to develop permanent venues catering to young persons from different social class backgrounds, with different tastes and preferences for dance music (Joe Laidler 2004).

Finally, while the dance drug experience in Hong Kong reflects global developments within the electronic dance music scene, developments in Hong Kong highlight the importance of considering local influences, being most obvious in the increasing attraction of ketamine. In fact, evidence exists to suggest that ketamine, once exclusively found within the dance scene, has become a feature of the more general youth lifestyle within Hong Kong (Joe Laidler, Hodson, & Day 2004).

Photograph courtesy of Simon Brockbank.

Chapter 9

In the Club Redux: Ecstasy Use and Supply in a London Nightclub

Bill Sanders

Attending nightclubs is a relatively prominent activity amongst young people today. According to the Home Office publication *Safer Clubbing*, an estimated four million young people each week attend the thousands of clubs in the UK (Webster, Goodman & Whalley 2002). They attend for a variety of reasons, such as socializing with friends, meeting new people, dancing to the music, to just 'chill out', and to use drugs (Measham, Aldridge & Parker 2001; Release 1997). One of the more popular 'dance' drugs, 'ecstasy', has been considered to go hand-in-glove within 'raves' and clubs (*inter alia* Redhead 1993; Shapiro 1999). The high rate of ecstasy use within clubs suggests these settings are ripe for the commercialization of this drug (Ruggiero & South 1995). *Safer Clubbing* acknowledges that the "single most important factor in tacking drug" selling in club land are the "door supervisors" (Webster, Goodman & Whalley 2002 p. 33; see also Morris 1998). But what if club security themselves are selling drugs, or at least allowing it, and what are the implications of this? The elements that make up 'club culture', on any one evening, may best be considered a variety of interacting cultures that 'make' the night (Gilbert & Pearson 1999; Redhead 1997; Thornton 1995; Stanley 1997). This manuscript analyses two vital elements of club culture: ecstasy use and ecstasy supply.

Club culture today is intrinsically linked with a drugs culture. Throughout the 20th century youth cultures in the UK, US and Australia have been associated with using specific drugs. Cocaine was used by punters at late night jazz venues in the 1920s, Mods and Rockers, skinheads and punks used amphetamines, 'hippies' championed cannabis and experimented with LSD, and the celebration of marijuana is a consistent theme within hip-hop (Brake 1985; Kohn 1997; Moore 1994; Shapiro 1999). Contemporary club culture, however, seems slightly different due to the exceptionally large percentage of young people who have used ecstasy within club settings. Researchers have found 53% (O'Hagan 1999; Release 1997) and 67% (Measham, Aldridge & Parker 2001) of clubbers admitting to using ecstasy, either that evening or within the past three months. The tight association of a drug (ecstasy) with a youth culture (raving/clubbing) within contemporary Western society seems somewhat unprecedented (Collin & Godfrey 1997; Parker, Measham & Aldridge

1995). But what is the context of ecstasy use within clubs? Does 'E' use within club land reflect the image of a drug using subculture (Cloward & Ohlin 1960)? Perhaps punters' recreational use of ecstasy and other 'dance' drugs is marked by its 'normalized' character (Parker, Measham & Aldridge 1995; Parker, Aldridge & Measham 1998)? The first part of this manuscript attempts to answer these questions.

The culture of 'drug selling' is another intrinsic aspect of club culture. Clubbing mainly occurs at night (and into the early hours of the morning), and buying and selling ecstasy and other 'dance' drugs is a prominent feature of an illicit night-time economy (Hobbs et al. 2003; Silverstone this volume; Winlow 2001). This dance drugs market is left wide open for exploitation to any entrepreneurial spirit with enough resources, backup, ability and gall for such an endeavor. As a 'team', bouncers are in an ideal position to capitalize on this market (Hobbs et al. 2003; Winlow 2001), and in a manner distinct from 'street' level drug selling operations. For instance, researchers (Ruggiero 1993, 2000; Ruggiero & South 1995) found evidence of drug cultures without drug economies in inner city London, where highly visible and highly identifiable young people engaged in risky behavior for relatively little money (cf. Venkatesh 2005). Drug sales within clubs potentially differ, and my data suggests a club environment containing a drug culture complete with a drug economy. The latter part of this manuscript explores and analyses the role of club security in regulating and managing this economy.

Methods

The information presented in this manuscript is based on observational data collected through my complete-participant role as a security guard or 'bouncer' at Sam's Club,[1] a large London nightclub, and in-depth interview material with seven security guards and a bar manager at this club. To an extent I became an 'insider' (Merton 1972; see also Measham & Moore this volume) amongst the bouncers at Sam's Club, but the same cannot be said of other 'cultures' within the club. The transient nature of club promoters and bar staff and the closed nature of many club managers, the sound and light engineers and the owner greatly hindered my access and, consequently, the information that could be gathered about them. My data are thus limited, concerning only the behaviors of 'the punters' en masse and those of the bouncers who worked on a more continual basis. The findings aim to challenge what we know about ecstasy users, ecstasy sellers and their relationship to one another within clubs. Further research would be required to test reliability.

My bouncer career was serendipitous in nature (see Adler 1993; Johnston 1990). While writing my doctorate on young people and 'crime' in inner city London (Sanders 2002, 2005), I befriended three individuals, Scott, Mike and Kelly, who

---

1   All of the names of people, businesses and organizations within this research have been changed. Also, and importantly, while the venue still remains, all of the bouncers, club managers, and bar staff that worked at Sam's Club are no longer there.

assisted in launching this career. Similarities in our personal tastes and personal histories formed the basis of our friendships, which, in turn, allowed for this research opportunity (see Armstrong 1993; Hobbs 1993).[2] When a security guard at Sam's Club failed to turn up in mid-June 1999, I received a last minute call to fill in, beginning my year and a half career as a club bouncer.

The general gist of bouncing at the club was: man a fire exit and make sure only staff use it; intervene in fights/help people who need it (e.g. those asleep or too intoxicated to move); make sure no one is using drugs (officially); ask those found doing so to be more discreet (in practice); report any of those selling drugs to head of security that night. However, the majority of the time working as a bouncer was spent standing around 'doing nothing' except watching the punters. Boredom was certainly a prominent feature of being a club security guard (Hobbs et al. 2003; Winlow 2001). The long spells of simply 'doing nothing' allowed for an ideal opportunity to record observations.

Initially, bouncing only served to generate a little extra cash and provide some friends with a free night out listening to some world-renown DJs. A couple of weeks into the job I decided to record field notes on various aspects of the club, including what drugs were used and the behaviors of the punters when 'high' on these drugs. Detailing and analyzing various aspects of club culture – particularly ecstasy use – from a researcher-cum-security guard's perspective were the original intentions of this research. After several nights working at Sam's Club, however, I became aware that some security guards were involved in selling ecstasy, and to a lesser degree cocaine. Aside from heavy ecstasy use, the use of other drugs, such as cocaine, amphetamine and marijuana, were also observed within this club. These experiences shaped the focus of the research.

I attempted to corroborate observational data on ecstasy use and ecstasy selling bouncers in Sam's Club with in-depth interviews with other security guards. After everyone in the security firm was made redundant, I drafted interview schedules based on my observations, contacted many other security guards, informed them about the research topic, and asked if I could interview them. Perhaps somewhat surprisingly, almost all of those contacted were very encouraging, and agreed to an interview, including the main players in the ecstasy and cocaine selling enterprise. However, pinning down these individuals proved very difficult, and I felt lucky to get seven to speak with me. Indeed, the difficulties of interviewing 'active offenders', let alone finding such individuals, are well-documented (e.g. Lee 1995; Maguire 2000). Aside from seven security guards, a club manager was also interviewed.

Security workers in pubs and clubs have been demonized within the media (Bloomfield 2001; Harris 2001; Winlow et al. 2001), and tempering these stereotypes is important. Generally speaking, bouncers are employed in a potentially dangerous job, as their working environment is riddled with various risks (Monaghan 2002a).

---

2 These researchers discussed similarities between their lives and the lives of the individuals they sought to study, and how this semblance aided their access into these individuals.

While these guardians of club land might be seen as glamorous by punters (Hobbs et al. 2003; Winlow 2001), the job was marked by its routine banality, sparingly interrupted by unpleasantness. Many of the other bouncers at Sam's Club seemed to be there for the same reason as I was: to earn a little extra cash. Likewise, these bouncers had other jobs, other lives, and most of them had nothing to do with selling ecstasy or other dance drugs. Other researchers have shown that bouncers tended to distance themselves from such activities (Hobbs et al. 2003). Only a small handful amongst dozens of bouncers at Sam's Club was involved in selling ecstasy and/or cocaine.

Researcher as Bouncer

My self-presentation as a bouncer was atypical, and my 'bodily capital' - the tattoos, muscles and scars often associated with the job (Hobbs et al. 2003; Monaghan 2002a, 2002b; Winlow et al. 2001), not self-evident. In other words, I did not necessarily look like a bouncer. At 6'0 and roughly 190 pounds, I was lightest bouncer in the club. Most of the other bouncers were physically threatening, some 'ripped' and 'cut' with muscles, others just huge. My role within this bouncer community was as the amicable lightweight. Ron, the head bouncer, sometimes commented on how he "needed someone responsible, someone he could trust" when he called me to work. Barry, the club's handyman and key holder, once remarked how I never had to hit anyone because I could "talk them out of any situation." Rather than muscles and menace, my reliability and conversational skills saw me through, demonstrating that I could do 'the job'.

My behavior as a bouncer at Sam's Club also differed significantly from most other bouncers. For one, I predominantly ignored the *blatant* drug use that occurred in the club, even when punters asked *me* if I could 'sort them out with some pills'. I called in a couple of people who I thought were selling ecstasy and cocaine in the club, but upon discovering that the bosses were involved in their own enterprise, stopped caring. Also, I confiscated punter's drugs only on a couple of occasions; several bouncers regularly sought out punter's drugs for *their* personal use (cf. Silverstone this volume). The ubiquity of drugs such as ecstasy and marijuana, and to a lesser degree cocaine, within this setting made policing their use futile. As Benny, a club manager, said, drugs such as ecstasy and cocaine "fuel" Sam's Club. Moreover, I never punched, kicked, pushed or restrained anyone, and attempted to discourage these behaviors amongst other bouncers when possible. If violence was ever needed (and indeed in several situations it was), I remained, for the most part, in waving distance from someone much larger, more capable, and, in some instances, totally willing to engage in violence.

From the offset, that the security firm at Sam's Club was pregnant with its own doom was clear. Numerous internal conflicts raged in that setting, much of it reportedly related to heavy drug use amongst the various sections of management and the bouncers. The club manager, head of the promotion team and the head bouncer all routinely used cocaine, and often argued and failed to get along. Other bouncers used a combination of anabolic steroids, ecstasy, cocaine, cannabis and/or alcohol, which occasionally encouraged violence towards the punters and sometimes amongst themselves. Even by their own standards, references such as 'hard men' and 'nutters' were appropriate (Monaghan 2002b). Several of the bouncers had histories of very serious offences and their capacities for violence (not to mention drinking and drug use) were great. In these respects, we differed, and I never pretended to act or be 'hard' like them (cf. Polsky 1969).

I did, however, befriend several bouncers. On numerous occasions we met outside working hours, usually on Sunday evening for a couple of drinks. We had fun. And while this was the case, I never failed to realize these relationships were fragile. Where we had been and where we were going were dissimilar, and a certain relief descended upon me when my bouncing career ended. Methodologically, my researcher role was somewhat similar to that of 'Marginal Man' – a cultural hybrid of an individual who is both 'the same' and 'different' from that researched (Linder 1996; Park 1950; Sanders 2005). Large, muscular, aggressive, 'hard', British, Afro-Caribbean, working-class: distinctions between some bouncers and me. Middle-class, lived in America, white, college-educated: similarities between us. Greater still, several of the bouncers and I shared similar tastes and experiences from which the foundation of our friendships grew. These friendships were genuine, not manufactured. Many of us talked about our personal lives, particularly relationships and future plans. Similarities in our lives allowed me to get close to them. Simultaneously, my researcher status and overall agenda placed a distance between us.

On a final note, should the authorities have been informed of the illegal activities that transpired at Sam's Club? The decision to report illegal activities that occur in plain view in the course of the research appears ultimately up to the researcher (see Jacobs 1998; Polsky 1969), and I did not call the police for a couple of reasons. For one, that people are using and selling ecstasy in clubs in inner city London would come as no surprise to the Metropolitan Police. If the Met wanted to sweep through Sam's Club with the aims of catching ecstasy and cocaine users and sellers, any visit during a Friday and Saturday night would have resulted in many arrests. However, whether arresting young people who use drugs within club venues is a priority for the police remains uncertain (Measham, Aldridge & Parker 2001). Many other offences were committed in plain view, such as violence, and perhaps a series of other legal infractions, such as overcrowding the venue, lack of proper ventilation, and utilizing unlicensed bouncers (of which I was one). Anyone could have reported such events. In terms of violence, the punters who were assaulted appeared to have brought it upon themselves. In the main, the punters who were beaten up, bloodied and dragged outside asked for it; they antagonized the bouncers either verbally or physically, usually while intoxicated (cf. Silverstone this volume). Levi, a bouncer, brought up this point when discussing the times he witnessed other bouncers become violent.

Have you ever seen any of the other security guards [push, punch, kick, harm or restrain] people?

I've seen a couple of them throw some punches, yeah. I think that only happened twice inside the club. Some of the guys that had worked there a long time. The punters didn't make any noise about it because they knew they were in the wrong anyway. It wasn't excessive. Because of the situation, it was warranted. They weren't listening and were getting aggressive towards the guard. It's more like the guard defending himself than becoming aggressive.

Reporting these assaults to the police would have been fruitless, and probably would have placed me in a precarious situation; it would have been my word and that of the individual who was assaulted versus that of several of the bouncers. In the situations where assaulted punters did lodge a complaint, the police always went on the word of the bouncers and never took any action against the club or staff members during my term as a bouncer.

A final reason the police were not called relates to the nature of research on crime and delinquency. Social scientists want to find out about certain 'causes', contexts, and subjective rationalizations of various law-breaking behaviors defined as 'crime'. In order to do this, and, indeed, to collapse the often wide gap between researcher of crime and deviance and those who engage in criminal and deviant acts (Neklen 1993), observing criminal acts and/or talking with those who commit them is crucial. Such observations and interviews should not be used to encourage or discourage routines that are occurring whether the researcher is present or not. Social scientists can aid decision makers only insofar as their inquiries are non-invasive, objective, and free from either personal or political agendas. My decision not to report 'crime' at Sam's Club was not siding with 'criminals' nor advocating revocation of certain criminal laws. Rather, the decision had to do what social scientists are charged with doing: observing and explaining patterns of social behavior.

The Normalised Character of Ecstasy at Sam's Club

Club culture has been described as fluid, fragmented, and difficult to consider 'subcultural' (Gilbert & Pearson 1999; Redhead 1997; Stanley 1997; Thornton 1995). Subcultures are marked by their difference to the 'general population' or the 'mainstream', both in terms of what they look like, their ideals and/or their values (Brake 1985; Hall & Jefferson 1976; Hebdige 1979; Redhead 1997). Contemporary club culture *is* mainstream youth culture. Clubs are 'time out' spaces, 'wild zones', pleasure centers where (young and young-ish) people ritualistically congregate on weekend nights in order to have 'a good time', to become released from the pressures of daily life, and, as such, are a contemporary element of the leisure landscape within the ongoing work/leisure nexus (Measham, Aldridge & Parker 2001; Presdee 2000; Rojek 2000). The fashion, music and practice of clubbing is promoted via mass media, not 'underground' magazines or 'word of mouth', as has been the reported case of earlier incarnations of 'rave' culture (Thornton 1995). Smaller, distinct club cultures do exist, which may possess more of a subcultural vibe, but the practice of clubbing more generally is difficult to capture in subcultural terms (Measham and Moore this volume; Silverstone this volume).

Sam's Club was not a large, unified 'culture', but a series of smaller, interacting cultures, including the dance culture, the 'management' culture (promoters, owners and club managers), and the DJ culture (Thornton 1995). Additional cultures at Sam's Club included the culture of the sound and light engineers, culture of the bar staff, the culture of those handing out flyers at the night's end, 'guest list' culture, and the culture of those who do not use illicit drugs. While factions within Sam's Club argued often over seemingly trivial matters (particularly the club's management with bouncers and bar staff), 'the night' always went ahead, the doors were always opened, and punters normally filled the venue beyond capacity. All kinds of punters attended, and no evidence emerged to support the notion that individuals who frequented Sam's Club were part of a distinct subculture. On the surface nothing distinguished the clubbers at Sam's from the rest of society. Based on their overall appearances, punters seemed to come from various socio-economic backgrounds, did not possess any discernible 'uniform', and would be difficult to consider a particular 'type' (Forsyth, Barnard & McKeganey 1997; Lenton, Boys & Norcross 1997; Measham, Aldridge & Parker 2001; Release 1997). The average age range was 18-35, with men and women equally represented. Clubbers were predominately 'white British', but an ethnically and culturally diverse range of people attended Sam's Club.

An omnipresent and observable aspect of club culture is the drug culture. At Sam's Club, drugs of various legal classifications were used by punters, including cocaine, speed, marijuana, alcohol, tobacco and a couple of instances individuals were found sniffing glue, smoking cocaine (crack or freebase) or injecting heroin. Ecstasy, however, was clearly the 'hard' drug of choice within this setting. Importantly, the use of ecstasy within Sam's was *not* subcultural, and ecstasy users who attended were not akin to the image of society's "double failures" (Cloward & Ohlin 1960). Just as no one 'type' of clubber emerged, no one 'type' of ecstasy user existed (Forsyth et al. 1997; Lenton, Boys & Norcross 1997; Hammersley, Khan & Ditton 2002; Measham, Aldridge & Parker 2001). The punters observed using ecstasy at Sam's Club were not radically different from those in the 'general population.' No noticeable consistencies amongst the ecstasy users at this venue suggested otherwise.

For the most part, DJs at Sam's Club played music that might generally be considered house, trance, techno and jungle. Hip hop played in the smaller room during the jungle night, and on occasion, hip hop would be the only music played in the club, particularly when local and popular artists or 'rappers' headlined. During such nights, more 'black'[3] people attended, and ecstasy use was less observed during the 'hip hop only' night (O'Hagan 1999; cf. Silverstone this volume). This observation

---

3   By 'black' people I refer to individuals whose ethnic heritage stems from Afro Caribbean, West African and East African countries.

also lends support to the idea that the music played within a venue acts as a rough indicator of the types of drugs consumed within that venue (Forsyth, Barnard & McKeganey, 1997; O'Hagan 1999). Ecstasy use appeared fairly consistent and the contexts of its use roughly similar for the remainder of the evenings, including the jungle/hip hop night. My argument regarding the normalized character of ecstasy use at Sam's Club does not apply to the 'hip hop only' nights.

Towards the end of the 20th century some significant changes in the conceptualizations of illegal drug use amongst young people occurred. Rather than being considered an activity amongst the few and marginalized, certain drugs have recently been considered "a *normal* part of the leisure-pleasure landscape" (Parker, Measham & Aldridge 1995 p. 25, original emphasis). This position is generally referred to as the 'normalization' thesis (Parker, Measham & Aldridge 1995, 1998; see also Measham, Aldridge & Parker 2001; Parker, Williams & Aldridge 2002). Howard Parker and colleagues have applied the concept of normalized recreational drug use to young people *in general*. According to them, normalization does not suggest that the use of any or all drugs is a 'normal' activity for young people. Rather, they argue how the use of certain drugs, particularly cannabis, but increasingly dance drugs, such as speed (amphetamine), cocaine and ecstasy (Measham, Aldridge & Parker 2001; Parker, Williams & Aldridge 2002), have come to be expected, something 'ordinary' and not necessarily 'deviant' (South 1999). The characteristics suggesting a drug's normalized character are its availability, its frequency of use, its social acceptability, and its supportive cultural references. Based on these conditions, ecstasy within Sam's Club was 'normalized'. At Sam's Club, ecstasy was available, many punters (and staff, including club security) were using it, few people found it a 'problem' (and management indirectly encouraged its use) and positive cultural references to ecstasy were apparent in the fashions of the punters, psychedelic club displays and lyrics of the music.

One quality about ecstasy that suggested its normalized character at Sam's Club was its availability. People selling ecstasy were evident on every night at the club. Before entering the venue young men in their late teens or early twenties were observed 'hanging around' outside asking punters if they wanted any 'Es' or 'pills'. These young men were not club security's concern, only those attempting to sell inside the club. Our job was never to apprehend those selling drugs in the club, just report this behavior to the head bouncer or someone else 'in charge.' As noted above, these head bouncers were involved in selling ecstasy themselves. Additional evidence of the availability of ecstasy were the white pills found frequently on the ground, which, given the amount of people selling ecstasy pills at Sam's Club and the tight association of ecstasy with clubs in general, were likely ecstasy. From those selling pills just outside the club, to the network of bouncers selling pills inside, to the amount of pills found on the dance floor, along the stairwells, in the lavatories, and around the cloakroom, ecstasy was certainly available at Sam's Club.

Another observation that suggested the normalized character of ecstasy at Sam's was the copious amounts of people using this drug. Bar staff, engineers, promoters, the owner, managers, and several club security guards were observed using ecstasy while working. Benny, a club manager, said "You could probably say each and every one of the bar staff were probably on pills." Kelly, a bouncer, even mentioned, "I took ecstasy a couple of times and I think that's why I got sacked [fired]." Furthermore, several club security, a club manager and I estimated that, on average, on any one night, the majority (more than half) of the punters at Sam's Club were using stimulant drugs, either ecstasy, amphetamine and/or cocaine. These estimates are based on observations of behaviors typical of ecstasy and other stimulant use, such as amphetamine and cocaine, not drug tests. The use of such drugs are observable in a number of different ways. Several behaviors amongst the clubbers indicated they might be using these drugs, particularly ecstasy. One of the more obvious ones was when they actually ingested pills in plain view. This happened with such frequency that Ron, the head of security, actually told us what to do in such cases.

> If people take pills in front of us, Ron said that we should have a word with them and tell them not to be so obvious. He said, "Because people are going to take pills, aren't they?" [field note Feb. 10, 2000]

Other behavioral indicators of stimulant drug use include certain physiological side-effects of these drugs, such as dilated pupils, wide-eyed stares, profuse sweating, slightly trembling hands and lips, and chattering teeth (*inter alia* Saunders 1997). Men dancing and roaming around without shirts and people carrying water bottles may also indicate ecstasy use, as do 'face orgasms' or 'gurning' – the licking of lips, eyes closed, head swaying to the music in a rollicking bliss (Shapiro 1999). Other bouncers also noticed these behaviors and associated them with ecstasy or other stimulant drug use. Hank, for instance, discussed how he could tell if people were using "Es or stuff":

> *Did you believe that people at the club were using drugs?*
> Yeah. Working through from clubs that I've been at, yeah. I could tell they were on Es or stuff just by the way they are. They get hot, they strip and they're constantly chewing their tongues. Eyes are all glassy. Loads of things you can tell. It's just something you just get to know through seeing them.
> *How often would you say that you saw someone using ecstasy?*
> Quite a lot really. There's quite a lot of people. I mean, a lot of people come to clubs now with just their own personal stuff, just to make themselves get high so they can have a good time. That's what they see as having a good time.

Ecstasy is an empathogen, and has been considered the 'luv drug' and its effects described as being 'luvd up' (Reynolds 1997; Shapiro 1999). Frequently, complete strangers at the club, who possessed the above noted visual (potential) indicators of ecstasy and other stimulant drug use, would come up and talk with me, asking about my well-being, what my name was, if I found the evening entertaining, if I wanted some gum or something to drink and so on. At times, these same individuals would shake my hand or give me hugs. Once, someone pulled a £10 note out of their wallet, handed it to me and said, 'Keep up the good work.' These behaviors were probably encouraged by the 'feel good' vibe associated with the use of ecstasy. The fact that I observed ecstasy being sold more in comparison to other 'dance' drugs also lends weight to the idea that these punters were likely using ecstasy. Furthermore, other security guards interviewed commented on how ecstasy pills were the most common drug they found punters in possession of. For instance Stuart, said, while working the front door that he, "confiscated, pills. A lot of pills were there. Sometimes Charlie, coke. But it was mainly pills."

Another consideration that suggested the normalized character of ecstasy within Sam's Club was its social acceptability and the tolerance displayed amongst club punters and staff towards its use (Measham, Aldridge & Parker 2001). Bouncers, managers, promoters, staff, and the owner all knew ecstasy and other drugs were being used at the club. Punters never voiced anything along the lines of ecstasy being unacceptable. Furthermore, the actual use of ecstasy was not considered a 'problem' or something that needed to be controlled by the club managers, the club promoters, the heads of security, or all but a couple of the bouncers interviewed. James, another bouncer, claimed that Martin, the club's general manager, actually told him to "turn a blind eye" to ecstasy use:

> Don't forget, I worked directly for Martin. His thing was: 'We know it goes on. Without it there wouldn't be a club. Just don't let it get too out of control and too obvious.'

Benny, a club manager, commented on how certain drugs were always going to be found within clubs or raves:

> I don't think the rave scene's ever going to be drug-free. Come on.
> *Why do you think that?*
> If fuels it, man. You don't get many people gong to a rave club or anything that are not on drugs.
> *What kind of drugs?*
> Whatever. Generally, it just depends on the night, you know what I mean? Basically, most of the time, it's just Es, speed or Charlie [cocaine]
> [later in the interview] *What was your boss's view on these drugs overall?*
> They always come in from the work aspect, you know, and the legal side, so they just don't want to see it, don't want to know. Out of sight, out of mind. They don't check anything and nothing bad happens. Everyone carries on, you know?

In some cases ecstasy use within the club might have actually been encouraged. As will be discussed further in the next section, several bouncers were involved in selling ecstasy to punters and staff at Sam's Club. For them, unofficially nurturing the use of drugs they sold is good business. Simultaneously, their 'official' 'no drugs will be tolerated' stance was a facade, serving only to suggest to the authorities that they 'did all they could' about drug use within the establishment. Ecstasy in Sam's Club was ubiquitous, seemingly a quality of club culture more generally (Collin & Godfrey 1997; Measham, Aldridge & Parker 2001). As Ron, a head of security, mentioned when punters come into the club "they're going to use pills, aren't they?"

This tolerance amongst the club's staff further suggests the normalized character of ecstasy within the club.

At Sam's Club the use of other drugs, particularly cannabis, was observed, as were other 'dance' drugs, such as amphetamine (speed), cocaine, and amyl nitrate (poppers), to a lesser degree. The use of ecstasy and marijuana was generally accepted within the club, but club security had much more critical attitudes towards the use of other drugs. In particular, open use of cocaine and heroin, if not their use in general, was not tolerated. Amongst staff, attitudes towards illicit drugs in general were sharply differentiated. Kelly, for instance, offered his opinion on the use of different drugs, which was typical of the view held by other bouncers:

> *How do you feel about them using cannabis or other drugs in the club?*
> I think it's good that they use weed in the club. It keeps them peaceful and quiet. If you want a quiet night and you don't want aggro [violence], it's better that they're smoking a joint than boozing it up. Then you have to deal with arseholes, but if they're smoking a joint they're usually mellow. If they're doing ecstasy, they're usually mellow. We never really went along with cocaine or crack. If we saw someone with that, they were out. If you saw someone with weed, you'd give them a warning. If they were on Es, that's fair enough because everybody is...But coke users, crack, out.

Clubs more generally provide an arena where ecstasy use seems not only acceptable, but ideal; both the music and atmosphere within clubs or raves have been suggested as being conducive to the effects of ecstasy (Rietveld 1993; Saunders 1997; Shapiro 1999). Clubbing is carnival (Presdee 2000; Rietveld 1993; Rojek 2000), and carnival licenses fun, play, 'losing' oneself and being intoxicated. From the pounding rhythmic music and hooked electronic samples, to the lasers and smoke, bells and whistles, lights and images, the club atmosphere encouraged and accommodated ecstasy use (Collin & Godfrey 1997; Saunders 1997; Shapiro 1999). Ecstasy use itself partially defines club culture (Measham, Aldridge & Parker 2001; Parker et al. 1998), and has for some time (Redhead 1993). Ecstasy use within club settings have occurred for more than 15 years, and ecstasy has remained the drug of choice in such settings (Collin & Godfrey 1997; Measham, Aldridge & Parker 2001; O'Hagan 1999; Release 1997). The cultural references to ecstasy use can be found in the music, the names of the DJs, the names of the songs, and the fashions of the punters (Gilbert & Pearson 1999; Reynolds 1997). Likewise, positive references to ecstasy were observed in the fashions of the punters at Sam's Club, such as on T-shirts, on the psychedelic displays and 'trippy' pictures throughout the club, and occasionally heard within the lyrics of the music played. The hypnotic beat of house, trance, jungle and techno music nourish ecstasy use. The machine-like march of the drums invites those using ecstasy to work off the drug's effects. Ecstasy has a dance factor (Shapiro 1999), and dancing to club music while using ecstasy can promote escapist ideals, where the beat of the music and the effects of the drug merge to promote a sense of loss of self amongst the user, perhaps a punter's ideal (Collin & Godfrey 1997; Rietveld 1993; Saunders 1997). The long history of ecstasy within club land, the references to ecstasy in the music and on punter's clothing, and the high-energy dancing that the music encourages: the combination of these "cultural accommodations of the illicit" (Parker, Aldridge & Measham 1998 p. 156) further suggested the normalized character of ecstasy at Sam's Club.

The Control and Supply of Ecstasy

Bouncer culture is a fundamental part of club culture (Hobbs et al. 2003), and may consist of several smaller cultures.[4] At Sam's Club one of these included the culture of bouncers who sold drugs. About eight bouncers, including the two head bouncers, were involved in selling ecstasy and to a lesser extent cocaine at the club. These individuals were physically intimidating, local hard-men-cum-bouncers with histories of offending, particularly violence (Hobbs et al. 2003; Winlow 2001; Winlow et al. 2001). The borough where the club is located has a long history of high crime rates, with robbery and burglary rates some of the highest in the country. Extensive heroin and crack use and sales are evident within a couple hundred yards of the club. Illicit drug sales more generally are part of a large and well-established informal economy within the borough. Other illegal activity went down within Sam's Club, such as the trading of stolen merchandise, the theft of large sums of money and dealings with unlicensed mini-cab drivers, but little information could be gathered about these activities.

Rather than robbing banks and holding up armored cars, selling controlled substances has become the contemporary 'street criminal's' offence of choice (Hobbs 1995; Ruggiero & South 1995). Clubs provide an ideal environment to market certain drugs, namely dance drugs (Ruggiero & South 1995), and club security, through their control of the doors and relative positions of power, are in an ideal position to capitalize on the potentially lucrative financial rewards selling these drugs (Hobbs et al. 2003; Winlow 2001). At Sam's Club, the efforts of eight security guards selling ecstasy and cocaine amounted to a 'retail enterprise', with "a manager employing people in a variety of specialist roles to distribute drugs to users" (Dorn & South 1990 p. 177; see also Measham, Aldridge & Parker 2001). These eight may be considered the 'inner circle' of bouncers at Sam's Club. This inner circle worked the door and the floor, meaning they monitored who entered the venue and combed the crowd for people selling and/or using drugs. Their knowledge of others involved in some sort of 'criminal enterprise' in the borough, including those selling illicit drugs, helped them keep such individuals out. These practices, in turn, enabled them to gain greater control of the market for ecstasy and cocaine within the club.

The bouncers who did *not* sell any drugs primarily worked the fire exists, but a couple 'roamed' the club floors. These 'regular' bouncers blindly adhered to 'the rules' of the club: no drug use or drug selling will be tolerated. They escorted people caught selling drugs out of the club, and warned those caught using to be more

---

4 For example, distinguishable cultures amongst the bouncers at Sam's Club included those who 'worked out', violent bouncers, women bouncers, foreign bouncers, one-off and occasional bouncers, bouncers who were athletes, and bouncers using drugs.

discreet. The 'regular' bouncers held the attitude that if they saw these things, they would attempt to stop them, not in order to further the drug enterprise of those in the inner circle, but because they felt it part of 'the job'. Levi, for instance, mentioned,

> I don't mind if people do their drugs outside the club as well. Don't bring the drugs inside the club because that gets us into trouble as well. Because that means we're not doing our job well. I don't like that. Whatever you do outside the club, do outside the club, but don't come inside the club and be silly. If I catch people with drugs inside, I just escort them out. I'm not going to take the drugs off people because then that means I'm responsible for the drugs and stuff. I just have to throw them out and be done with it.

In addition, several bouncers only worked occasionally, others just once. These 'temporary' bouncers also followed 'the rules' and seemed unaware those in the inner circle were selling drugs. The 'regular' bouncers knew those in the inner circle were selling ecstasy and cocaine, but 'got on' with 'the job' as it provided an important source of (somewhat legitimate) income. This brings up an important point: regardless of drug selling, *all* the bouncers exhibited a sense of solidarity to the extent we 'had each others backs' and everyone roughly got along. Such relations are requirements of 'the job'. The 'regular' and 'temporary' bouncers who kept their jobs did as the bosses within the inner circle asked and remained quiet. For them, keeping the job was more salient than the outcome of the illegal activities committed by the inner circle. Outside the inner circle, most bouncers did what might be considered a 'normal' job and related to the punters in a 'typical' fashion. Some did use drugs such as marijuana, ecstasy and/or anabolic steroids, but failing that, no other illicit or illegal activities emerged amongst them.

The culture of drug selling was extensive at Sam's Club. Some working behind the bar sold marijuana, an engineer sold speed and another who occasionally worked as a bouncer sold anabolic steroids. However, these individuals only sold these drugs to fellow staff members, not to the punters, and the amounts observed and reported were relatively small, not interfering with the inner circle's drug selling 'enterprise.' Ron and Tom were head of the club's security, and they, along with Ray, formed the core of the inner city and controlled the sales of ecstasy and cocaine. According to other bouncers, they earned a total of between £1000 to £1500 each night largely from selling ecstasy to the club's punters, as the majority of the cocaine was infrequently sold to other staff members, the general manager and the club owner. As Kelly said, they sold "mostly ecstasy." In order to get the drugs to the punters, Ray's girlfriend, Tanya, along with four bouncers, Stuart, Chris, Mike and Kelly, 'worked' for Ron, Tom and Ray in 'specialist roles' by selling ecstasy, and, to a lesser extent, cocaine at Sam's Club. These five carried amounts of ecstasy pills and/or cocaine powder in either half gram or gram 'wraps' (cocaine wrapped in glossy paper), and circulated through the club asking punters if they wanted 'pills' or 'coke.' Ecstasy pills were sold for £5 each or £20 for 5; half gram wraps of cocaine sold for £25 and grams for £50. All five of these 'specialists' were supplied pills and wraps by either Ron, Tom or Ray, and they only carried a certain amount of money and drugs on them at any one point for security reasons. As Mike mentioned, "If a bust went down, one person wasn't left holding everything. So then they'd get a minor offence for maybe having the stuff, but it wouldn't be enough to consider it as trafficking or pushing or dealing." James confirmed this.

> The person's who's selling it won't have the drugs on him. It'll be his mate or his mate's mate stood six people away in a busy club, so they'll just pass it from one to the next. So the person who is obviously lurking is selling. He's not the person who actually has the goods…The people you buy off of are not the people who hold the drugs because of the risk of losing it all and getting arrested.

Inside the club, the 'job' of some bouncers, particularly Mike, Kelly, Chris and Stuart, was to eject others attempting to sell drugs from the club. Such activities assisted in gaining further control of ecstasy and cocaine within the club. When these four caught others selling or using drugs, they sometimes took the drugs off of these individuals and then sold them on to punters. In other cases, these bouncers used the drugs themselves. Stuart talked about this:

> *Have you ever confiscated drugs?*
> Yes. The idea was, we'd take the drugs off them. We were supposed to put them in the office and then they'd go off to the police. But what happens is, they'd take the drugs and a lot of the time the managers would go and then take the drugs themselves. So we decided, because we're using and selling, that we would take the drugs and put a tiny bit in there [a 'drugs box' in the office] or keep them ourselves. At first we gave a tiny bit back, but then we decided never to give any.

Stuart was not the only bouncer using the drugs he was selling. Mike, Kelly, Chris, and particularly Ron, head of security, used ecstasy, cocaine and/or cannabis when working at the club. These practices went against the edict of 'not getting high on your own supply', and other research has shown that individuals do not use the drugs they sell, particularly if they sell crack cocaine (Ruggiero & South 1995). The drug using drug seller also lies outside Dorn and South's (1990) conceptualization of the 'retail specialist.' They claimed that "the important organisational consideration" of the retail specialists "is that they are not 'stoned' while working (being stoned would impair efficiency)" (1990 p. 182). While these bouncers were often 'high' on the drugs they sold, they still (temporarily) managed their retail enterprise. Their 'taking care of business' demeanor while using these drugs countered the stereotype of the dozing, incapacitated drug using 'junkie' (Ruggiero & South 1995). In fact, most of the club security (and club staff more generally) were observed using a drug at some point, usually cannabis, and seemed capable of doing their job properly.

Bouncers and Violence

Those in the inner circle had great capacities for violence, which somewhat assisted in their retail drug enterprise. All but two of these bouncers were physically large 'nutters' or 'hard men' (Monaghan 2002b), and could inflict significant damage with their fists alone. These capacities for violence were useful, effective and, perhaps, required in order to profit from selling illegal drugs in a competitive environment (Bourgois 1995; Hobbs 1995). Stuart, for instance, used force "loads of times, hundreds of times" to take drugs off of those selling. He continued:

> I'm a nice person. I would take the drugs. If [the punter selling drugs] gave me any attitude at all, at that time, when I was high, I would beat them up and then throw them out and take their drugs.

However, given the thousands of punters who attended each weekend, and the copious amounts of alcohol and stimulant based drugs they consumed, violent incidents in the club involving bouncers were relatively infrequent (cf. Silverstone this volume). James, for instance, who had worked extensively in clubs and bars in Northern England, mentioned that, in comparison, Sam's Club was a "pussycat club." Stanley, the largest of the bouncers at 6'6" and 360 pounds, concurred:

> I think our club was quite a mellow club. People just really wanting to enjoy themselves. You had times where you had an element on certain nights when guys would come in, you had to direct certain people. All of a sudden they'd get a bit lairy [surly] and you'd have to bark at them really. The only time I've had to push or restrain people is because they're drunk or off their heads on drugs.

For several bouncers, intakes of large quantities of amphetamine based drugs (cocaine, ecstasy), at times alongside continued use of anabolic steroids, encouraged violent bursts or erratic behavior (cf. Adler 1993). One of these bouncers was Kelly. During my bouncer career, Kelly was the closest person to me, both when working and outside of the club. Kelly also had a particular reputation for violence, being partially related to his occasional use of steroids and binge drinking. I witnessed Kelly violent with punters on numerous occasions, but these had little to do with the drug 'business' operating in the club. Kelly, for instance, became violent with punters who disrespected him.

> If they're drinking, they usually get obnoxious. They can get a bit stirred up and they can get in your face and to them all you are is just some guy who is just a security guard. You're worthless, so they talk to you sometimes like that. And I feel, for £8 an hour, I'm not going to listen to that shit. For £8 an hour, how professional can you be?...You're getting paid £8 and you're getting threatened that you're going to get knifed or fucking shot or whatever and you've got some jackass who's nobody and he's telling you that he's going to do this and that to you. You lose your patience. You don't have to listen to that shit from people.

Clearly, Kelly's reasons for violence towards punters stem more from insults directly at his 'manhood' or those which he felt challenged his 'respect' (Anderson 1999; Kennedy & Forde 1999: Messerschmidt 1993, 2000), as opposed to those associated with the drug's operations. In fact, violence, while closely linked to drug 'businesses' in some form, is not necessarily 'good' for business (Dorn & South

1990; Hobbs 1995; Ruggiero 2000), particularly within club environments. Violence amongst drug sellers in clubs attracts unnecessary attention, and violence directed at punters can undermine profits. Indeed, due to Kelly's reputation for violence, he became unpopular amongst other bouncers, being referred to as a "fucking psycho" or "steroid schizo", and eventually lost his job and was banned from the club.

'If you want anything, you go to a bouncer'

Drug selling bouncers justified selling ecstasy and cocaine to an extent. Those in the inner circle expressed that selling ecstasy and cocaine was filling a void, providing a service, and giving people what they desired. Several bouncers expressed how if they failed to sell punters these drugs, someone else would, and that they might as well pocket the lucrative monetary rewards. Mike, for instance, said:

> Yeah, basically the way it works in most English clubs is the doormen try and control the drug trade One: because there's a lot of money to be made. And two: if they control the drug trade then they know who they are up against - themselves. It's an on-going battle between the dealers and the doormen. So, basically, if you kick out all the dealers and just have the doormen doing it then you make all the money and you've got none of the trouble.

Stuart also mentioned.

> It's known. If you want anything, you go to a bouncer…If I was on the front door, people would come up. I didn't know them. 'Have you got any pills?' That's what they'd say to me. I'd check them out and say, 'I don't but I can get some for you.'
> *How often?*
> All the time….loads of people would come up to me. They thought I was a drug dealer. So they would come up all the time. So, I could either sell it to them, or…

In this way, bouncers legitimized selling ecstasy and cocaine in the club. Their reasoning for doing so echo Sykes and Matza's (1957) 'techniques of neutralization' – rationalizations that 'deflect' negative feelings associated with illegal or 'deviant' behaviors – but could be much more than this. Rather than having negative feelings towards these behaviors they knew were illegal, evidence suggests they truly felt nothing 'wrong' was being done, that their positions as bouncers in a club *allowed* them to sell ecstasy and cocaine, and that, as club bouncers, they *should* be selling these dance drugs. Additional evidence suggests punters who frequented Sam's Club believed security guards were appropriate figures from which to purchase ecstasy. Whether this relates to these punters' general perceptions or their perceptions of this particular club is uncertain. Nonetheless, numerous times punters approached me and inquired about 'pills.'

> Someone asked if I 'had any pills' or 'knew where I could get some.' I asked if he had ever been to a club before and if he realised that I was security. He seemed a bit out of it and I told him to be careful and not ask those wearing all black carrying around walkie-

talkies as they were most likely security guards. He thanked me. I sent him on his way and he seemed happy. Later I told Mike how someone came up and asked if I had any pills or if I knew where he could get some, thinking he would laugh it off or something like that. He said that I should have sent the guy to him because he was now selling pills [field note Oct. 9, 1999].

At Sam's Club, ecstasy users and ecstasy sellers mutually benefited, making this setting a particular drugs environment. The ecstasy selling bouncers made money, and by buying pills many punters who come to the club to use ecstasy were ensured a 'good night' was going to be had. Club organizers, promoters, managers, bouncers and the club's revelers all participated in an economically prosperous and exciting drugs culture. Sam's Club was an environment where ecstasy was bought, sold and ingested, an environment that actually encouraged its consumption. Ecstasy, and to a lesser extent other dance drugs, were relatively accepted in this environment. Furthermore, people could use these drugs at Sam's Club without fear from reprisals by the authorities. Strongly enforcing an ecstasy free environment within a setting where the use of ecstasy is one of its defining features is a difficult endeavor (Hobbs et al. 2003). Police officers rarely visited the club, perhaps on two separate recorded occasions, which amounted only to a quick stroll around the dance floors. In terms of dance drug use and sales within club land in general, the police seem to have "neither the resources nor the inclination" (Measham, Aldridge & Parker 2001 p. 185) to stop such behaviors. This point was supported by Mike, a bouncer, who mentioned the police only came to the club a couple of times.

We had the police there a couple of times. As far as undercover goes, I don't know. It was rumored, but, the thing is that you've got to think that the town that this happened in was a great tolerant town, and the police didn't really care about drugs in this town. They had bigger fish to fry. What it was, I don't know, but they never really bothered us, and everything that was going on in this club was pretty blatant. It was widely publicized. It was a very large club in a town and basically it was known. It was high profile people. And that kind of thing goes on in clubs anyway and the police do nothing about it. As a matter of fact there was even a couple of instance where they said, 'We're not really bothered with drug use in clubs.'

Sam's Club contained a drug economy complete with a drug culture. Ruggeiro (1993, 2000) discussed how drug economies exist without drug cultures and vice versa. A drug economy lacking a drug culture is hidden from the authorities, where money is being made by those selling drugs, but no "distinctive, visible attitudes among both suppliers and customers" emerge (Ruggeiro 1993 p. 84). A drug culture without a drug economy is a well-known, highly visible, yet poorly regulated endeavor, where little money is generated and suppliers and users are stigmatized and targeted for intervention by the police. The former conjures up images of an efficient establishment where drugs are sold, where 'customers' buy their drugs and leave to use them elsewhere (Williams 1992). The latter is the reality of crack and heroin street level 'dealing' in poor, inner city environments (Ruggeiro 1993, 2000; Ruggeiro & South 1995; cf. Venkatesh 2005).

As a drug culture complete with a drug economy, Sam's Club was an environment that authorized and even advocated both the use and supply of ecstasy and other dance drugs. In this setting club security controlled a considerable section of the market for these drugs and made money in the process. Sam's Club was self-contained, self-policed and self-sufficient. The image of the security guards supplying ecstasy and cocaine in the venue was not one of the 'pusher', not one of an individual tempting 'impressionable youth' into using 'hard' drugs, but rather of a valued commodity, an important element within club land's leisure landscape. Several punters were even comfortable enough to actually ask club security if they could supply them with their night's drugs, and several security guards capitalized on this market by answering the demand.

Importantly, by giving ecstasy users what they want, several bouncers not only encouraged their own illicit 'retail enterprise', but also aided in the club's overall longevity by doing so. Punters whose idea of a 'good night out' relies on using ecstasy are likely to return to a venue where this drug can be procured. Ruggeiro (1993, 2000) discussed how true drug economies pump some profits into local legal enterprises. No evidence emerged to suggest any of the bouncers involved in selling ecstasy or cocaine at Sam's Club did anything like this. Nonetheless, in actuality, these bouncers implicitly invested their efforts in what was perhaps the most important legitimate aspect of this entire culture: the club's punters. By providing ecstasy to many of the clubbers, the security guards enabled them to have a 'good time', which may encourage their return. Consequently, this would help keep Sam's Club open for business, with punters and those who work at the venue reciprocating in a lively drug culture and prosperous drug economy.

Conclusions

Ecstasy was 'normalized' at Sam's Club. Many people used this drug, ecstasy was available from a couple of sources, those within the club found ecstasy use acceptable, even non-users, and the club's overall atmosphere accommodated and encouraged ecstasy use. Within the existing literature on ecstasy use and contemporary clubbing, these qualities are evident. Academic and journalistic research has recorded some or all of the characteristics associated with ecstasy's normalization in club land (e.g. Collin & Godfrey 1997; Measham, Aldridge & Parker 2001; Shapiro 1999). The prospect of ecstasy being normalized in sections of club land raises some important questions related to this drug, such as those surrounding the safety of ecstasy using clubbers and the drug's legal classification. Ecstasy's current status effectively criminalizes thousands of young people who appear otherwise law-abiding. Moreover, if ecstasy is normalized, then such widespread use of this drug is a public health concern. Further efforts at educating these young people with the health risks of ecstasy use may promote safer clubbing.

Bouncer culture at Sam's Club, similar to club culture more generally, was not a homogenous culture, but a fragmented series of interacting ones. One tangent of bouncer culture within the club included those who sold ecstasy and cocaine. This manuscript has demonstrated the operational processes these bouncers exhibited when selling these drugs and the overall context of this processes. I endeavored to explain that ecstasy and cocaine use and sales at Sam's Club produced a particular drugs environment, where dance drug using punters, dance drug sellers and club staff participated in a vivacious and modern drug culture complete with a successful and somewhat protected drug economy. If these behaviors are similar in other club settings, this raises some important questions concerning the conceptualization of dance drug suppliers, their relationship with dance drug users and their overall role within dance culture. This chapter[5] also raises some important questions surrounding bouncers. Background checks compiled by local authority organizations may help screen out individuals with severe violent and/or criminal histories.

5   Reprinted by permission of Sage Publications Ltd. from Bill Sanders, 'In the Club: Ecstasy Use and Supply in a London Nightclub', Copyright *Sociology*, 2005, vol. 39, no. 2, pp. 241-258.

Chapter 10

Pub Space, Rave Space and Urban Space: Three Different Night-Time Economies

Daniel Silverstone

In the United Kingdom, the night-time economy is now a hugely profitable and contentious phenomenon. As a sociological term, the night-time economy has come to encapsulate the tension between profit, crime and leisure and at its broadest it can be used to describe our ever growing use of the night (Kreitzman 1999). In this chapter, this economy refers to the burgeoning night club industry, currently estimated to be contributing £2 billion (Hobbs 2000) to the economy and employing about 130,000 people (Ullswater 1997). British youth have always been at the forefront of reinventing, revitalising and exporting night-time cultures. The imminent arrival of twenty four hour licensing (Department for Culture, Media and Sport 2005) promises them an opportunity to transform the night again, though it is provoking fierce political disagreement between the government and opposition over its potential for unrest (Guardian 2005).

The term night-time economy implies a singular entity that is structurally determined, failing to take into account the varied drug cultures and youth cultures clearly evident in the UK (Willis 1977; Blackman 2004). Recent work has reduced the social structure of the night to a Marxist clash between exploitative capital, exploited proletariat and weak local government (Hobbs et al. 2003). However, other research suggests that recent accounts of youth cultures have tended to ignore any structural determinants and stress personal choice within the night accessed through individual consumption and leisure (Melchi 1993; Muggleton 1997, 2000). Little attention has been given to the limiting variables of class, ethnicity or locale. This chapter argues that the different sociological criteria of race, class and gender still exist and predetermine the kinds of spaces that people inhabit. In turn, these characteristics produce environments with varying degrees of danger for those who attend and work within them. Moreover, these environments are treated very differently by the state and have different relationships with the dominant capitalist hegemony.

One of these environments is 'rave space'. Data about rave space is drawn from a recent ethnography at Club Mix (a pseudonym) – a late licensed dance club based in London that stayed open until six in the morning and catered for 750 or more punters. It had musically themed nights, such as trance, house or jungle/drum and bass nights. The club's most singular characteristic was the normalized acceptance of both ecstasy selling and taking (Sanders this volume; Silverstone in press). This club existed as a contemporary venue for 'rave culture'. As a criminal and exciting place, Club Mix was seemingly the antithesis to the kinds of boring branded drinking establishments featured in other ethnographies (e.g. Hobbs et al. 2003). These other branded drinking establishments have been characterized by Measham (2004a) as 'pub space', which are archetypically large pubs where alcohol rather than illicit drugs are favored. Furthermore, the music played is 'mainstream' or 'pop' and the licensing hours are more limited.

The people who attended Club Mix were also visible different from those who routinely attend pub space (Silverstone in press). It is likely that such individuals were more affluent (Bean 2004) with more white people in attendance than that in the local pub space (CRE 2001). Yet, to separate the night-time time economy into this dichotomy ignores a third group whom I became aware of when researching the market and those who use illegal firearms both locally and nationally. In the first of these studies, we looked at how guns were used in the Borough of Brent, which has the fifth highest rate of gun crime in London, and interviewed fifteen young people convicted of gun offences (Hales & Silverstone 2005). We then interviewed 81 convicted firearm offenders in London, the West Midlands, Greater Manchester, and Nottinghamshire. These interviews were done solely with young offenders drawn from urban environments[1] and the interviewees were heterogeneous but disproportionably black.[2] Attending night clubs and clubbing was very important for these young people. For instance, in the latter project only six out of 80 young people said they did not go clubbing (Hales, Lewis & Silverstone 2006). Yet these young people did not regularly attend rave space nor pub space though they did in their own words "go raving." These young people followed black British artists and musical genres (principally UK garage, but also R& B, reggae and hip-hop), disdained from taking large amounts of either ecstasy or alcohol and often frequented private parties (cf. Sanders 2005). These spaces hosted inner city crowds that were not exclusively Afro-Caribbean, but were disproportionately so. Unlike those people who attend rave space, violence was anticipated. For instance, comments such as, "I've seen loads of fights at raves" were common. Moreover, many youth anticipated danger and voiced concerns such as, "if we were going partying, there would be 15 or 20 people cos we would feel safer." Such elements of these youth need to be looked at separately, and I use the title 'urban space' to describe the environments these young people frequent.

Overall, various night-time economies have emerged in different locales, catering to different crowds and somewhat distinct tastes. In this chapter, I categorize these different aspects of the night-time economy as 'rave space', 'pub space' and 'urban space' using four different criteria: capitalism, violence, policing and control.

---

1   One was conducted in the London borough of Brent and in the other, 80% of the sample came from urban areas.

2   In project one, 60% were black, (defined as either Black British, Black Caribbean, Black African or Black other) 13% were mixed race and in project two, 35% identified themselves as black and another 13.8% as mixed race (a number of whom were mixed black and white).

Capitalism

As Hobbs et al. noted (2003 p.36) "the night-time economy is as dependent upon hedonistic drives cultivated in the alcohol/youth nexus as industrial society was on the motive power of coal and steam." The recent accounts of the alcohol driven night time economy have focused on the existence of neo-liberal capitalism and the position of the breweries within the market place to transform the urban landscape (Hobbs et al. 2003). In their pursuit of profit, breweries managed to seduce cash-strapped councils into granting numerous licenses to drinking establishments, which have then offered drink in quantities and varieties of novel ways (Measham 2004a). For instance, in Manchester 1,500 capacity venues cater to 100,000 revelers each weekend. As dramatic as has been the rise in the mutation of the physical pub spaces, so too has been a change in gender dynamics. The drinking environment now is rarely an all male preserve. For instance, figures from the Health Survey for England showed that 23% of women aged between 16 and 24 drank over 21 units a week, 14% higher than nine years ago. Moreover, the survey indicated that the number of women drinking double the recommended daily level has also increased.

The marketization of the night has grown and encroached on spaces where drug use once   predominated. Indeed, one of the key finding from a Home Office study on the normalisation of drug use amongst 760 club-goers was that most of them had drunk alcohol on the night of the interview, with two-thirds classified as hazardous drinkers (Deehan & Saville 2004). Moreover, their presence in pubs at least three times a week is one the key factors that now predicts taking illegal drugs (Roe 2005). In relation to the movement of capital, not only is this the triumph of big business imposed from above, but the kind of culture being promoted is reminiscent of the nineteenth century (Golby & Purdue 1999). These arguments provoke the same sanctimonious concern over licentiousness and weakness of the people, yet no concerns from elites or interest from theorists concerning its challenge to existing inequalities or capitalist hegemony have emerged. Instead, pub space is marked neither by dissidence nor protest, and approximates the critique of the cultural industry's characterization of popular culture. Indeed, alcohol has rarely been associated with cultural innovation. As Jock Young (1971 p. 137) observed, "the subversive properties of alcohol are still subsumed by the work ethic; a drug used to relax and refresh before the inevitable return to reality."

The rise in ecstasy use within clubs would seem to be the antithesis of big business because its origin came from the creativity of youth who used and misused old machines such as turntables, samplers, microphones (Rose & Ross 1994), and medical drugs such as ketamine and ecstasy to create novel social interaction and psychological highs (Saunders 1995)[3]. Rave culture also initially utilized the multi-media to publicise their events, including the Internet and pirate airwaves (see Collin

---

3　As Beck (1992 p.154) has observed, science "is no longer concerned with the liberation from pre-existing dependencies, but with the dissemination and distribution of errors and risks which were produced by itself."

& Godfrey 1997; Reynolds 1998). Initially, in relation to capitalism the culture was at best non-committal, and with free raves being held in the open air, they could be considered the 21st century's manifestation of Bahktin's carnival (Hayward 2004; Presdee 2000). Even the activities of early drug sellers, normally the most mercenary of people, were described in other, more amiable terms as groups of "trading charities or mutual societies" (Dorn, Murji & South 1992 p. xiii).

Early rave years were a richly creative period for British youth, which also contained an anti-consumerist idealism that was picked up by theorists whose attention was turned away from previous debates on 'subcultures' and who started to examine and rework the new oddities observed on the dance floor. In particular, cultural studies took an overactive interest in the symbolism of dance fashions (see McRobbie 1994; Richard & Kruger 1998) extrapolating elaborate symbolism from new styles of dance-floor dress. Others, such as Steve Redhead (1993) and Mike Presdee (2000), saw in the rise of ecstasy driven clubbing the old modern constraints of five to eleven drinking subcultures disappearing into the effervescent lure of the morning hours. For these researchers, such night-clubs had become an unbridled playground of mixed identities, blurred boundaries and amorphous sexualities. Here was something that seemed to be popular, and anti-consumerist, experimental and challenging to the status quo.

As time passed, 'rave culture' also changed significantly. Sarah Thornton (Thornton 1995) was the first to recognise this in *Club Cultures*, noting the existence of cultures of distinction and the denigration of the mainstream from within them. Indeed, upon close observation, the actions of the club goers were somewhat ordered. For instance, ecstasy purchases have been planned in advance, ways of dealing with ecstasy induced 'come downs' were anticipated, and particular spots were reserved for dancing and talking in the club (Panagopoulos & Ricciardelli 2005; cf. Perrone this volume). The weekend took on a routine with everything being done over and over again, until the participants started to tire from the magic of the drugs. Meanwhile, some would progress further into heavier dosages or into new drugs (Simpson 2003).[4]

The rave scene underwent a profound mutation best summarized as a "commercialization of a cultural space (the unlicensed rave) into the commodification of a criminal culture (within licensed places)" (Measham 2003 p.342). At the same time mainstream breweries attempted to sideline rave culture by sponsoring dance clubs, promoting reduced drink prices, and introducing a new range of alcopops aimed at young drinkers. This left club space encroached upon, and for many its challenging relationship to capital has been neutered.

In clubs, however, where there still exist nights where over 70% of the crowd expect to use an illegal drug (Deehan & Saville 2004), the relationship to consumerism

---

4   Here, Simpson quite correctly asks academics and drug workers to move "away from the complete reliance upon the dichotomous model of recreational-dependent use currently favoured in the UK" (2003 p.317). Instead, the importance is to look at the links between the two groups dependent on local social environments.

is still markedly different. This was best articulated by Malbon (1999)[5] who argues that drug induced night clubbing seems closer to play as opposed to pursuing status or the opposite sex. For Malbon, those who attend these clubs and especially those who use other drugs, are instead trying to reach states which he calls "oceanic" and "playful" vitality. Here, oceanic vitality refers to the "sensations of extraordinary and transitory euphoria, joy and empathy .. that can be experienced as a result of the intensive sensory stimulation of the dance floor" and playful vitality as "vitality that is experienced and can, through dancing take the form of a sense of individual and communal euphoria" (Malbon pp. 105 and 161). Certainly, this culture is not without obvious consumption, as drug use is the gateway into enjoying 'rave space' (O'Malley & Mugford 1994). However, these clubbers are trying to achieve a mental high, and are much more attuned to pushing the boundaries of experience than conforming to traditional prescribed forms of action as in pub space, nor displaying conspicuous items of consumption as in urban space.

Those who attended urban space most frequently made reference to conspicuous items of consumption (cf. Hayward 2004; Stanley 1997). For instance, the value of Avirex jackets, Moet Champagne, and Nike Shox shoes were extolled by our sample as markers of status and of symbolic importance to attracting the opposite sex. These themes have been explored elsewhere as indicative of hyper-capitalist culture displayed and flaunted by successful American rappers (Hayward 2004). This narrative is normally combined with the negative impact of urban music's lyrics in reference to the glorification of violence (cf. Howells 2003; Livingstone 2005). Overall, despite the impoverished background of those who attend rave space, its relationship to capitalism is remarkably supportive, providing a forum for wealth and consumerism often denied to its participants elsewhere (cf. Sanders 2005).

The culture of urban space, however, as it primarily pertains to Afro-Caribbean youth, cannot be seen as either racially distinctive or as entirely new. Such particulars of this culture have been observed before in Mods, whose over-exaggerated consumption patterns and flamboyant fetishisation of mainstream consumerist products seems to be an accurate precursor to the modern urban scene (Hebdige 1976). The compelling fantasy of the 'weekend', combined with materialistic obsession, contrasted strongly with the often miserable daily lives of the working–class, predominantly white youth (cf. Cohen 1972; Willis 1977). As Hebdige (1976 p. 90) observed, "Every Mod was existing in a ghost world of gangsterism, luxurious clubs, and beautiful women even if reality only amounted to a draughty Parker Anorak, a beaten up Vespa, and fish and chips out of a greasy bag." At the time, this was counter-posed by the existence of a more overtly political and anti-capitalist black youth culture encapsulated as Rastafarian (Cashmore 1984; Hebdige 1976; Pryce 1979).

There does not seem to be a political aspect of the culture of urban space. Yet, it may be too hasty to condemn the scene as entirely acquiescent to consumer hegemony. Certainly, urban space is privy to the most ostentatious types of consumption that

---

5   Though he does not give the importance of ecstasy and other drugs sufficient importance, nor does he explain why people cease clubbing.

inadvertently advertise luxury brands (Hallsworth 2004). Nonetheless, our research (Hales & Silverstone 2005) indicated some tensions not normally mentioned in other analyses. For instance, American hip-hop, which is seen as the pre-eminent example of this culture by those outside of it, was actually often looked down on for being inauthentic and overly showy. Those 'in the know' preferred British offerings and ventured into urban spaces that played this music. Garage and UK based hip-hop was seen as being more realistic, being both made and played outside of mainstream music industry. Such music offers its listeners a chance to express themselves and to reflect on their own culture in un-commercial spaces where they are the majority. This music is genuinely more cynical and critical, containing elements of anger and politicisation against the racial and consumer inequalities in mainstream capitalism (George 1998). Thus, a tension was experienced by those who were active participants in urban space between doing materially well and being able to keep the right to be critical.

Violence

In pub space, beyond the rising drunken egalitarianism, the predominance of routine violence is the key aspect of this culture. Here Hobbs et al. (2003) are at their most trenchant and have the greatest empirical support. For them the night time economy has metamorphosed not "into a post-modern playground … but more akin to a pre-modern battleground" (Hobbs et al. 2003 p.36). The statistics are stark, as crime has generally fallen in the United Kingdom (BCS 2005), including incidences of violence.[6] Yet, at the same time in Manchester City Centre between 1998 and 2001, the capacity of licensed premises increased by 240%, which was accompanied by an increase of 225% in the number of assaults reported to the Greater Manchester Police (Hobbs et al. 2003 p.39).

More generally, evidence from the Home Office indicates that in nearly half of all violent events, victims believe that the offender was under the influence of alcohol (Home Office 2005). Furthermore, as Mott (1990 p.26) observed, "evidence from a number of studies, specifically looking at licensed premises, associates disorderly conduct offences to be in or near licensed premises in 20-30 % of cases. The time of such offences is likely to follow the end of licensing hours, and to occur on a Friday or Saturday night and involve young men" (cited from South 1997 p.950). And the violence is serious. For instance, Deehan (1999 p.9) calculated that "half of the facial injuries sustained by persons between 15 and 25 years of age were the result of assaults, nearly half were in or near bars and 40% were severe enough to necessitate specialist surgery." Indeed, such is the gravity of the situation that it is estimated that the fear of violence is driving ordinary citizens away from city centers and the police are voicing an unwillingness of being an outnumbered rapid reaction force (Hobbs et al. 2000).

---

   6   Though this is disputed, see the difference between the BCS figures and the latest police figures.

It may be that club space is being encroached on by pub space, which means a confusing picture exists. Ecstasy is now more inexpensive than ever (Drugscope 2005), and people are reputably taking more than ever at once (Mixmag 2004), yet the numbers using it are on the decline (Chivite-Matthews et al. 2005; Drugscope 2005). However there still exists, as mentioned previously, monthly club events where over 70% of the crowd expect to use an illegal drug (Deehan & Saville 2004). In these spaces in particular, the atmosphere is very different from that mentioned in pub space.

People are positively attracted to peaceful atmospheres. Indeed, one of the most positive and consistent outcomes to emerge from a variety of research methods has been the lack of violence in rave space (see, e.g., Henderson 1993; Newcombe 1991, 1992). These early studies also stressed the way women felt accepted and able to express themselves without the predatory attacks of drunken men. Subjectively, those indulging in ecstasy use stressed the importance of empathy and love (Release 1997), and were less interested in winning confrontations than avoiding them. One of the most revealing empirical pieces of evidence from these studies was highlighted in Measham, Aldridge & Parker's (2001 p.164) study that indicated that "eight in ten clubber's felt safe or very safe in club-land and discuss clubs with specific reference to feeling safe and at home by comparison with work, their domestic lives, or out and about on the streets."

Urban space, on the other hand, is neither characterized by endemic alcohol induced violence, nor is it known to be peaceful. How often and what sort of violence prevails within urban space is unclear. It is, however, interesting to note that statistics taken from Operation Trident,[7] which recorded the location of black on black shootings in London, indicated that about a fifth of such incidents occurred in night-clubs, bars, parties or raves (Brown 2003). In one of our studies, almost all of the interviewees had experienced or witnessed violence in and around nightclubs; half reported having seen guns, including guns fired into the ceiling and fired at people. A significant minority, including three that had worked in door security roles, reported door security staff being targeted and shot (Hales, Lewis & Silverstone 2006 p.75). However, asking how representative those episodes are and what causes them is reasonable. It would seem from our work, far from originating in a distinct black subculture with an overly attuned notion of respect (Pearson & Hobbs 2003), such events arise due to conflicts between two or more pre-existing criminal groups all frequenting similar places.

Our respondents did not articulate a widespread unease in going to urban spaces in general, but were aware that other groups similar to them might be there and, if seen, a confrontation would happen. Events that had been reported as trivial and that exploded into violence either involved pre-existing conflicts or, alternatively involved a small amount of criminals who were previously involved in drug selling. The fact that those involved in violence had prior criminal involvements suggest

---

7   London's Metropolitan police specialist black on black gun crime unit. Shootings recorded from January 2002 through December 2002.

that the violence is not endemic within the community. However, the conspicuous consumption on display (e.g. designer clothes, jewelry) that was liable to provoke jealousy or 'red eye', as the youths called it, could be a motivation for violence between two or more groups of youth committed to offending at the same venue.

Policing

Doormen or 'bouncers' are seen as part of the genealogy of working class muscle caught within the competing demands of de-industrialization and rapid growth in criminal opportunities, with an occupational culture not dissimilar to the British bobby on steroids (Hobbs et al. 2003; Holdaway 1983; Monaghan 2002a, 2002b; Winlow 2001). According to Hobbs et al. (2003 p.147), these men and women experience violence unparalleled outside of "military and penal institutions" and, in turn often inflict assaults that go unpunished. The academics who have worked as bouncers (Hobbs et al. 2003; Monaghan 2002a 2002b; Winlow 2001) have been sympathetic to the vulnerable position of bouncers in pub spaces, providing in depth accounts of how bouncers have had to respond 'manfully' to the inadequacies of policing placed upon them, emphasising their frequent use of their physical prowess.

Within rave space, however, ethnographic research reads very differently (Sanders this volume; Silverstone 2003). Having worked in a big 'club space' first as a member of the bar staff and then as part of the security team, I only witnessed one physical fight and this was started and finished by two drunken friends who set upon each other (cf. Sanders this volume). This was not due to the vigilance of the security teams who, as Sanders pointed out, were often too busy selling drugs. In fact the team's main pre-occupation was to stop the drug taking becoming too blatant, apprehending other dealers who were taking away customers, or pouncing upon unsuspecting users who could be fleeced of their substances.

In terms of policing these spaces, violence was a rarity, as a working drug market did not want the police attention that might come with routine violence (see Dorn & South 1990; Pearson & Hobbs 2001; Ruggiero & South 1995). However, others would argue that punters are increasingly cynical of door staff and such is the current availability of recreational drugs that they no longer need to buy them from security teams (see Shewen, Dalgarno & Reith 2000). Yet, it should not be underestimated that even if most clubbers choose to get their drugs beforehand the value of the internal market is high. The club space itself with its security team, bar staff and promoters makes up a lucrative drug market (see Sanders this volume).

The Home Office was concerned that security teams were also significant forces in their local drug market (Morris 1999). Due to the fragmented state of British disorganised crime (Hobbs 1995) this could indeed be a possibility. If the recent histories of British organized criminals are reviewed, it would appear that many have served their apprenticeship as bouncers (Kray 2004; Thompson 2005). However, graduating to a wider patch requires both cosmopolitan ability and a strong desire for confrontation. Many security teams may only be comfortable selling in their own clubs, unwilling to engage with more treacherous and ably policed drugs or drug markets (see Hobbs 1998; Stelfox 1998).

Regarding urban space, working on a door where garage and/or hip-hop music predominates raises its own problems. In my experience in policing these events, having door-staff that are knowledgeable about local criminal groups is useful, as they are drawn from this part of the milieu and are likely to visit the club (cf. Sanders this volume). Secondly, a racial predominance existed, which meant, in my experience, black door staff were at a premium. It was vital that those stopping and searching clubbers at the door were a different ethnicity from the local police and that the surveillance that did exist was careful to avoid the kind of antagonistic confrontations often provoked by police stop and searches carried out on the street (Fitsgerald 2001).

Control

For the British government, bouncers have been the folk devil of choice. The existence of criminal security firms with well known figures, self-confessed or otherwise, from the British underworld at their helm has prompted action (see Courtney 2001; Walsh 2004). Chief among them has been the Private Securities Act 2001 (Button 2002). This Act is a substantial development in a previously sporadically regulated trade. It has meant that the criminal histories and provenance of prospective bouncers is monitored and demands that their training meets national standards. The Private Securities Act affects all doorstaff regardless of whether they appear in pub, rave or urban spaces. However, it may impact more positively in rave space by keeping away criminal doormen who would otherwise be orchestrating a criminal drug trade. Moreover, the Act might have less of an impact on those policing pub space or urban space who might no longer have the criminal know-how or physical ability to deal with those frequenting such venues.

Hobbs et al. (2003) see the reliance on private security as one example of a broader neo-liberal solution to the problems of the market that relies on the "polluter pays" principle. Once again Hobbs et al. (2003) seem to be accurate in describing the actions in regards to pub space, with the recently self-introduced ban on Happy Hours by publicans being a good case in point. However, the kinds of control imputed onto these three aspects of the night-time economy have been vastly divergent.

David Garland (2001 p.186)[8] has provided a most comprehensive, post-Foucauldian account of the way the state has responded to spiraling crime rates. Garland proposes that the state cannot accept a limit on its sovereignty, and, instead, responds to crime at its broadest in two ways:-it either acts out by imposing "control from the outside in the form of legal threats and moral exhortations and condemns and excludes all those who fail to take heed"; or with a "piecemeal development of a network of unobtrusive situational controls, retrofitted to modify existing routines

---

8   See Taylor (1999) Young (1999) for some important recent exceptions.

situational and technological solutions" (2001 p.186). These latter sorts of strategies emphasize that the public should share responsibility for crime control, while the first emphasizes expressive punishment that demonizes the criminal.

By employing Garland, we can better differentiate the strands of state control. Hobbs et al. (2003) may be right to suggest that the government's decision to restrict happy hours is evidence of the market principle in action, as no regulatory framework exists for enforcement, and such action has been done on the behest of the British Beer and Pub Association. However, it is harder for Hobbs et al. to explain the numerous studies that have been commissioned on the situational factors that might spark or lessen violence, and it is now clearer which venues represent the safest layout for pub space (MCM 1990). But there are also reactions of the frightened sovereign state. The Licensing Act of 2003 has introduced penalty notices or on the spot fines for anti-social behaviour, and the beleaguered police are expected to act as human traffic wardens. Meanwhile, the proposed Violent Crime Reduction Bill (2005) indicates a raft of immanent punitive measures, including alcohol disorder zones, orders to leave a locality, and exclusions from licensed premises.

When it comes to rave space, the state's response, far from encouraging the culture, which was seen to threaten the boundaries and monopoly of leisure capital, was to license it (Shapiro 1999). Both of Garland's (2001) two pronged approach are equally evident. Firstly and most publicly, the state responded by acting out, with the far reaching Criminal Justice Act of 1994 that effectively tackled the phenomena of outdoor 'rave' events. This was soon followed by the Public Entertainment Licences Drug Act of 1997, which gave the Local Council and the police the authority to close clubs if "there was a serious problem relating to the supply or use of controlled drug at the place or nearby which is controlled by the holder of the license" (Drug Forum Focus 1997). This has been further strengthened by the amendment to Section Eight of the Misuse of Drug Act, which now makes it a criminal offence for people to knowingly allow premises they own, manage, or have responsibility for, to be used by any other person for administration or use of any controlled drug. Finally, and most recently, the state has exercised control by employing a closure order under Section 1 of the Antisocial Behavior Act of 2003, which was essentially set up to shut down on 'crack houses'. Indeed, a very similar approach has been used by the Americans with the RAVE Act, which eventually culminated in the Illicit Drug Proliferation Act of 2003.

In recognition of the government's impotence is a piecemeal development of a network of unobtrusive situational controls, in the form of the widely publicized *Safer Clubbing* (Webster et al. 2002). This is based around the supply of clean drinking water, the provision of first aid, and cool "chill out rooms" where over heated clubbers can convalesce. What is interesting here, and this can be seen as criticism of Garland, is to look at how this legislation is enforced. Research indicates it is very rare for police officers to frequent clubs, and it is only on exceptional circumstances that this might be so (Sanders this volume). Indeed, those who operate outside of the club spaces and principally deal with different drugs who are most likely to be arrested and incarcerated (see, e.g., Ruggerio 1993, 2000; Ruggerio and South 1995).

In terms of urban space, the same situational controls have been inputted. For instance *Safer Clubbing* refers to the importance of fitting metal detectors in all nightclubs, something which the police have also reiterated. This kind of initiative forms one aspect of a much broader initiative to try and reduce gun violence in particular within the black communities. However, finding an expressive reaction is not difficult. The now disbanded urban collective 'So Solid Crew', have had their tour stopped from the fear of provoking further violence and there are further allegations that clubs in the centre of London are reluctant to put on urban music nights. Certainly, when interviewed, people who attended such events spoke about the importance of private venues that would play the music as alternatives to licensed spaces (Hales & Silverstone 2005). These spaces, however, were completely unregulated.

Conclusion

The night time economy is a paradigmatic theoretical example of the world we live in. The increased choice on offer, the rapid speed (Berman 1983) in which trends change, the globalisation of youth cultures (Giddens 1999), and the ever present sense of risk (Beck 1992) are all inherent aspects of our world. The failure of the state to gain control of this space is symptomatic of the state's failure to get to grips with crime (Garland 2001). Yet, the night-time economy is far from uniform. Most broadly these different spaces have divergent relationships to both capital and control, which will range from the acquiescent to the antagonistic. In this regard, it seems urban space will be the most profoundly ambivalent, extolling some of out most expensive products yet providing a voice for some of the most excluded. It will remain the most tightly regulated and a space for spectacular violence but is as yet under researched. Pub space will stay the dominate night-time economy. However, the falling price of cocaine (Home Office 2005), the lengthening of the licensing hours, endemic violence, and newly regulated door teams may provoke a more restrictive regime. In the UK, rave space remains on the decline with anything resembling resistance reduced, but is still a more peaceful space than that that dreamt up by big business. The new extended licensing hours may mean that all three spaces are set to mutate and change again.

Bibliography

Achilles, N 1967, 'The development of the homosexual bar as an institution', in J Gagnon & B Simon (eds.), *Sexual deviance*, Harper & Row, New York, pp. 228-244.

Adam, B 1987, *The rise of a gay and lesbian movement*, Twayne, Boston, MA.

Addiction Research and Theory 2001, Special editions on qualitative drugs research, vol. 9, no. 4 & 5.

Adlaf, E & Smart, RG 1997, 'Party subculture or dens of doom? an epidemiological study of rave attendance and drug use patterns among adolescent students', *Journal of Psychoactive Drugs*, vol. 29, no. 2, pp. 193-198.

Adler, PA 1993, *Wheeling and dealing: an ethnography of an upper-level drug-dealing and smuggling community*, 2nd ed., Columbia University Press, New York.

Agar, M 1985, 'Folks and professionals: different models for the interpretation of drug use' *The International Journal of the Addictions*, vol. 20, no. 1, pp. 173-182.

Agar, M 1996 'Recasting the "ethno" in "epidemiology"', *Medical Anthropology*, vol. 16, pp.391-403.

Ahmed, SN & Petchkovsky, L 1980, 'Abuse of ketamine', *British Journal of Psychiatry*, vol. 37, pp. 303.

Akers, RL 1985, *Deviant behavior: a social learning approach*, 3rd ed., Wadsworth Publishing Company, Belmont, CA.

Allaste, AA & Lagerspetz, M 2002, 'Recreational drug use in Estonia: the context of club culture', *Contemporary Drug Problems*, vol. 29, pp.183-200.

Anderson, E 1999, *Code of the streets: decency, violence, and the moral life of the inner city*, WW Norton and Co., New York.

Anderson, R, Flynn, N, Clancy, L, Anglin, D, & Kano, N 1994, 'HIV prevention: reaching out-of-treatment high risk drug users in jail', poster presented at the Tenth International Conference on AIDS, Yokohama, 7-12 August.

Andrews, JA, Tildesley, E, Hops, H, & Li, F 2002, 'The influence of peers on young adult substance use', *Health Psychology*, vol. 21, no. 4, pp. 349-357.

Armstrong, G 1993 'Like that Desmond Morris?' In D Hobbs & T. May (eds.), *Interpreting the field: accounts of ethnography*, Clarendon Press, Oxford, pp. 3-39.

Arria, AM, Yacoubian, GS, Jr., George, S, Jr., Fost, E, & Wish, ED 2002, 'Ecstasy use among club rave attendees', *Archives of Pediatrics and Adolescent Medicine*, vol. 156, no. 3, pp. 295-296.

Associated Press (AP) 2001, 'Ecstasy selling penalties stiffened' 21 March, viewed 22 March 2001, <http://www.cbsnews.com>.

Avni, S 2002, 'Ecstasy begets empathy', *Salon.com*, viewed 15 November 2005, <http://www.salon.com/mwt/feature/2002/09/12/grob_interview/>

Baggott, M & Mendelson, J 2001, 'Does MDMA cause brain damage?' in J Holland (ed.), *Ecstasy: the complete guide*, Park Street Press, Rochester, VT, pp. 110-145.

Barnett, J 2005 'Meth panel demands leadership', *The Oregonian*, 27 July, viewed 27 July, 2005, <http://www.oregonlive.com/printer/printer.ssf?/base/front_page>

Baudrillard, J 1995, *Simulacra and simulation,* translated by Sheila Faria Glaser, University of Michigan Press, Ann Arbor.

Bauman, KE & Ennett, ST 1996, 'On the importance of peer influence for adolescent drug use: commonly neglected considerations', *Addiction*, vol. 91, no. 2, pp. 185-198.

Baxter, D, Campbell, D, Cooper, D, Crawford, J, Kippax, S, Prestege, G & Van de Ven, P 1997, 'Factors associated with unprotected anal intercourse in gay men's casual partnerships in Sydney, Australia', *AIDS Care*, vol. 9, no. 6, pp. 637-649.

BBC Online 2003, 'Gun law shake-up unveiled', viewed 1st November, 2005, <http://newswww.bbc.net.uk/1/hi/uk_politics/2631097.stm>

Bean, P 2004, *Drugs and crime*, 2nd ed., Willan, Cullompton.

Beck, J & Rosenbaum, M 1994, *Pursuit of ecstasy: the MDMA experience*, State University of New York Press, Albany.

Beck, U 1992, *Risk society: towards a new modernity*, Sage, London.

Becker, HS 1963, *Outsiders: studies in the sociology of deviance*, Free Press of Glencoe, London.

Becker, H 1967, 'Whose side are we on?', *Social Problems*, vol. 14, pp. 239-47.

Becker, H 1971, *Sociological work*, Allen Lane, London.

Behar, R 1996, *The vulnerable observer: anthropology that breaks your heart*, Beacon, Boston.

Bellis, MA, Hughes, K, Bennett, A & Thomson, R 2003, 'The role of an international nightlife resort in the proliferation of recreational drugs', *Addiction*, vol. 98, pp. 1713-1721.

Bennett, A 1999, 'Subcultures or neo-tribes? Rethinking the relationship between youth, style and musical taste', *Sociology*, vol. 33, no. 3, pp. 599-617.

Bennett, A 2002, 'Researching youth culture and popular music: a methodological critique', *British Journal of Sociology*, vol. 53, no. 3, pp. 451-467.

Bennett, A 2003, 'The use of insider knowledge in ethnographic research', in A Bennett, M Cieslik and S Miles (eds.), *Researching youth*, Palgrave, Basingstoke.

Bennett, A & Peterson, R 2004, *Music scenes: local, translocal and virtual*, Vanderbilt University Press, Nashville, TN.

Benson, ML 2002, *Crime and the life course: an introduction*, Roxbury Publishing Company, Los Angeles.

Bentham, M & Temko, N 2005, 'Lord Winston in tirade on drink laws', *The Observer*, 4th September.

Berger, PL & Luckmann, T 1966, *The social construction of reality: a treatise in the sociology of knowledge*, New York, Anchor.

Bergman, SA 1999, 'Ketamine: review of its pharmacology and its use in pediatric anesthesia', *Anesthesia Progress,* vol. 46, pp. 10-20.

Berman, M 1983, *All that is solid melts into air: the experience of modernity*, Verso, London.

Bhopal, R 2002, *Concepts of epidemiology: an integrated introduction to the ideas, theories, principles and methods of epidemiology*, Oxford Univ. Press, Oxford.

Biernacki, P 1986, *Pathways from heroin addiction: recovery without treatment*, Temple University Press, Philadelphia.

Biernacki, P & Watters, JK 1989, 'Targeted sampling: options and considerations for the study of hidden populations', *Social Problems*, vol. 36, pp. 416-430.

Bion, JF 1984, 'Infusion analgesia for acute war injuries: a comparison of pentazocine and ketamine', *Anesthesia*, vol. 39, pp. 560-564.

Blackman, S 2004, *Chilling out: the cultural politics of substance consumption, youth and drug policy*, Open University Press, Maidenhead.

Blackman, S 2005, 'Youth subcultural theory: a critical engagement with the concept, its origins and politics, from the Chicago School to postmodernism', *Journal of Youth Studies*, vol. 8, no. 1, pp. 1-20.

Bloomfield, R 2001, 'Door to door disservice', *Time Out: London*, October 24-31.

Boardman, JD, Finch, BK, Ellison, CG, & et al 2001, 'Neighborhood disadvantage, stress, and drug use among adults', *Journal of Health and Social Behavior*, vol. 42, pp. 151-165.

Boeri, MW 2002, "I'm an addict, but I ain't no junkie': an ethnography analysis of the drug career of baby boomers', *Dissertation Abstracts International*, vol. 63, no. 6, pp. 2371A-2372A.

Bourgois, P 1995, *In search of respect: selling crack in El Barrio*, Cambridge University Press, Cambridge.

Boyd, CJ, McCabe, SE, & d'Arcy, H 2003, 'Ecstasy use among college undergraduates, gender, race, and sexual identity', *Journal of Substance Abuse*, vol. 24, no. 3, pp. 209-215.

Bradford, J & Ryan, C 1987, *Mental health implications: national lesbian health care survey*, National Lesbian and Gay Health Foundation, Washington DC.

Brake, M 1985, *Comparative youth culture: the sociology of youth cultures and youth subcultures in American, Britain and Canada*, Routledge, London.

Brewer, NT 2003, 'The relation of internet searching to club knowledge and attitudes', *Psychology & Health*, vol. 18, pp. 387-401.

Bronski, M 1993, 'How sweet and sticky it was', in J Preston (ed.), *Flesh and the world 2*, Plume, New York.

Brown, A 2003, *Insights from Operation Trident*, Youth Justice Board, London.

Buchbunger, S, Colfax, GM, Guzman, R, Mansergh, G, Marks, G & Rader, M 2001, 'The circuit party men's health survey: findings and implications for gay and bisexual men', *American Journal of Public Health*, vol. 91, no. 6, pp. 953-958.

Buffum, J & Moser, C 1986, 'MDMA and human sexual function', *Journal of Psychoactive Drugs*. vol. 18, no. 4, pp. 355-360.

Burke, R & Sunley, R 1998, 'Post-modernism and youth subcultures in Britain in the 1990s', in K Hazelhurst & C Hazelhurst (eds.), *Gangs and youth subcultures: international explorations*, Transaction, London, pp. 35-65.

Button, M 2002, *Private policing*, Willan, Cullumpton.

Calvey, D 2000, 'Getting on the door and staying there: A covert participant observational study of Bouncers', in G Lee-Treweek and S Linkogle (eds.), *Danger in the field: risks and ethics in social research*, Routledge, London, pp. 43-60.

Camilleri, AM & Caldicott, D 2005, 'Underground pill testing, down under', *Forensic Science International*, vol. 151, no. 1, pp. 53-58.

Carlson, R, McCaughan, JA, Falck, RS, Wang, J, Siegal, HA, & Daniulaityte, R 2004, 'Perceived adverse consequences associated with MDMA/ecstasy use among young adults in Ohio: implications for intervention', *International Journal of Drug Policy*, vol. 15, pp. 265-274.

Cashmore, EE 1984, *No future: youth and society*, Heinemann, London.

Cavacuiti, CA 2004, 'You, me ... and drugs – a love triangle: important considerations when both members of a couple are abusing substances', *Substance Use & Misuse*, vol. 39, pp. 645-656.

Central Registry of Drug Abuse (CRDA) 2005, *53rd Report*, Narcotics Division, Hong Kong Government.

Cerbone, FG & Larison, CL 2000, 'A bibliographic essay: the relationship between stress and substance use', *Substance Use & Misuse*, vol. 35, no. 5, pp. 757-786.

Chang, L, Grob, CS, Ernst, T, Itti L, Mishkin FS, Jose-Melchor R, & Poland RE 2000, 'Effect of ecstasy (3,4-methylenedioxymethamphetamine [MDMA]) on cerebral blood flow: a co-registered SPECT and MRI study', *Psychiatry Research*, vol. 98, pp. 16-28.

Chivite-Matthews, N, Richardson, A, O'Shea, J, Becker, J, Owen, N, Roe, S & Condon, J 2005, *Drug misuse declared: findings from the 2003/04 British Crime Survey*, England & Wales, Home Office, London.

Clatts, MC, Welle, DL & Goldsamt. LA 2001, 'Reconceptualizing the interaction of drug and sexual risk among MSM speed users: notes toward an ethno epidemiology', *AIDS and Behavior*, vol. 5, pp. 115-29.

Clatts, MC, Goldsamt, L, Neaigus, A, & Welle, DL 2003, 'The social course of drug injection and sexual activity among YMSM and other high-rish youth: an agenda for future research, *Journal of Urban Health: Bulletin of the New York Academy of Medicine*, vol. 80, no. 4 (Supplement 3), pp. iii26-iii29.

Clatts, MC, Goldsamt, L & Huso, Y 2005, 'Club drug use among young men who have sex with men in NYC: a preliminary epidemiological profile', *Substance Use & Misuse*, vol. 40, pp.1317-1330.

Cleckner, PJ 1979, 'Freaks and congnoscenti: PCP use in Miami', in HW Feldman, M Agar & GM Beschner (eds.), *Angel dust: an ethnographic study of PCP users*, Lexington Books, Lexington, MA.

Cloward, R & Ohlin, L 1960, *Delinquency and opportunity: a theory of delinquent gangs*, Collier-Macmillian, London.

Cohen, A 1955, *Delinquent boys: the culture of the gang*, Free Press, New York.

Cohen, P 1972, 'Sub-cultural conflict and working class culture', *Working Papers in Cultural Studies, vol.* 2, University of Birmingham, pp. 5-51.

Cohen, S 1972, *Folk devils and moral panics: the creation of the Mods and Rockers*, MacGibbon and Kee, London.

Cohen, S, Mermelstein, R, Kamarck, T & Hoberman, HM 1985, 'Measuring the functional components of social support,' in IG Sarason & BR Sarason (eds.), *Social support: theory, research and applications*, Martines Nijhoff, The Hague, Holland, pp. 73-94.

Collin, M & Godfrey, J 1997, *Altered state: the story of ecstasy culture and acid house*, Serpent's Tail, London.

Comerci, GD & Schwebel, R 2000, 'Substance abuse: an overview', *Adolescent Medicine*, vol. 11, no.1, pp. 79-101.

Commission of Racial Equality (CRE) 2005, *Race equality impact assessment: healthcare statistics*, viewed 1st November, 2005, <www.cre.gov.uk/duty/reia/ statistics_health.html>

Community Epidemiology Work Group (CEWG) 2003, *Epidemiologic trends in drug abuse. Volume 1: highlights and executive summary*, National Institute on Drug Abuse, NIH Publication No. 04-5364, Washington DC.

Community Epidemiology Working Group (CEWG) 2005, *Epidemiologic trends in drug abuse. Volume 1: highlights and executive summary*, NIH Publication No. 05-5364A, National Institute of Health, Division of Epidemiology and Prevention Research, National Institute of Drug Abuse, Bethesda, MD.

Connelly, JC, Coyne, L, Lohrenz, LJ & Spare, KE 1978, 'Alcohol problems in several Midwestern homosexual communities', *Journal of Studies on Alcohol*, vol. 39, pp. 1959-1963.

Coomber, R, Morris, C & Dunn, L 2000, 'How the media do drugs: quality control and the reporting of drug issues in the UK print media', *International Journal of Drug Policy*, vol. 11, pp. 217-225.

Copeland, J & Dillon, P 2005, 'The health and psycho-social consequences of ketamine use', *International Journal of Drug Policy*, vol.16, pp.122-131.

Corbin, J & Strauss, A 1998, *Basics of qualitative research: techniques and procedures for developing grounded theory*, Sage Press, Thousand Oaks, CA.

Corssen, G & Domino, EF 1966, 'Dissociative anesthesia: further pharmacologic studies and first clinical experience with the phencyclidine derivative CI-581', *Anesthesia and Analgesia Current Researches*, vol. 45, no. 1, pp. 191-199.

Courtney, D 1999, *Stop the ride I want to get off*, Virgin Publishing, London.

Crank, S, Dugdill, L, Peiser, B & Guppy, A 1999, 'Moving beyond the drugs and deviance issues: rave dancing as a health promoting alternative to conventional physical activity', paper presented at Club Health 2000, 1st International Conference on Nightlife, Substance Use and Related Health Issues, Royal Tropical Institute, Amsterdam, 10-12 November.

Curran, HV & Travill, RA 1997, 'Mood and cognitive effects of 3,4-methylenedioxymethamphetamine (MDMA, Ecstasy): weekend "high" followed by mid-week low' *Addiction*, vol. 92, pp. 821-831.

Curran, V & Morgan, C 2000, 'Cognitive, dissociative and psychotogenic effects of ketamine in recreational users on the night of drug use and 3 days later', *Addiction*, vol. 95, no. 4, pp. 575-590.

Dalgarno, PJ & Shewan, D 1996, 'Illicit use of ketamine in Scotland', *Journal of Psychoactive Drugs*, vol.28, no.2, pp.191-99.

Davies, JB 1992, *The myth of addiction*, Harwood, Reading.

Decorte, T 2000, *The taming of cocaine: cocaine use in European and American cities*, VUB University Press, Brussels.

Decorte, T 2001a, 'Drug users' perceptions of 'controlled' and 'uncontrolled' use', *International Journal of Drug Policy,* vol. 12, pp. 297-320.

Decorte, T 2001b, 'Quality control cocaine users: underdeveloped harm reduction strategies', *European Addiction Research,* vol. 7, pp. 161-175.

DeCrescenzo, TA, Fifield, L & Lathan JD 1975, *On my way to nowhere: alienated, isolated, drunk: an analysis of gay alcohol abuse and an evaluation of alcoholism*, Rehabilitation Services for the Los Angeles Gay Community, Gay Community Services Center and Office of Alcohol Abuse and Alcoholism, Los Angeles, CA.

Deehan, A 1999, *Alcohol and crime: taking stock*, Home Office, London.

Deehan, A & Saville, E 2003, *Calculating the risk: recreational drug use among clubbers in the South East of England*, Home Office Online Report 43/03, Home Office, London.

Degenhardt, L, Darke, S & Dillon, P 2002, 'GHB use among Australians: characteristics, use patterns and associated harm', *Drug and Alcohol Dependence,* vol.67, pp. 89-94.

Degenhardt, L, Barker, B & Topp, L 2003, 'Patterns of ecstasy use in Australia: findings from a national household survey', *Addiction*, vol. 99, pp. 187-195.

Degenhardt, L & Topp, L 2003, 'Crystal meth' use among polydrug users in Sydney's dance party subculture: characteristics use patterns and associated harm', *International Journal of Drug Policy*, vol.14, pp. 17-24.

Degenhardt, L, Copeland, J & Dillion, P 2005, 'Recent trends in the use of 'club drugs': an Australian review', *Substance Use & Misuse*, vol. 40, pp. 1241-1256.

Delph, EW 1978, *The silent community: public homosexual encounters*, Sage, Beverly Hills CA.

De Micheli, D & Formigoni, ML 2002, 'Are reasons for the first use of drugs and family circumstances predictors of future use patterns?', *Addictive Behaviors*, vol. 27, no. 1, pp. 87-100.

D'emilio, J 1983*, Sexual politics, sexual communities: the making of a homo-sexual minority in the United States, 1940-1970*, University of Chicago Press, Chicago.

Denscombe, M 2001, 'Uncertain identities and health-risking behaviour: the case of young people and smoking in late modernity', *British Journal of Sociology*, vol. 52, no. 1, pp.157-177.

Denzin, N K 1997, *Interpretive ethnography: ethnographic practices for the 21st century*, Sage, London.

Department for Culture, Media and Sport 2005, *The new licensing laws have come into effect*, viewed 24th November, 2005 <http://www.culture.gov.uk/alcohol_and_entertainment/licensing_act_2003/ default.ht>

Derzon, JH & Lipsey, MW 1999, 'What good predictors of marijuana use are good for: a synthesis of Research', *School Psychology International*, vol. 20, no.1, pp. 69-85.

Des Jarlais DC, Diaz, T, Perlis, T, Vlahov, D, Maslow, C, Latka, M, Rockwell, R, Edwards, V, Friedman, SR, Monterroso, E, Williams, I & Garfein, RS 2003, 'Variability in the incidence of human immunodeficiency virus, hepatitis B virus, and hepatitis C virus infection among young injecting drug users in New York City', *American Journal of Epidemiology*, vol. 157, no. 5, pp. 467-471.

Dillon, P, Copeland, J & Jansen, K 2003, 'Patterns of use and harms associated with non- medical ketamine use', *Drug and Alcohol Dependence*, vol. 69, pp. 23-28.

Ditman, D, Eggan, F & Reback, C 1996, 'Methamphetamine use among gay male drug users: an ethnographic study', paper presented at the 11th International Conference on AIDS, Vancouver, 7-12 July.

Domino, EF, Chodoff P & Corssen, G 1965, 'Pharmacologic effects of CI-581, a new dissociative anesthetic, in man', *Clinical and Pharmacological Therapeutics*, vol. 6, pp. 279-291.

Donovan, D, Gorman, M, Gunderson, R & Marlatt, A 1996, 'HIV risk among gay and bisexual methamphetamine injectors in Seattle', paper presented at the 11th International Conference on AIDS, Vancouver, 7-12 July.

Dorn, N & South. N 1990 'Drug markets and law enforcement', *British Journal of Criminology*, vol. 30, no. 2, pp. 171-88.

Dorn, N, Murji, K & South, N 1992, *Traffickers: drug markets and law enforcement*, Routledge, London.

Dotson, JW, Ackerman, DL & West, LJ 1995, 'Ketamine abuse', *Journal of Drug Issues*, vol. 25, no. 4, pp. 751-757.

Douglas, J 1972, 'Observing deviance' in *Research on deviance*, Random House, New York, pp. 3-34.

Douglas, M 1992, *Risk and blame: essays in cultural theory*, Routledge, New York.

Drug Abuse Warning Network (DAWN) 2004, *The DAWN report: amphetamine and methamphetamine emergency department visits, 1995-2002*, US Department of Health and Social Services, Rockville, MD.

Drug Enforcement Administration (DEA) 2001, 'Drug intelligence brief, club drugs: an update September 2001', viewed 7th October 2005, <http://www.usdoj.gov/dea/pubs/intel/01026/ index.html>.

Drug Enforcement Administration (DEA) 2002, 'DEA to launch 'operation x-out': new club and predatory prevention initiative', viewed 21st November 2002, <http://www.cbsnews.com>

Drugscope 2005, *10 years on from Leah Betts: 20 years of ecstasy in the UK*, viewed 1st November 2005, <www.drugscope.org.uk >

Ellinwood, EH, Eibergen, RD & Kilbey, MM 1976, 'Stimulants: interaction with clinically relevant drugs', *Annals of the New York Academy of Sciences*, vol. 281, pp. 393-408.

Ellis, C & Bochner, AP 2003, 'Autoethnography, personal narrative, reflexivity: researcher as subject', in NK Denzin and YS Lincoln (eds.), *Collecting and interpreting qualitative materials*, 2nd revised ed., Sage, London, pp. 199-258.

Enarson, MC, Hays, H, Woodroffe, MA 1999, 'Clinical experience with oral ketamine', *Journal of Pain Symptom Management*, vol. 17, no. 5, pp. 384-386.

Erickson, PG & Cheung, YW 1999, 'Harm reduction among cocaine users: reflections on individual intervention and community social capital', *International Journal of Drug Policy*, vol. 10, pp. 235-246.

Esbensen, F & Elliot, DS 1994, 'Continuity and discontinuity in illicit drug use: patterns and antecedents', *Journal of Drug Issues*, vol. 24, pp. 75-97.

Ettorre, E 1992, *Women and substance use*, Macmillan, Basingstoke.

European Monitoring Centre for Drugs and Drug Addiction (EMCDDA) 2004, *Statistical bulletin 2004*, viewed 1st August 2005, <http://stats04.emcdda.eu.int/index.cfm?fuseaction=public.Content&nNodelID=5328>

Fehintola, L 2000, *Charlie says ... don't get high on your own supply*, Scribner, London.

Felson, M & Clarke, RV 1998, *Opportunity makes thief: practical theory for crime prevention*, Home Office, London.

Fendrich, M, Wislar, JS, Johnson, TP & Hubbell, A 2003, 'A contextual profile of club drug use among adults in Chicago', *Addiction*, vol. 98, pp. 1693-1703.

Fendrich, M & Johnson, TP 2005, 'Editors' introduction to this special issue on club drug epidemiology', *Substance Use & Misuse*, vol. 40, pp. 1179-1184.

Ferrell, J & Hamm, MS (eds.) 1998, *Ethnography at the edge: crime, deviance and field research*, Northeastern University Press, Boston.

Fine, PG 1999, 'Low-dose ketamine in the management of opioid nonresponsive terminal cancer pain', *Journal of Pain Symptoms Management*, vol. 17, no. 4, pp. 296-300.

Finnegan, D & McNally, E 1987, *Dual identities*, Hazelden, Center City, MN.

Fitsgerald, M 2001, 'Ethnic minorities and community safety', in R Matthews & J Pitts (eds.), *Crime disorder and community safety*, Routledge, London.

Fitzgerald, F 1986, *Cities on a hill*, Simon and Schuster, New York.

Flom, PL, Friedman, SR, Jose, B & Curtis, R 2001, 'Peer norms regarding drug use and drug selling among household youth in a low-income 'drug supermarket' urban neighborhood', *Drugs: Education, Prevention & Policy*, vol. 8, pp. 219-232.

Forsyth, A 1995, 'Ecstasy and illegal drug design: a new concept in drug use', *International Journal of Drug Policy*, vol. 6, no. 3, pp. 193-209.

Forsyth, A 1996a, 'Places and patterns of drug use in the Scottish dance scene', *Addiction*, vol. 91, no. 4, pp. 511-521.

Forsyth, A 1996b, 'Are raves drug supermarkets?', *International Journal of Drug Policy*, vol. 7, no. 2, pp. 105-110.

Forsyth, AJM, Barnard, M & McKeganey, NP 1997 'Musical preference as an indicator of adolescent drug use', *Addiction*, vol. 92, no. 10, pp. 1317-1325.

Friedman, SR & Aral, S 2001, 'Social networks, risk-potential networks, health, and disease', *Journal of Urban Health*, vol. 78, no. 3, pp. 411-418.

Friedman SR, Maslow C, Bolyard M, Sandoval M, Mateu-Gelabert P & Neaigus A 2004, 'Urging others to be healthy: "intravention" by injection drug users as a community prevention goal,' *AIDS Education & Prevention*, vol. 16, no. 3, pp. 250-63.

Frosch, D, Shoptaw S, Huber A, Rawson RA, & Ling W 1996, 'Sexual risk among gay and bisexual male methamphetamine abusers', *Journal of Substance Abuse Treatment*, vol. 13, no. 6, pp. 483-486.

Fyvel, TR 1963, *The insecure offenders*, Penguin, Harmondsworth.

Gamma, A, Buck, A, Berthold, T, & Vollenweider, FX 2001, 'No difference in brain activation during cognitive performance between ecstasy (3,4-methylenedioxymethamphetamine) users and control subjects: a positron emission tomography study', *Journal of Clinical Psychopharmacology*, vol. 21, no. 1, pp. 66-71.

Gamma, A, Frei, E, Lehmann, D, Pascual-Marqui, RD, Hell, D, & Vollenweider, FX 2000, 'Mood state and brain electric activity in ecstasy users', *Neuroreport*, vol. 11, no. 1, pp. 157-162.

Garland, D 2001, *The culture of control: crime and social order in contemporary society*, Oxford University Press, Oxford.

Geertz, C 1983, *Local knowledge: further essays in interpretive anthropology*, Basic Books, New York.

George, N 1999, *Hip hop America*, Penguin, London.

Gibson, C & Pagan, R 2001, *Rave culture in Sydney, Australia: mapping youth spaces in media discourse*, viewed 4 June 2005, <http://www.cia.com.au/peril/youth>

Giddens, A 1999, *Runaway world: how globalisation is reshaping our lives*, Profile Books, London.

Gilbert, J & Pearson, E 1999, *Discographies*, Routledge, London.

Gill, JR & Stajic, M 2000, 'Ketamine in non-hospital and hospital deaths in New York City', *Journal of Forensic Science*, vol. 45, no. 3, pp. 655-658.

Gill JR, Hayes JA, deSouza IS, Marker E, & Stajic M 2002, 'Ecstasy (MDMA) deaths in New York City: a case series and review of the literature', *Journal of Forensic Sciences*, vol. 47, no. 1, pp. 121-126.

Gilman, M 1992, 'Beyond opiates … and into the '90s', in M Ashton (ed.), *The ecstasy papers: a collection of ISDD's publications on the dance drugs phenomenon*, ISDD, London, pp. 16-21.

Gilmour, HB 1977, *Saturday Night Fever*, Bantam, New York.

Golby, J & Purdue, A 1999, *The civilization of the crowd: popular culture in England, 1750-1900*, Sutton Publishing, London.

Goldstein, PJ 2004, 'The drugs/violence nexus: a tripartite conceptual framework', in JA Inciardi & K McElrath (eds.), *The American drug scene: an anthology*, 4th ed., Roxbury, Los Angeles, pp. 384-394.

Gordon, D, Harris, NV, McGough, JP & Thiede, H 1993, 'Risk factors for HIV infection among injecting drug users: results of blinded surveys in drug treatment centers, King County, Washington 1988-1991', *Journal of Acquired Immune Deficiency Syndromes*, vol. 6, no. 11, pp. 1257-1282.

Gottfredson, MR & Hirschi, T 1990, *A general theory of crime,* Stanford University Press, Palo Alto.

Gouzoulis-Mayfrank, E, Daumann, J, Tuchtenhagen, F, Pelz, S, Becker, S, Kunert, H, Fimm, B & Sass, H 2000, 'Impaired cognitive performance in drug free users of recreational ecstasy (MDMA)', *Journal of Neurology, Neurosurgery & Psychiatry*, vol. 68, no. 6, pp. 719-725.

Green, SM, Rothrock, SG, Lynch, EL, Ho, M, Harris, T, Hestdalen, R, Hopkins, GA, Garrett, W & Westcott, K 1998, 'Intramuscular ketamine for pediatric sedation in the emergency department: safety profile in 1,022 cases', *Annals of Emergency Medicine*, vol. 31, no. 6, pp. 688-697.

Greenfield, SF, Manwani, SG, & Nargiso, MA 2003, 'Epidemiology of substance use disorders in women', *Obstetrics and Gynecology Clinics of North America*, vol. 30, pp. 413-446.

Grob, C 1998, 'MDMA research: preliminary investigations with human subjects', *International Journal of Drug Policy*, vol. 9, no. 2, pp. 119-124.

Grob, C 2000, 'Deconstructing ecstasy: the politics of MDMA research', *Addiction Research*, vol. 8 pp. 549-588.

Gross, J & McCaul, ME 1991, 'A comparison of drug use and adjustment in urban adolescent children of substance abusers', *International Journal of Addiction*, vol. 25, no. 4A, pp. 495-511.

Gross, SR, Barrett, SP, Shestowsky, JS, & Pihl, RO 2002, 'Ecstasy and drug consumption patterns: a Canadian rave population study', *Canadian Journal of Psychiatry*, vol. 47, no. 6, pp. 546-551.

Grund, JPC 1993, *Drug use as a social ritual: functionality, symbolism and determinants of self-regulation*, IVO Reeks Series, Rotterdam.

The Guardian 2005, 'Open galleries later to cut binge drinking', viewed 11 November, 2005   <http://society.guardian.co.uk/drugsandalcohol/story/0,8150,1647482,00. html>

Gyarmathy, VA, Neaigus, A, Miller, M, Friedman, SR, & Des Jarlais, DC 2002, 'Risk correlates of prevalent HIV, hepatitis B virus, and hepatitis C virus infections among noninjecting drug heroin users', *Journal of Acquired Immune Deficiency Syndrome*, vol. 30, no. 4, pp. 448-456.

Halbert, RJ, Simon, RR & Nasraty, Q 1988, 'Surgical theatre in rural Afghanistan', *Annals of Emergency Medicine*, vol. 17, no. 8, pp. 775-778.

Hales, G & Silverstone, D 2005, 'Interviews with 15 convicted offenders', in G. Hales (ed.), *Gun crime in Brent*, University of Portsmouth, Portsmouth, pp. 57-110.

Hales, G, Lewis, C & Silverstone, D 2006, *The market in and use of illegal firearms: interviews with 80 convicted firearms offenders*, Home Office, London.

Halkitis, P, Parsons, J & Stirratt, M 2001, 'A double epidemic: crystal methamphetamine drug use in relation to HIV transmission among gay men', *Journal of Homosexuality*, vol. 41, no. 2, pp. 17-35.

Halkitis, P & Parsons, J 2002, 'Recreational drug use and HIV-risk sexual behavior among men frequenting gay social venues', *Journal of Gay and Lesbian Social Services*, vol. 14, pp. 19-38.

Hall, JN 1996, 'Drug use in Miami (Dade County), Florida', *Proceedings of the Community Epidemiology Work Group Public Health Service, NIDA*, vol.2, pp. 113-129.

Hall, S & Jefferson, T (eds.) 1976, *Resistance through rituals: subcultures in post-war Britain*, Hutchinson, London.

Hallsworth, S 2005, *Street crime*, Willan, Cullompton.

Halpern, JH, Harrison, G, Pope, HG, Jr., Sherwood, AR, Barry, S, Hudson, JI, & Yurgelun-Todd, D 2004, 'Residual neuropsychological effects of illicit 3,4-methylenedioxymethamphetamine (MDMA) in individuals with minimal exposure to other drugs', *Drug and Alcohol Dependence*, vol. 75, no. 2, pp. 135-147.

Hamil-Luker, J, Land, KC & Blau, J 2004, 'Diverse trajectories of cocaine use through early adulthood among rebellious and socially conforming youth', *Social Science Research,* vol. 33, pp. 300-321.

Hammersley, M & Atkinson, P 1995, *Ethnography: principles in practice*, 2nd ed., Routledge, London.

Hammersley, R, Ditton, J, Smith, I & Short, E 1999, 'Patterns of ecstasy use by drug users', *British Journal of Criminology*, vol. 39, no. 4, pp. 625-647.

Hammersley, R, Khan, F & Ditton, J 2002, *Ecstasy and the rise of the chemical generation*, Routledge, London.

Hammersley, R & Reid, M 2002, 'Why the pervasive addiction myth is still believed', *Addiction Research & Theory,* vol. 10, no. 1, pp. 7-30.

Hammond, N 1986, 'Chemical abuse in lesbian and gay adolescents', paper presented at the Symposium on Gay and Lesbian Adolescents, Minneapolis, 30-31 May.

Hansen, D, Maycock, B & Lower, T 2001, "Weddings, parties, anything...', a qualitative analysis of ecstasy use in Perth, Western Australia', *International Journal of Drug Policy*, vol. 12, pp. 181-199.

Hansen, G, Jensen, SB, Chandresh, L & Hilden, T 1988, 'The psychotropic effect of ketamine', *Journal of Psychoactive Drugs*, vol. 20, no. 4, pp. 419-425.

Harding, S (ed.) 1987, *Feminism and methodology: social science issues*, IUP, Indianapolis.

Harris, S 2001, 'Backhand gang', *Time Out: London*, October 24-31, pp. 20-24.

Hayward, KJ 2004, *City limits: crime, consumer culture and the urban experience.* Glasshouse Press, London.

Heather, N & Robertson, I 1981, *Controlled drinking*, Methuen, London.

Hebdige, D 1976, 'The meaning of Mod', in S Hall & T Jefferson (eds.) *Resistance through ritual: youth subcultures in post-war Britain*, Hutchinson, London, pp. 87-98.

Hebdige, D 1979, *Subculture: the meaning of style*, Routledge, London.

Heischober, B & Miller, A 1991, 'Methamphetamine abuse in California', *NIDA Research Monographs*, vol. 115, pp. 60-71.

Hemment, D 1998, 'Dangerous dancing and disco riots: the northern warehouse parties', in McKay (ed.), *DiY culture: party and protest in nineties Britain*, Verso, London, pp. 208-227.

Henderson, S 1993a, 'Fun, fashion and frisson', *International Journal of Drug Policy*, vol. 4, no. 3, pp.122-129.

Henderson, S 1993b, *Young women, sexuality and recreational drug use: a research and development project*, Final Report, Lifeline, Manchester.

Henderson, S 1993c, 'Luvdup and de-elited: responses to drug use in the second decade', in P Aggleton, P Davies and G Hart (eds.), *AIDS: Facing the Second Decade*, Falmer, London, pp. 119-131.

Henderson, S 1997, *Ecstasy: case unsolved*, Pandora, London.

Henry, JA 1992, 'Ecstasy and the dance of death', *British Medical Journal*, vol. 305, pp. 5-6.

Henry, JA, Jeffreys, KJ, & Dawling, S 1992, 'Toxicity and deaths from 3,4 methylenedioxymethamphetamine ("ecstasy")', *Lancet*, vol. 340, pp. 384-387.

Henry, JA & Rella, J 2001, 'Medical risks associated with MDMA use', in J Holland (ed.), *Ecstasy: the complete guide*, Park Street Press, Rochester, Vermont, pp. 71-86.

Hesmondhalgh, D 2005, 'Subculture, scenes or tribes? None of the above', *Journal of Youth Studies*, vol. 8, no. 1, pp. 21-40.

Hill, A 2002, 'Acid house and Thatcherism: Noise, the mob and the English countryside', *British Journal of Sociology*, vol. 53, no. 1, pp. 89-105.

Hinchliff, S 2001, 'The meaning of ecstasy use and clubbing to women in the late 1990s', *International Journal of Drug Policy*, vol. 12, pp. 455-468.

Hirota, K & Lambert DG, 1996, 'Ketamine: it's mechanism(s) of action and unusual clinical uses', *British Journal of Anesthesia*, vol. 17, no. 4, pp. 441-444.

Hirschi, T 1969, *Causes of delinquency*, University of California Press, Berkeley.

HNCR Group, Mattison, AM, Ross, MW & Wolfson, DF 2001, 'Circuit party attendance, club drug use, and unsafe sex in gay men', *Journal of Substance Abuse*, vol. 13, pp. 119-126.

Ho, E, Karimi-Tabesh, L, & Koren, G 2001, 'Characteristics of pregnant women who use ecstasy (3, 4-methylenedioxymethamphetamine)', *Neurotoxicol Teratol*, vol. 23, no. 6, pp. 561-567.

Hobbs, D 1988, *Doing the business: entrepreneurship, the working-class and detectives in the East End of London*, Oxford University Press, Oxford.

Hobbs, D 1993, 'Peers, careers, and academic fears: writing as field work', in D Hobbs & T May (eds.), *Interpreting the field: accounts of ethnography*, Clarendon Press, Oxford.

Hobbs, D 1995, *Bad business: professional crime in modern Britain*, Oxford University Press, Oxford.

Hobbs, D 1998, 'Going down the local: the local context of organised crime', *The Howard Journal,* vol. 37, no. 4, pp. 407–422.

Hobbs, D & May, T (eds.) 1993, *Interpreting the field: accounts of ethnography,* Oxford: Clarendon.

Hobbs, D, Lister, S, Hadfield, P, Winlow, S & Hall, S 2000, 'Receiving shadows: governance and liminality in the night-time economy', *British Journal of Sociology,* vol. 51, no. 4, pp.701-718.

Hobbs, D, Hadfield, P, Lister, S & Winlow, S 2003, *Bouncers: violence and governance in the night-time economy,* Oxford University Press, Oxford.

Hodkinson, P 2002, *Goth: identity, style and subculture,* Berg, Oxford.

Hodkinson, P 2005, 'Insider research' in the study of youth cultures', *Journal of Youth Studies,* vol. 8, no. 2, pp. 131-149.

Holdaway, S 1983, *Inside the British Police,* Basil. Blackwell, Oxford

Home Box Office (HBO) 2002, *America undercover: small town ecstasy.*

Hope, B, McKirnan, DJ & Ostrow, DG 1996, 'Sex, drug and escape: a psychological model of HIV-risk sexual behaviours', *AIDS Care,* vol. 8, pp. 655-669.

Howells, K 2003, cited in The Guardian online 2003 *Minister labelled racist after attack on rap 'idiots',* viewed 1st November, 2005, <http://www.guardian.co.uk/ gun/Story/0,2763,869428,00.html>

Howes, D 1996, 'Introduction: commodities and cultural borders', in D Howes (ed.), *Cross-cultural consumption: global markets, local realities,* Routledge, London, pp. 1-16.

Huba, GJ, Melchior, LA, Staff of The Measurement Group, and HRSA/HAB's SPNS Cooperative Agreement Steering Committee 1997, *Module 24: brief substance abuse history form.* The Measurement Group. Adapted from work used in the NIDA Risk Behavior Assessment (RBA), viewed 21 March 2001, < http://www. themeasurementgroup.com/modules/mods/module24.htm>

Humphreys, L 1970, *Tearoom trade: impersonal sex in public places,* Aldine, Chicago.

Hunt, D 2004, 'Rise of hallucinogen use', in JA Inciardi & K McElrath (eds). *The American drug scene: an anthology,* 4th ed., Roxbury, Los Angeles, pp. 288-301.

Hunt, G & Evans, K 2003, 'Dancing and drugs: a cross-national exploration', *Contemporary Drug Problems,* vol. 30, pp. 779-814.

Hwang I, Daniels AM, & Holtzmuller KC 2002, '"Ecstasy"-induced hepatitis in an active duty soldier', *Military Medicine,* vol. 167, no. 2, pp. 155-156.

Inciardi, JA 1993, 'Some considerations on the methods, dangers and ethics of crack-house research', Appendix, in JA Inciardi, D Lockwood & AE Pettieger (eds.), *Women and crack cocaine,* Macmillan, New York.

International Journal of Drug Policy, 2002/3, Special editions on ethnographic methods in drugs research, vol. 13. no. 4 2002, and vol. 14, no. 1 2003.

Jacobs, A 2002, 'In clubs, a potent drug stirs fear of an epidemic', *The New York Times,* Volume CLI, 29 January, p. B1.

Jacobs, BA 1998, 'Researching crack dealers: dilemmas and contradictions', in J Ferrell & MS Hamm (eds.), *Ethnography at the edge: crime, deviance, and field research*, Northeastern Press, Boston, pp. 160-203.

James, M 1997, *State of bass - jungle: the story so far*, Boxtree, London.

Jansen, KLR 1998, 'Ecstasy (MDMA) dependence', *Drug and Alcohol Dependence*, vol. 53, no. 2, pp. 121-124.

Jansen, K 2001, *Ketamine: dreams and realities*, Multidisciplinary Association for Psychedelic Studies, Sarasota, FL.

Jayakody, R, Danziger, S, & Pollack, H 2000, 'Welfare reform, substance use, and mental health', *Journal of Health Politics, Policy and Law*, vol. 25, no. 4, pp. 623-651.

Jayanthi, S, Ladenheim, B, Andrews, AM, & Cadet, JL. 1999, 'Overexpression of human copper/zinc superoxide dismutase in transgenic mice attenuates oxidative stress caused by methelyenedioxymethamphetamine (Ecstasy)', *Neuroscience*, vol. 91, pp. 1379-1387.

Jefferson, DJ 2005, 'America's most dangerous drug', *Newsweek*, 8 August, vol. 146, no. 6, pp. 40-48.

Jenkins, P 1999, *Synthetic panics: the symbolic politics of designer drugs*, New York University Press, New York.

Joe Laidler, K 2004, 'Globalization and the illicit drug trade in Hong Kong', in C Sumner (ed.), *The Blackwell companion to criminology*, Blackwell Press, MA.

Joe Laidler, KA 2005, 'The rise of club drugs in a heroin society: the case of Hong Kong', *Substance Use & Misuse*, vol. 40, pp. 1257-1278.

Joe Laidler, K, Day, J & Hodson, D 2001, *Final report on the study of the psychotropic drug abuse problem in Hong Kong for the action committee against narcotics*, report to the Narcotics Division, Hong Kong Government, Center for Criminology, University of Hong Kong.

Joe Laidler, K with Hodson, D & Day, J 2004, *Final report on the initiation, continuation and consequences of drug use among women*, report to the ACAN, Narcotics Division, Hong Kong Government, Center for Criminology, University of Hong Kong.

Joe Laidler, K, with Hodson, D &Traver, H 2000, *Report on the Hong Kong drug market*, report to the United Nations Drug Control Program and United Nations Institute Interregional Crime and Justice.

Johnston, JC 1990, *Selecting Ethnographic Informants*, Sage, Newbury Park.

Johnston, LD & O'Malley, PM 2001, *Monitoring the future, 1999*, The University of Michigan, Ann Arbor, MI. Viewed 10 November 2000, <http://www.monitoringthefuture.org>

Johnston, LD, O'Malley, PM, & Bachman, JG 2001, *National Results on Adolescent Drug Use from Monitoring the Future: Overview of Key Findings*, National Institute on Drug Abuse, Bethesda, MD.

Johnston, LD, O'Malley, PM, Bachman, JG & Schulenberg, JE 2003, *Ecstasy use falls for second year in a row, overall teen drug use drops*, University of Michigan

News and Information Services, Ann Arbor, MI., Viewed 22 January 2004, <www.monitoringthefuture.org>

Johnston, LD, O'Malley, PM, & Bachman, JG 2002, *Ecstasy use among American teens drops for the first time in recent years, and overall drug and alcohol use also decline in the year after 9/11.* University of Michigan News and Information Services, Ann Arbor, MI. viewed 22nd January, 2004, <www.monitoringthefuture. org>

Johnston, LD, O'Malley, PM, Bachman, JG & Schulenberg, JE 2005, *Monitoring the future: national result on adolescent drug use: overview of key findings, 2004,* US Department of Health and Human Services, Washington DC.

Johnston, LD, O'Malley, PM, Bachman, JG & Schulenberg, JE 2005, *Monitoring the future national survey results on drug use, 1975-2004. Volume I: Secondary school students,* NIH Publication No. 05-5727, National Institute on Drug Abuse, Bethesda, MD.

Julien, RM 1992, *A primer of drug action: a concise, non-technical guide to the actions, uses and side effects of psychoactive drugs,* W.H. Freeman and Company, New York.

Kandel, DB & Davies, M 1990, 'Friendship networks of illicit drug users in adulthood: a comparison of two competing theories', *Criminology,* vol. 29, pp. 441-469.

Kane, S 1998, 'Reversing the ethnographic gaze: experiments in cultural criminology', in J Ferrell & MS Hamm (eds.), *Ethnography at the edge: crime, deviance and field research,* Northeastern University Press, Boston, pp. 132-145.

Kennedy, LW & Forde, DR 1999, *When push comes to shove: a routine conflict approach to violence,* New York, State University of New York Press, New York.

Ketcham, DW 1990, 'Where there is no anesthesiologist: the many uses of ketamine', *Tropical Doctor,* vol. 20, pp. 163-166.

Khan-Harris, K 2004, 'Unspectacular subculture? Transgression and mundanity in the global extreme metal scene', in A Bennett and K Khan-Harris (eds.), *After subculture: critical studies in contemporary youth culture,* Palgrave, London.

Klitzman, RL, Pope, HG, Jr., & Hudson, JI 2000, 'MDMA (ecstasy) abuse and high-risk sexual behaviors among 169 gay and bisexual men', *American Journal of Psychiatry,* vol. 157, no. 7, pp. 1162-1164.

Kohn, M 1997, 'Cocaine girls', in S Redhead (ed.) with D Wynne & J O'Connor , *The clubcultures reader: readings in popular cultural studies,* Blackwell, Oxford, pp. 137-147.

Koopman, C, Rosario, & Rotheram-Borus, MJ 1991, 'Minority youths at high risk: gay males and runaways', in ME Colten & S Gore (eds.), *Adolescent stress: causes and consequences,* Harper Collins, New York, pp. 181-200.

Kray, K 2000, *Hard bastards,* Blake publishing, London.

Krebs, CP & Steffey, DM 2005 'Club drug use among delinquent youth', *Substance Use & Misuse,* vol. 40, pp. 1363-1379.

Kreitzman, L 1999, *The 24 hour society,* Profile books, London.

Kronz, CS 2000, 'A 30-year old woman with possible unknown ingestion of date rape drugs', *Journal of Emergency Nursing*, vol. 26, no. 6, pp. 544-548.

Kuhn, C, Swartzwelder, S & Wilson, W 1998, *Buzzed: the straight facts about the most used and abused drugs from alcohol to ecstasy*, WW Norton Co, New York.

Kus, R 1985, 'Gay alcoholism and non-acceptance of self: the critical link', paper presented at the Nursing Research Conference, Honolulu, 8 April.

LaMontagne, DS, Fine, DN, & Marrazzo, JM 2004, 'Chlamydia trachomatis infection in asymptomatic men', *American Journal of Preventive Medicine*, vol. 24, no. 1, pp. 36-42.

Landry, MJ 2002, 'MDMA: a review of epidemiologic data', *Journal of Psychoactive Drugs*, vol. 34, no. 2, pp. 163-169.

Lankenau, SE & Clatts, MC 2002, 'Ketamine injection among high risk youths: preliminary findings from New York City', *The Journal of Drug Issues*, vol. 32, no. 3, pp. 893-905.

Lankenau, SE & Clatts, MC 2004, 'Drug injection practices among high-risk youth: the first shot of ketamine', *Journal of Urban Health*, vol. 81, pp. 232-48.

Lankenau, SE & Clatts, M 2005, 'Patterns of polydrug use among ketamine injectors in New York City', *Substance Use & Misuse*, vol. 40, pp. 1381-1398.

Lankenau, SE & Sanders, B 2004, 'Becoming a ketamine injector: a preliminary analysis of high-risk youth in New York City', paper presented at the 99th annual meeting of the American Sociological Association, San Francisco, 14-17 August.

Lankenau, SE, Clatts, MC, Goldsamt, LA, & Welle, D 2004, 'Crack cocaine injection practices and HIV risk: findings from New York and Bridgeport', *Journal of Drug Issues*, vol. 34, pp. 319-32.

Lankenau, SE, Sanders, B, Bloom, JJ, Hathazi, D, Alarcon, E, Tortu, S & Clatts, MC 2005, 'Ketamine injection initiation among young injection drug users (IDUs) in three U.S. cities', paper presented at the 133rd annual meeting of the American Public Health Association, Philadelphia, 10-14 December.

Latkin, CA, Forman, V & Knowlton, A 2002, 'Concordance between drug users' and their network members' reported drug use and HIV status: implications to HIV prevention', *Advances in Medical Sociology*, vol. 8, pp. 151-164.

Latkin, CA, Forman, V & Knowlton, A & Sherman, S 2003, 'Norms, social networks, and HIV-related risk behaviors among urban disadvantaged drug users', *Social Science and Medicine*, vol. 56, pp. 465-476.

Leavitt, F 2003, *The real drug abusers*, Rowman and Littlefield Publishers, Inc, New York.

Lee, JK, Jennings, JM. & Ellen, JM 2004, 'Discordant sexual partnering: a study of high-risk adolescents in San Francisco', *Sexually Transmitted Diseases*, vol. 30, no. 3, pp. 234-240.

Lee, R 1995, *Dangerous fieldwork*, Sage, London.

Lenton, S, Boys, A & Norcross, K 1997, 'Raves, drugs and experience: drug use by a sample of people who attend raves in Western Australia', *Addiction*, vol. 92, no.10, pp. 1327-37.

Lenton, S & Davidson, P 1999, 'Raves, drugs, dealing and driving: qualitative data from a West Australian sample', *Drug and Alcohol Review,* vol. 18, pp. 153-161.

Leonard, L & Ross, M 1997, 'The last sexual encounter: the contextualization of sexual risk behaviour', *International Journal of STD & AIDS,* vol. 8, pp. 643-645.

Leri, R, Bruneau, J & Stewart, J 2003, 'Understanding polydrug use: review of heroin and cocaine co-use', *Addiction,* vol. 98, pp. 7-22.

Letherby, G 2000, 'Dangerous liaisons: auto/biography in research and research writing', in G Lee-Treweek & S Linkogle (eds.), *Danger in the field: risks and ethics in social research*, Routledge, London, pp. 91-113.

Levine, M 1998, *Gay macho: the life and death of the homosexual clone*, New York University Press, New York.

Levy, KB, O'Grady, KE, Wish, ED & Arria, AM 2005, 'An in-depth qualitative examination of the ecstasy experience: results of a focus group with ecstasy-using college students', *Substance Use & Misuse,* vol. 40, pp. 1427-1441.

Lewis, CE, Robins, E & Saghir, MT 1982, 'Drinking patterns in homosexual and heterosexual women', *Journal of Clinical Psychiatry,* vol. 43, pp. 277-279.

Lewis, LA & Ross, MW 1995, *A select body: the gay dance party subculture and the HIV=AIDS pandemic*, Cassell, London.

Li, J 1971, 'Editorial', *Anesthesia,* vol. 26, no. 2, pp. 125-126.

Liechti, ME & Vollenweider, FX 2000, 'Acute psychological and physiological effects of MDMA ("Ecstasy") after haloperidol pretreatment in healthy humans', *European Neuropsychopharmacology,* vol. 10, pp. 289-295.

Linder, R 1996, *The reportage of urban culture.* (translated by Adrian Morris), Cambridge University Press, Cambridge.

Livingstone, K 2005, cited in The Times online 2005 *Mayor blames rap for deaths,* viewed 1st November, 2005 <http://www.timesonline.co.uk/article/0,,2-1854985,00.html>

Loughery, J 1998, *The other side of silence. Men's lives and gay identities: a twentieth century history*, Own Books, New York.

Lua, AC, Huei RL, Te YT, An RH & Pei, CY 2003, ' Profiles of urine samples from participants at rave party in Taiwan: prevalence of ketamine and MDMA abuse', *Forensic Science International,* vol. 136, pp. 47-51.

Luckman, S 2000 'Mapping the regulation of dance parties', in R Nile (ed.), *The beautiful and the damned: Journal of Australian Studies, no. 64,* API network UQP, St. Lucia, pp. 217-223.

Luhmann, N 1993, *Risk: a sociological theory*, De Gruyter Press, New York.

Lyng, S 1998, 'Dangerous methods: risk taking and the research process', in J Ferrell and MS Hamm (eds.), *Ethnography at the edge: crime, deviance and field research*, Northeastern University Press, Boston, pp. 221-251.

McDermott P, Matthews, A & Bennett, A 1992, 'Responding to recreational drug use: why clubbers need information, not outreach', *Druglink,* vol. 7, no. 1, pp. 12-13.

McElhatton, PR, Bateman, DN, Evans, C, Pughe, KR, & Thomas, SH 1999, 'Congenital anomalies after prenatal ecstasy exposure', *Lancet*, vol. 352, no. 9188, pp. 1441-1442.

McKirnan, DJ & Peterson, PL 1989, 'Alcohol and drug use among homosexual men and women', *Addictive Behaviours*, vol. 14, pp. 545-553.

McMahon, JM & Tortu, S 2003, 'A potential hidden source of hepatitis C infection among noninjecting drug users', *Journal of Psychoactive Drugs,* vol. 35, no. 4, pp. 455-460.

McRobbie, A 1994, *Postmodernism and popular culture*, Routledge, London.

Maguire, M 2000, 'Researching "street criminals": a neglected art', in R King & E Wincap (eds.), *Doing research on crime and justice*, Oxford University Press, Oxford, pp. 121-152.

Maher, L 2002, 'Don't leave us this way: ethnography and injecting drug use in the age of AIDS', *International Journal of Drug Policy*, vol. 13, pp. 311-325.

Malbon, B 1998, 'Clubbing: consumption, identity and the spatial practices of every-night life', in T Skelton & G Valentine (eds.), *Cool places: geographies of youth cultures*, Routledge, London, pp. 266-286.

Malbon, B 1999, *Clubbing: dancing, ecstasy and vitality*, Routledge, London.

Malotte, CK, Rhodes, R & Woods, MM 1996, 'Pilot study of drug-using men who have sex with men: access and intervention strategies', paper presented at the 11th International Conference on AIDS, Vancouver, 7-12 July.

Mansergh, G, Colfax, GN, Marks, G, Rader, M, Guzman, R & Buchbinder, S 2001, 'The circuit party men's health survey: findings and implications for gay and bisexual men,' *American Journal of Public Heath*, vol. 91, no. 6, pp. 953-958.

Martins, SS, Mazzotti, G & Chilcoat, HD 2005, 'Trends in ecstasy use in the United States from 1995-2001: comparison with marijuana users and association with other drug use', *Experimental and clinical psychopharmacology*, vol. 13, no. 3, pp. 244-252.

Mas, M, Farre, M, de la Torre, R, Roset P, Ortuno J, Segura J, & Cami J 1999, 'Cardiovascular and neuroendocrine effects and pharmacokinetics of 3,4-methylenedioxymethamphetamine in humans', *Journal of Pharmacology and Experimental Therapeutics*, vol. 290, pp. 136-145.

Mass Observation 1987, *Pub and the people*, Ebury Press, London.

Mattison, AM, Ross, MW, Wolfson, T, Franklin, D, & HNRC Group 2001, 'Circuit party attendance, club drug use, and unsafe sex in gay men,' *Journal of Substance Abuse*, vol. 13, pp. 119-126.

Maxwell, JC & Spence, RT 2005, 'Profiles of club drug users in treatment', *Substance Use & Misuse,* vol. 40, pp. 1409-1426.

May, T 1998, 'Reflections and reflexivity', in May, T & Williams, M (eds.), *Knowing the social world*, Open University Press, Buckingham, pp. 157-166.

Mayer, KH, McCusker, J, Stoddard, AM, Westenhouse, J, Zapka, JG & Zorn, MW 1990, 'Use of drugs and alcohol by homosexually active men in relation to sexual practices', *Journal of Acquired Immune Deficiency Syndromes*, vol. 3, no. 7, pp. 729-736.

Maynard, M & Purvis, J 1994, *Researching women's lives from a feminist perspective*, Taylor and Francis, London.

MCM Research, 1990 *Conflict and violence in the pub*, MCM Research, Oxford.

Measham, F 1988, 'Men buy the beer and the leer: a case study of women and bar work', unpublished Masters thesis, University of Warwick, Warwick.

Measham, F 1996, 'The 'Big Bang' approach to sessional drinking: changing patterns of alcohol consumption amongst young people in North West England', *Addiction Research*, vol. 4, no. 3, pp. 283-299.

Measham, F 2002, "Doing gender' – 'doing drugs': conceptualising the gendering of drugs cultures', *Contemporary Drug Problems*, vol. 29, no. 2, pp. 335-373.

Measham, F 2004a, 'Play space: historical and socio-cultural reflections on drugs, licensed leisure locations, commercialisation and control', *International Journal of Drug Policy*, Special Edition: Social theory in drug research and harm reduction, vol. 15, no. 5-6, pp. 337-345.

Measham, F 2004b, 'Drug and alcohol research: the case for cultural criminology', in J Ferrell, K Hayward, W Morrison and M Presdee (eds.), *Cultural criminology unleashed*, Glasshouse, London, pp. 207-218.

Measham, F 2004c, 'The decline of ecstasy, the rise of 'binge' drinking and the persistence of pleasure', *Probation Journal, Special Edition: rethinking drugs and crime*, vol. 51, no. 4, pp. 309-326.

Measham, F 2005, '"Damned if you do, damned if you don't": clubs, criminality and reluctant reflexivity', paper presented to American Society of Criminology Annual Meeting, Toronto, 15-19 November.

Measham, F in press, 'The new policy mix: alcohol, harm minimisation and determined drunkenness in contemporary society', *International Journal of Drug Policy*, Special edition: Alcohol and harm reduction.

Measham, F, Aldridge, J & Parker, H 2001, *Dancing on drugs: risk, health and hedonism in the British club scene*, London: Free Association Books.

Measham, F & Brain, K 2005, 'Binge' drinking, British alcohol policy and the new culture of intoxication, *Crime, Media, Culture: An International Journal*, vol. 1, no. 3, pp. 262-283.

Melechi, A 1993, 'The ecstasy of disappearance', in S Redhead (ed.), *Rave off politics and deviance in contemporary youth culture*, Avebury, Aldershot, pp. 29-40.

Mendelson, B & Harrison, L 1996, 'Drug use trends in Denver and Colorado', *Proceedings of the Community Epidemiology Work Group Public Health Service, NIDA*, vol. 2, pp. 52-67.

Merton, RK 1938, 'Social structure and anomie', *American Sociological Review*, vol. 3, pp. 672-682.

Merton, RK 1957, *Social theory and social structure*, revised and enlarged ed., Glencoe Free Press, London.

Merton, RK 1972, 'Insiders and outsiders: a chapter in the sociology of knowledge', *American Journal of Sociology*, vol. 78, pp. 9-47.

Messerschmidt, JW 1993, *Masculinities and crime: critique and reconceptualization of theory*, Rowman and Littlefield, Lanham, MD.

Messerschmidt, JW 2000, *Nine lives: adolescent masculinities, the body, and violence*, Westview, Oxford.

Metcalfe, S 1997, 'Psychedelic warriors and ecstasy evangelists', in A Melechi (ed.), *Psychedelia Britannica: hallucinogenic drugs in Britain*, Turnaround, London, pp. 166-184.

Milani, RM, Parrott, AC, Turner, JJD, & Fox, HC 2004, 'Gender differences in self-reported anxiety, depression, and somatization among ecstasy/MDMA polydrug users, alcohol/tobacco users, and nondrug users', *Addictive Behaviors*, vol. 29, pp. 965-971.

Miles, S 2000, *Youth lifestyles in a changing world*, Open University Press, Buckingham.

Miller, M & Neaigus, A 2001, 'Networks, resources and risk among women who use drugs', *Social Science Medicine*, vol. 52, no. 6, pp. 967-978.

Mitchell, J 2001,'The moral panic about raves: newspaper transmission and legislation', unpublished masters thesis, Humboldt State University, Humboldt, CA.

Mixmag 1994, *What's in your E?*, vol. 2. no. 43, December.

Mixmag 2004, *Drug Britain: a nation of caners - what state are you in?*, vol. 33, no. 55, February.

Moeller, FG, Dougherty, DM, Steinberg, JL, Swann, AC, Silverman, PB, Ruiz, P & Barratt, ES 2002, 'Heavy ecstasy use is associated with increased impulsivity', *Addictive Disorders and their Treatment*, vol. 1, no. 2, pp. 47-52.

Moffit, TE 1993, 'Adolescent-limited and life-course persistent antisocial behavior: a developmental taxonomy', *Psychological Review*, vol. 100, pp. 674-701.

Monaghan, LF 2002a, 'Opportunity, pleasure, and risk: an ethnography of urban male heterosexualities', *Journal of Contemporary Ethnography*, vol. 31, no. 4, pp. 440-77.

Monaghan, LF 2002b 'Hard men, shop boys and others: embodying competence in a masculinist occupation, *The Sociological Review*, vol. 50, no. 3, pp. 334-55.

Moore, D 1994, *The lads in action: social processes in an urban youth subculture*, Ashgate, Aldershot.

Moore, D 1995, 'Raves and the bohemian search for self and community: a contribution to the anthropology of public events', *Anthropological Forum*, vol. 7, no. 2, pp. 193-214.

Moore, K 1998, 'Notions of recovery amongst former anorexia sufferers', unpublished Masters thesis, University of East Anglia, Norwich.

Moore, K 2003a, 'E-heads vs beer monsters: researching young people's drug consumption in dance club settings', in A Bennett, S Miles and M Cielslik, (eds.), *Researching Youth*, Palgrave, London.

Moore, K 2003b, '"Proper mashed like": spectacular and mundane aspects of hard house, funky house and trance clubbing in Manchester, UK, BSA Youth Study Group Conference, University of Northampton, UK, 11-13 November.

Moore, K 2004, 'A commitment to clubbing', *Peace Review: A Journal of Social Justice*, vol. 16, no. 4, pp. 459-465.

Moore, K 2005, '"Sort drugs, make mates": the use and meanings of mobiles in club culture', in B Brown & K O'Hara (eds.), *Reinventing music: social and collaborative aspects of new music technology*, Hewlett Packard Labs, Bristol, pp. 211-239.

Moore, NN & Bostwick, JM 1999, 'Ketamine dependence in anesthesia providers', *Psychosomatics*, vol. 40, no. 4, pp. 356-359.

Morgan, CJ, Monaghan, L & Curran, HV 2004, 'Beyond the K-hole: a 3-year longitudinal investigation of the cognitive and subjective effects of ketamine in recreational users who have substantially reduced their use of the drug', *Addiction*, vol. 99, no. 11, pp. 1450-1461.

Moran JP, 2000, *Teaching sex: the shaping of adolescence in the 20th century*, Harvard University Press, Cambridge, MA.

Morgan, MJ 1998, 'Recreational use of "ecstasy" (MDMA) is associated with elevated impulsivity,' *Neuropsychopharmacology*, vol. 19, pp. 252-264.

Morral, AR, McCaffrey, DF, & Paddock, SM 2002, 'Reassessing the marijuana gateway effect', *Addiction*, vol. 97, no. 12, pp. 1493-1505.

Morris, S 1998, *Clubs, drugs and doormen*, Police Research Group, London.

Mott, J 1990 *Young people alcohol and crime*, Home Office Research Bulletin, Research and Statistics Department, 28, pp. 24-8.

Mueller, PD & Korey, WS, 1998, 'Death by "ecstasy": the serotonin syndrome?', *Annals of Emergency Medicine*, vol. 32, pp. 377-380.

Muggleton, D 1997, 'The post-subculturalist', in S Redhead (ed.) with D Wynne and J O'Connor, *The club cultures reader: readings in popular cultural studies*, Blackwell, Oxford, pp. 185-203.

Muggleton, D 2000, *Inside subcultures: the postmodern meaning of style*, Berg, London.

Mungham, G & Pearson, G 1976 (eds.) *Working class youth culture*, Routledge & Kegan Paul, London.

Murji, K 1998, 'The agony and the ecstasy: drugs, media and morality', in R Coomber (ed.), *The control of drugs and drug users: reason or reaction?*, Harwood Academic Publishers, Amsterdam, pp. 65-85.

Murphy, S & Rosenbaum, M 1997, 'Two women who used cocaine too much: class, race, gender, crack and coke', in C Reinarman & HG Levine (eds.), *Crack in context: demon drugs and social justice*, University of California Press, Berkeley, pp. 98-112.

Murray, S 1996, *American gay*, University of Chicago Press, Chicago.

Najavits, LM Weiss, RD, & Shaw, SR 1997, 'The link between substance abuse and posttraumatic stress disorder in women. A research review', *American Journal of the Addictions*, vol. 6, no. 4, pp. 273-283.

Nardi, PM 1982, 'Alcoholism and homosexuality: a theoretical perspective', *Journal of Homosexuality*, vol. 7, no. 4, pp. 9-25.

Narvaez, R 2001, 'MDMA in combination: 'trail mix' and other powdered drug combinations', paper presented at MDMA/Ecstasy Research: Advances, Challenges, Future, Bethesda, 19-20 July.

National Center on Addiction and Substance Abuse (CASA) at Columbia University 2004, *You've got drugs! Prescription drug pushers on the Internet*, Columbia University, New York.

National Center on Addiction and Substance Abuse (CASA) at Columbia University 2005, *Under the counter: the diversion and abuse of controlled prescription drugs in the US*, Columbia University, New York.

National Drug Strategy Household Survey (NDSHS) 2002, The Australian National University, Canberra.

National Institute of Justice (NIJ) 2003, *2000 Arrestee Drug Abuse Monitoring: annual report*, US Department of Justice, Washington DC.

National Survey on Drug Use and Health (NSDUH) 2005, *The NSDUH report: substance use among past year ecstasy users*, US Department of Health and Human Services, Washington DC.

Neaigus, A, Miller, M, Friedman, SR, & Des Jarlais, DC 2001, 'Sexual transmission risk among noninjecting heroin users infected with human immunodeficiency virus or hepatitis C virus', *Journal of Infectious Disease*, vol. 184, no. 3, pp. 359-363.

Nelken, D 1993, 'Reflexive criminology?', in D Nelken (ed.), *The futures of criminology*, Sage, London, pp. 7-42.

Negrusz, A & Gaensslen, RE 2003, 'Analytical developments in toxicological investigation of drug-facilitated sexual assault', *Annals of Bioanalytical Chemistry*, vol. 376, pp. 1192-1197.

Newcombe, R 1987, 'High time for harm reduction', *Druglink*, vol. 2, pp.10-11.

Newcombe, R 1988, 'Serious fun: drug education through popular culture', *Druglink*, vol. 3, no. 6, pp. 11-14.

Newcombe, R 1991, *Raving and dance drugs: house music clubs and parties in north-west England*, Rave Research Bureau, Liverpool.

Newcombe, R 1992a, 'A researcher reports from the rave', in M Ashton (ed.), *The ecstasy papers: a collection of ISDD's publications on the dance drugs phenomenon*, ISDD, London.

Newcombe, R 1992b, *The use of ecstasy and dance drugs at rave parties and nightclubs: some problems and solutions*, 3D Research Bureau, Liverpool.

Newcombe, R 1994a, *Drug use by young people at a rave club in North West England: The Empire, Morecambe, 1994*, 3D Research Bureau, Liverpool.

Newcombe, R 1994b, *Safer dancing: guidelines for good practice at dance parties and nightclubs*, 3D Research Bureau, Liverpool.

Newcombe, R & Johnson, M 1999, 'Psychonautics: a model and method for exploring the effects of psychedelic drugs', paper presented at Club Health 2000: 1st International conference on night-life, substance use and related health issues, Amsterdam, 10-12 November.

Newcombe, R & Woods, S 2002, 'How risky is ecstasy? A model for comparing the mortality risks of ecstasy use, dance parties and related activities', *Drugtext*, viewed 12 December 2002 <http://www.drugtext.org/library/articles/newcombe.html.>

Noell, J & Ochs, L 2001, 'Relationship of sexual orientation to substance use, suicidal ideation, suicide attempts, and other factors in a population of homosexual adolescents', *Journal of Adolescent Health*, 29 July, vol. 1, pp. 31-36.

Novoa, RA, Ompad, DC, Wu, Y, Vlahov, D & Galea, S 2005, 'Ecstasy use and its association with sexual behaviors among drug users in New York City', *Journal of Community Health*, vol. 30, no. 5, pp. 331-343.

Nuttal, J 1970, *Bomb culture*, Paladin, London.

O'Hagan, C 1999, *British dance culture: sub-genres and associated drug use,* Release, London.

O'Malley, P & Mugford, S 1994, 'Crime, excitement and modernity' in G Barak (ed.), *Varieties of criminology: readings from a dynamic discipline*, Praeger, London, pp. 189-211.

O'Shea, E, Granados, R, Esteban, B, Colado, MI, & Green, AR 1998, 'The relationship between the degree on neurodigestion of rat brain 5-HT nerve terminals and the dose and frequency of administration of MDMA (ecstasy)', *Neuropharmacology*, vol. 37, pp. 919-926.

O'Sullivan, LF 1995, 'Less is more: effects of sexual experience on judgments of men's and women's personality characteristics and relationship desirability', *Sex Roles*, vol. 33, pp. 159-181.

Oakley A 1981, 'Interviewing women: a contradiction in terms', in H Roberts (ed.), *Doing feminist research*, Routledge, London, pp. 30-61.

Office of Applied Studies (OAS) 2003, *Emergency department trends from the drug abuse warning network, final estimates 1975-2002*, Substance Abuse and Mental Health Services Administration, Rockville, MD.

Office of National Drug Control Policy (ONCDP) 2004, *National synthetic drugs action plan: the federal government response to the production, trafficking, and abuse of synthetic drugs and diverted pharmaceutical products*, Executive Office of the President, Washington, DC.

Oliver, MB & Sedikides, C 1992, 'Effects of sexual permissiveness on desirability of partner as a function of low and high commitment to relationship', *Social Psychology Quarterly*, vol. 55, pp. 321-333.

Ompad, DC, Galea, S, Fuller, CM, Edwards, V & Vlahov, D 2005, 'Ecstasy use among Hispanic and black substance users in New York City', *Substance Use & Misuse*, vol. 40, pp. 1399-1407.

Ornoy, ASJ, Bar-Hamburger, R & Greenbaum, C 2001, 'Developmental outcome of school-age children born to mothers with heroin dependency: importance of environmental factors', *Developmental Medicine & Child Neurology*, vol. 43, no. 10, no. 668-675.

Ostrow, DG 1996, 'Substance use, HIV, and gay men', *Focus*, vol. 11, no. 7, pp. 1-4.

Panagopoulos, I & Ricciardelli, LA 2005, 'Harm reduction and decision making among recreational ecstasy users', *International Journal of Drug Policy*, vol. 16, pp. 54-64.

Park, R 1950, *The collected papers of Robert Ezra Park: race and culture, volume on*, edited by Hughes, E, Johnson, C, Masuoka, J, Redfield, R & Wirth, L, Free Press. Glencoe, Ill.

Parker, H, Bakx, K & Newcombe, R 1988, *Living with heroin: the impact of a drugs 'epidemic' on an English community*, Open University Press, Milton Keynes.

Parker, H, Measham, F & Aldridge, J 1995, *Drugs futures: changing patterns of drug use amongst English youth*, Institute for the Study of Drug Dependence, London.

Parker, H, Aldridge, J & Measham, F 1998, *Illegal leisure: the normalization of adolescent recreational drug use*, Routledge, London.

Parker, H, Williams, L, & Aldridge, J 2002, 'The normalization of 'sensible' recreational drug use: further evidence from the North West England Longitudinal Study', *Sociology*, vol. 36, no. 4, pp. 941-964.

Parker, H & Williams, L 2003, 'Intoxicated weekends: young adults' work hard-play hard lifestyles, public health and public disorder', *Drugs: Education, Prevention and Policy*, vol. 10, pp. 345-367.

Parks, KA & Kennedy, CL 2004, 'Club drugs: reasons for and consequences of use', *Journal of Psychoactive Drugs*, vol. 36, pp. 295-302.

Parks, KA & Scheidt, DM 2000, 'Male bar drinkers' perspective on female bar drinkers', *Sex Roles*, vol. 43, pp. 927-941.

Parrott, AC 2001, 'Human psychophamacology of Ecstasy (MDMA): a review of 15 years of empirical research', *Human Psychopharmacology - Clinical and Experimental*, vol. 16, pp. 557-577.

Parrott, AC & Lasky, J 1998, 'Ecstasy (MDMA) effects upon mood and cognition: before, during, and after a Saturday night dance', *Psychopharmacology*, vol. 139, no. 3, pp. 261-268.

Parrott, A, Milani, R, Parmar, R 2001, 'Recreational ecstasy/MDMA and other drug users from the UK and Italy: psychiatric symptoms and psychobiological problems', *Psychopharmacology*, vol. 159, no. 1, pp. 77-82.

Parrott, AC, Buchanan, T, Scholey, AB, Heffernan, T, Ling, J, & Rodgers, J 2002, 'Ecstasy/MDMA attributed problems reported by novice, moderate and heavy recreatonal users', *Human Psychopharmacology*, vol. 17, no. 6, pp. 309-312.

Pearson, G 1983, *Hooligan: a history of respectable fears*, MacMillian, London.

Pearson, G, Ditton, J, Newcombe, R & Gilman, M 1992, 'Everything starts with an E: an introduction to ecstasy use by young people in Britain', in M Ashton (ed.), *The ecstasy papers: a collection of ISDD's publications on the dance drugs phenomenon*, ISDD, London.

Pearson, G & Hobbs, D 2001, *Middle market drug distribution*, Home Office Research Study 227, Home Office, London.

Pedersen, W & Skrondal, A 1999, 'Ecstasy and new patterns of drug use: a normal population study', *Addiction*, vol. 94, no. 11, pp. 1695-1706.

Piacentini, L 2005, 'Cultural talk and other intimate acquaintances with Russian prisons', *Crime, Media, Culture*, vol. 1, no. 2, pp. 189-208.

Pini, M 2001, *Club cultures and female subjectivity: the move from home to house*, London, Palgrave.

Polsky, N 1967; 1998, *Hustlers, beats and others: expanded edition of the classic study of deviance*, updated with a new chapter and foreword, The Lyons Press, New York.

Pope, HG, Jr, Ionescu-Pioggia, M, & Pope, KW 2001, 'Drug use and life style among college undergraduates: a 30-year longitudinal study', *The American Journal of Psychiatry*, vol. 158, no. 9, pp. 1519-1521.

Preble, E, & Casey, L 1969, 'Taking care of business: the heroin user's life on the streets', *Journal of the Addictions*, vol. 4, pp. 1-24.

Presdee, M 2000, *Cultural criminology and the carnival crime*, Routledge, London.

Pryce, K 1979, *Endless pressure: a study of West Indian lifestyles in Britain*, Penguin, Harmondsworth.

Public Broadcasting System (PBS) 2001, *In the mix: ecstasy*, funded by the National Institute of Drug Abuse.

Pulse Check 2004, *Trends in drug abuse: advanced report December 2003*, Executive Office of the President, Office of National Drug Control Policy, Washington DC.

Pumariega, AJ, Rodriguez, L, & Kilgus, MD 2004, 'Substance abuse among adolescents: current perspectives', *Addictive Disorders and Their Treatment*, vol. 3, no. 4, pp. 145-155.

Reback, CJ 1997, *The social construction of a gay drug: methamphetamine use among gay and bisexual males in Los Angeles*, Report funded by the City of Los Angeles, AIDS Coordinator.

Redhead, S 1993, 'The politics of ecstasy', in *Rave off: politics and deviance in contemporary youth culture*, Avebury, Aldershot, pp. 7-27.

Redhead, S (ed.) 1993, *Rave off: politics and deviance in contemporary youth culture*, Avebury, Aldershot.

Redhead, S 1997, *Subculture to clubcultures: an introduction to popular cultural studies*, Blackwell Publishers, Oxford.

Reier, C 1971, 'Ketamine-'dissciative agent' or hallucinogen? (letter)', *New England Journal of Medicine*, pp. 791-792.

Reighley, KB 2000, *Looking for the perfect beat: the art and culture of the DJ*, Simon and Schuster Adult Publishing Group, New York.

Reinarman, C & Levine, HG 1997, 'Crack in context: America's latest demon drug', in C Reinarman & HG Levine (eds.), *Crack in context: demon drugs and social justice*, University of California Press, Berkeley, pp. 1-17.

Release 1997, *Drugs and dance survey: an insight into the culture*, Release, London.

Remafedi, G 1987, 'Adolescent homosexuality: psychosocial and medical implications', *Pediatrics*, vol. 79, pp. 331-337.

Reneman, L, Booij, J, de Bruin, K, Reitsma, JB, de Wolff, FA, Gunning, WB, den Heeten, GJ, & den Brink, WV 2001, 'Effects of dose, sex, and long-term abstention from use on toxic effects of MDMA (ecstasy) on brain serotonin neurons', *Lancet*, vol. 358, pp. 1864-1869.

Reynolds, S 1997, 'Rave culture: living dream or living death?' in S Redhead (ed.) with D Wynne & J O'Connor, *The clubcultures reader: readings in popular cultural studies*, Blackwell, Oxford, pp. 84-93.

Reynolds, S 1998, *Energy flash: a journey through rave music and dance culture*, Macmillan, London.

Reynolds, S 1999, *Generation ecstasy*, Routledge, New York.

Rhodes, T & Moore, D 2001, 'On the qualitative in drugs research: part one', *Addiction Research & Theory*, vol. 9, no 4, pp. 279-297.

Rich, JD, Dickinson, BP, Carney, JM, Fisher, A & Heimer, R 1998a, 'Detection of HIV-1 nucleic acid and HIV-1 antibodies in needles and syringes used for non-intravenous injection', *AIDS*, vol. 12, pp. 2345-2350.

Richard, B & Kruger, H 1998, 'Ravers paradise? German youth cultures in the 1990's', in T Skelton & G Valetine (eds.), *Cool places: geographies of youth cultures*, Routledge, London, pp. 161-174.

Rietveld, H 1991, 'Living the dream: analysis of the rave phenomenon in terms of ideology, consumerism and subculture', Ain't Nothing But a House Party seminar working paper, Unit for Law and Popular Culture, Manchester Polytechnic, Manchester.

Rietveld, H 1993, 'Living the dream', in S Redhead (ed.), *Rave off: politics and deviance in contemporary youth culture*, Avebury, Aldershot, pp. 41-71.

Rietveld, H 1998, 'Repetitive Beats: free parties and the politics of contemporary DiY dance culture in Britain', in G McKay (ed.), *DiY culture: party and protest in nineties Britain*, Verso, London, pp. 243-268.

Riley, SC & Hayward, E 2004, 'Patterns, trends, and meanings of drug use by dance-drug users in Edinburgh, Scotland', *Drugs: education, prevention and policy*, vol. 11, pp. 243-262.

Robins, D & Cohen, P 1978, *Knuckle sandwich: growing up in the working-class city*, Penguin, Harmondsworth.

Robins, LN, Davis, DH & Goodwin, DW 1974, 'Drug use in US army enlisted men in Vietnam: a follow up on their return home', *American Journal of Epidemiology*, vol. 99, pp. 235-249.

Roe, S 2005, *Drug misuse declared: findings from the 2004/05 British Crime Survey*, Home Office, London.

Rogers, A 2001, 'HIV research in American youth', *Journal of Adolescent Health*, vol. 29, no. 3S, pp. 1-4.

Rojek, C 2000, *Leisure and culture*, MacMillian, London.

Rose, A & Ross, T 1994, *Microphone fiends: youth music and youth culture*, Routlege, London.

Rosenbaum, M 2002, 'Ecstasy: America's new "reefer madness"', *Journal of Psychoactive Drugs*, vol. 34, no. 2, pp. 137-142.

Ruggiero, V 1993, 'Brixton, London: a drug culture without a drug economy?', *The International Journal of Drug Policy*, vol. 4, no. 2, pp. 83-90.

Ruggerio, V 1995, '*Drugs in central Lambeth; an exploratory study*', Research Bulletin 37, pp. 51-55.

Ruggiero, V 2000, *Crime and markets: essays in anti-criminology*, Oxford University Press, Oxford.

Ruggiero, V & South, N 1995, *Eurodrugs: drug use, markets, and trafficking in Europe*, UCL Press, London.

Ruggerio, V & South, N 1997, 'The late modern city as a bazaar: drug markets, illegal enterprise and the barricades', *British Journal of Sociology*, vol. 48, pp. 54-70.

Rusch, M, Lampinen, TM, Schilder, A, Hogg, RS 2004, 'Unprotected anal intercourse associated with recreational drug use among young men who have sex with men depends on partner type and intercourse role', *Sexually Transmitted Disease*, vol. 31, no. 8, pp. 492-498.

Saldanha, A 2002, 'Music, space, identity: geographies of youth culture in Bangalore', *Cultural Studies*, vol. 16, no. 3, pp. 337-350.

Sack, AR, Keller, JF & Hinkle, DE 1981, 'The sexual double standard: how prevalent today?', *College Student Journal*, vol. 15, pp. 47-52.

Sampson, RJ & Laub, J 1993, *Crime in the making: pathways and turning points in the life course*, Harvard University Press, Cambridge.

Sanders, B 2005, *Youth crime and youth culture in the inner city*, Routledge, London.

Sanders, B, Lankenau, SE, Jackson Bloom, J & Hathazi, D 2005, 'Non-Medical prescription drug use amongst young injection drug users in New York City,' paper presented to the 55th annual Society for the Study of Social Problem Conference, Philadelphia, 12-14 August.

Saunders, N 1993, *E for ecstasy*, Nicholas Saunders, London.

Saunders, N 1995, *Ecstasy and the dance culture*, Nicholas Saunders, London.

Saunders, N 1997, *Ecstasy reconsidered*, Nicholas Saunders, London.

Saunders, N & Doblin, R 1996, *Ecstasy: dance, trance, and transformation*, Quick American Archives, Oakland, CA.

Sanders, T 2004, 'Controllable laughter: managing sex work through humour,' *Sociology*, vol. 38, no. 2, pp. 273-291.

Sanders, T 2005, "It's just acting': sex workers' strategies for capitalizing on sexuality', *Gender, Work and Organisation*, vol. 12, no. 4, pp. 319-342.

Sanders, WS 2002, 'Breadren: exploring the group context of young offenders in an inner city English borough', *International Journal of Comparative and Applied Criminal Justice*, vol. 26, no. 1, pp. 101-113.

SAS Institute Inc. 2004, *SAS/STAT 9.1: User's guide*, SAS Institute, Cary, NC.

Scholey, AB, Parrott, AC, Buchanan, T, Heffernan, T, Ling, J, & Rodgers, J 2004, 'Increased intensity of ecstasy and polydrug usage in the more experienced recreational ecstasy/MDMA users: a WWW study', *Addictive Behaviors*, vol. 29, pp. 743-752.

Schuster, P, Lieb, R, Lamertz, C, & Wittchen, HU 1998, 'Is the use of ecstasy and hallucinogens increasing?', *European Addiction Research*, vol. 4, pp. 75-82.

Schwartz, RH & Miller, NS 1997, 'MDAM (Ecstasy) and the rave: a review', *Pediatrics*, vol. 100, no. 4, pp. 705-708.

Selzer, C 1997, 'Second thoughts: 'conflicts of interest and 'political science'', *Journal of Clinical Epidemiology*, vol. 50, pp. 627-629.

Shankaran, M, Yamamoto, BK, & Gudelsky, GA 1999, 'Involvement of the serotonin transporter in the formation of hydroxyl radicals induced by 3,4-methylenedioxymethamphetamine' *European Journal of Pharmacology*, vol. 385, pp. 103-110.

Shapiro, H 1999, 'Dances with drugs: pop music, drugs and youth culture', in N South (ed.), *Drugs: cultures, controls and everyday life*, Sage, London, pp. 17-35.

Sherlock, K & Conner, M 1999, 'Patterns of ecstasy use amongst club-goers on the UK 'dance scene'', *International Journal of Drug Policy*, vol. 10, pp. 117-129.

Shewan, D, Dalgarno, P & Reith, G 2000, 'Perceived risk and risk reduction among ecstasy users: the role of drug, set, and setting', *International Journal of Drug Policy*, vol. 10, pp. 431-453.

Shover, N 1996, *Great pretenders: pursuits and careers of persistent thieves*, Westview Press, Boulder.

Shukla, RK 2003, 'A rational choice analysis of decision-making and desistance from marijuana use', *Dissertation Abstracts International*, vol. 64, no. 4, p. 1417-A.

Shulgin, AT & Shulgin, A 1991, *PIHKAL: a chemical love story*, Transform, Berkeley.

Siegel, RK 1978, 'Phencyclidine and ketamine intoxication: a study of recreational users', in RC Peterson & R C Stillman (eds.), *Phencyclidine abuse: an appraisal*, National Institute on Drug Abuse Research Monograph 21, National Institute on Drug Abuse, Rockville, MD., pp. 119-140.

Silverstone, D in press, *Night-clubbing: drugs, clubs and regulation*, Willan, Cullompton.

Silverstone, D 2003, 'The ecstasy of consumption', unpublished PhD thesis, London School of Economics, London.

Simpson M 2003, 'The relationship between drug use and crime: a puzzle inside an enigma', *International Journal of Drug Policy*, vol. 14: 307-319.

Singer, LT, Linarres, TJ, Ntiri, S, Henry, R, & Minnes, S 2004, 'Psychosocial profiles of older adolescent MDMA users', *Drug and Alcohol Dependence*, vol. 74, pp. 245-252.

Sloan III, JJ 2001, 'It's all the rave: 'flower power' meets technoculture'', in J Inciardi & K McElrath (eds.) *The American drug scene: an anthology*, 3rd ed., Roxbury, Los Angeles, pp. 293-300.

Snow, M 1973, 'Maturing out of narcotic addiction in New York City', *International Journal of the Addictions*, vol. 8, pp. 921-938.

Sobell, LC, Kwan, E, & Sobell, MB 1995, 'Reliability of a drug history questionnaire (DHQ)', *Addictive Behaviors*, vol. 20, pp. 233-241.

Solowij, N, Hall, W, & Lee, N 1992, 'Recreational MDMA use in Sydney: a profile of "Ecstasy" users and their experiences with the drug', *British Journal of Addiction*, vol. 87, pp. 1161-1172.

Song, M & Parker, D 1995, 'Commonality, difference and the dynamics of discourse in in-depth interviewing', *Sociology*, vol. 29, no. 2, pp. 241-256.

South, N 1997, 'Drugs: use, crime and control', in M. Maguire, R. Morgan & R.Reiner (eds.), *The Oxford handbook of criminology*, Oxford University Press, Oxford, pp. 925-960.

South, N 1999, 'Debating drugs and everyday life: normalisation, prohibition and 'otherness'', in *Drugs: cultures, controls and everyday life*, Sage, London, pp. 1-15.

Southgate, E & Hopwood, M 2001, 'The role of folk pharmacology and lay experts in harm reduction: Sydney gay drug using networks', *International Journal of Drug Policy*, vol. 12, pp. 321-335.

Stall, R & Wiley, J 1988, 'A comparison of alcohol and drug use patterns of homosexual and heterosexual men', *Drug and Alcohol Dependence*, vol. 33, pp. 63-73.

Stanley, C 1997, 'Not drowning but waving: urban narratives of dissent in the wild zone', in S Redhead (ed.) with D Wynne & J O'Connor, *The clubcultures reader: readings in popular cultural studies*, Blackwell Publishers, Oxford, pp. 36-54.

Stanley, L (ed.) 1990, *Feminist praxis: research, theory and epistemology in feminist sociology*, Routedge, London.

Stanley, L & Wise, S 1993, *Breaking out again: feminist ontology and epistemology*, Routledge, London.

Strathdee, SA & Sherman, SJ 2003, 'The role of sexual transmission of HIV infection among injection and non-injection drug users', *Journal of Urban Health*, vol. 80, no. 4 (Supplement 3), pp. iii7-iii14.

Strauss, A & Corbin, J 1998, *Basics of qualitative research: grounded theory procedures and techniques*, 2nd ed., Sage Publications, Newbury Park, CA.

Stelfox, P 1998 'Policing lower levels of organised crime in England and Wales', *The Howard Journal*, vol. 37, no. 4, pp. 393-406.

Sternbach, H 1991, 'The serotonin syndrome', *American Journal of Psychiatry*, vol. 148, pp. 705-713.

Substance Abuse and Mental Health Services Administration (SAMHSA) 2001, *2001 National Household Survey on Drug Abuse Questionnaire*, Office of Applied Studies, Rockville, MD.

Substance Abuse & Mental Health Services Administration (SAMHSA) 2003a, *Results from the 2002 National Survey on Drug Use and Health: national findings*, Office of Applied Studies, Rockville, MD.

Substance Abuse & Mental Health Services Administration (SAMHSA) 2003b, 'The NHSDA report: Ecstasy Use', *National Household Survey on Drug Abuse*, Office of Applied Studies, Rockville, MD.

Substance Abuse & Mental Health Services Administration (SAMHSA) 2004a, *Results from the 2003 National Survey on Drug Use and Health: national findings*, Office of Applied Studies, Rockville, MD.

Substance Abuse & Mental Health Services Administration (SAMHSA) 2004b, *The club drugs scene: the myths and truths*, SAMSHA's National Clearinghouse for Alcohol and Drug Information, Rockville, MD.

Substance Abuse & Mental Health Services Administration (SAMHSA) 2005, *Results from the 2004 National Survey on Drug Use and Health: national findings*, Office of Applied Studies, Rockville, MD.

Sullivan, G 2000, 'Raving on the Internet', *Canadian Medical Association Journal*, vol. 162, no. 3, p. 1864.

Sutherland, EH & Cressey, DR 1966, *Principles in criminology*, 7th ed., JB Lippincott, Philadelphia.

Sykes, G & Matza, D 1957, 'Techniques of neutralization: a theory of delinquency', *American Sociological Review*, vol. 22, pp. 664-670.

Syme, SL 2000, 'Foreward' in LF Berkman & I Kawachi (eds.), *Social epidemiology*, Oxford Univ. Press, Oxford, pp. ix-xii.

Taylor, I 1999, *Crime in context: a critical criminlogy of market societies*, Blackwell, London.

Teal, D 1971, *Gay militants*, Stein & Day, New York.

Temple, MT, Leigh, BC, & Schafer, J 1993, 'Unsafe sexual behavior and alcohol use at the event level: results of a national survey', *Journal of Acquired Immune Deficiency Syndromes*, vol. 6, pp. 393-401.

Ter Bogt, T & Engels R 2005, '"Partying" hard: party style, motives for and effects of MDMA use at rave parties', *Substance Use & Misuse*, vol. 40, pp. 1479-1502.

Ter Bogt, T, Engels, R, Hibbel, B, Van Wel, F & Verhagen, S 2002, '"Dancestasy": dance youth and MDMA use in Dutch youth culture', *Contemporary Drug Problems*, vol. 29, pp.157-181.

Tewksbury, R 1995, 'Adventures in the erotic oasis: sex and danger in men's same-sex public sexual encounters', *Journal of Men's Studies*, vol. 4, no. 1, pp. 9-24.

Thompson, T 2004, *Gangs: a journey into the heart of the British underworld*, Hodder & Stoughton, London.

Thornberry, TP 1987, 'Toward an interactional theory of delinquency', *Criminology*, vol. 25, pp. 863-891.

Thornton, S 1995, *Club cultures: music, media and subcultural capital*, Wesleyan University Press, Hanover.

The Times Online 2005, *Mayor blames rap for deaths*, viewed 1 November, 2005, <http://www.timesonline.co.uk/article/0,,2-1854985,00.html>

Tomlinson, L 1998, '"This ain't no disco"...or it it? Youth culture and the rave phenomenon', in JS Epstein (ed.), *Youth culture: identity in a postmodern world*, Blackwell, Oxford, pp. 195-211.

Topp, L, Hando, J, Dillon, P, Roche, A, & Solowij, N 1999, 'Ecstasy use in Australia: patterns of use and associated harm', *Drug & Alcohol Dependence*, vol. 55, nos. 1-2, pp. 105-115.

Topp, L, Degenhard, L, Kaye, S & Darke S 2002, 'The emergence of potent forms of methamphetamine in Sydney, Australia: a case study of the IDRS as a strategic early warning system', *Drug and Alcohol Review*, vol. 21, no. 4, pp. 341-348.

Tori, SP 1996, *Ketamine abuse 'Special K'*, Middle Atlantic-Great Lakes Organized Crime Law Enforcement Network (MAGLOCLEN), Newtown, PA.

Travis, A 2005, 'Special K, the horse pill taking over from ecstasy among clubbers', *The Guardian (London)*, 6 September, p. 3.

Turner, DM 1994, *The essential guide to psychedelics*, Panther Press, San Francisco.

Turner, RJ & Avison, WR 2003, 'Status variations in stress exposure: implications for the interpretation of research on race, socioeconomic status, and gender', *Journal of Health and Social Behavior*, vol. 44, no. 4, pp. 488-505.

United Nations Office on Drugs and Crime (UNODC) 2003, *Ecstasy and amphetamine: global survey 2003*, United Nations, New York.

Urberg, KA, Luo, Q, Pilgrim, C, & Degirmencioglu, SM 2004, 'A two-stage model of peer influence in adolescent substance use: individual and relationship-specific differences in susceptibility to influence', *Addictive Behaviors*, vol. 29, no. 3, pp. 1243-1256.

van de Wijngaart, RB, Braam, R, De Bruin, D, Fris, M, Maalste, NJM & Berbraeck, HT 1999, 'Ecstasy use at large-scale dance events in the Netherlands', *Journal of Drugs Issues*, vol. 29, pp. 679-702.

van der Rijt, G, d'Haenens, L & van Straten, P 2003, 'Subcultural grounding of teenage smoking, drinking, and use of drugs', *Communications*, vol. 28, pp. 1-15.

Veblen, T 1899; 1994, *The theory of the leisure class*, Penguin Books, New York.

Venkatesh, SA 2005, 'Community justice and the gang: a life-course perspective', viewed 24 July 2005, <http://www.jcpr.org/porsem/ventatesh _paper.pdf >

Verheyden, SL, Hadfield, J, Calin, T, & Curran, HV 2002, 'Sub-acute effects of MDMA (3,4-methylenedioxymethamphetamine, "ecstasy") on mood: evidence of gender differences', *Psychopharmacology*, vol. 161, pp. 23-31.

Verheyden, SL, Henry, JA, & Curran, HV 2003, 'Acute, sub-acute and long-term subjective consequences of "ecstasy" (MDMA) consumption in 430 regular users', *Human Psychopharmacology - Clinical and Experimental*, vol. 18, no. 7, pp. 507-517.

Verheyden, SL, Maidment, R & Curran, HV 2003, 'Quitting ecstasy: an investigation of why people stop taking the drug and their subsequent mental health', *Journal of Psychopharmacology*, vol. 17, pp. 371-378.

Viscount Ullswater 1997, *UK Hansard*, HMSO, available at , <www.publications. parliament.uk/ pa/ld199697/ldhansrd/vo970206/text/70206-10.htm - 63k>

von Sydow, K, Lieb, R, Pfister, H, Hofler, M, & Wittchen, HU 2002, 'Use, abuse and dependence of ecstasy and related drugs in adolescents and young adults - a transient phenomenon? Results from longitudinal community study', *Drug and Alcohol Dependence*, vol. 66, no. 2, pp. 147-159.

Waldorf, D, Reinarman, C & Murphy, S 1991, *Cocaine changes: the experience of using and quitting*, Temple University Press, Philadelphia.

Walker, AK 1972, 'Intramuscular ketamine in a developing country', *Anesthesia*, vol. 27, no. 4, pp. 408 -414.

Walsh, P 2005, *Gang war: the inside story of the Manchester gangs*, Milo Books, Lytham St. Annes.

Warner, J, Room, R & Adlaf, EM 1999, 'Rules and limits in the use of marijuana among high-school students: the results of a qualitative study in Ontario', *Journal of Youth Studies*, vol. 2, pp. 59-76.

Warner, M 1997, 'We're queer, remember?', *The Advocate*, vol. 30, p. 7.

Warr, M 2002, *Companions in crime: the social aspects of criminal conduct*, Cambridge University Press, Cambridge.

Webster, R Goodman, M & Whalley, G 2002, *Safer clubbing: guidance for licensing authorities, club managers and promoters*, Home Office Drug Prevention Advisory Service, London.

Weil, A & Rosen, W 1983, *Chocolate to morphine: understanding mind-active drugs*, Hougton Mifflin Company, Boston.

Weinberg, M & Williams, CJ 1975, 'Gay baths and the social organization of impersonal sex', *Social Problems*, vol. 23, pp. 124-136.

Weiner, AL, Vieira, L, McKay, CA & Bayer, MJ 2000, 'Ketamine abusers presenting to the emergency department: a case series', *Journal of Emergency Medicine*, vol. 18, no. 4, pp. 447-451.

Weir, E 2000, 'Raves: a review of the culture, the drugs and the prevention of harm', *Canadian Medical Association Journal*, vol. 162, no. 13, pp. 1843-1848.

West, B & Hager, S 1993, 'Rave new world', *High Times*, May, no. 213, pp. 36-39.

Wibberley, C 2003, Book Review: 'Drugs for dancing?', *Addiction Research and Theory*, vol. 11, no. 3, pp. 207-208.

Wijngaart, Gvd, Braam, R, Bruin, Dd, Fris, M, Maalsté, N & Verbraeck, H 1998, *Ecstasy and the Dutch rave scene: a socio-epidemiological study on the nature and extent of, and the risks involved in using ecstasy and other party drugs at dance events*, Addiction Research Institute, Utrecht University, Utrecht, Holland.

Williams, L & Parker, H 2001, 'Alcohol, cannabis, ecstasy and cocaine: drugs of reasoned choice amongst young adult recreational drug users in England', *International Journal of Drug Policy*, vol. 12, pp. 397-413.

Williams, T 1992, *Crackhouse: notes from the end of the line*, Addison-Wesley Publishing Company, Inc., Reading, MA.

Willis, P 1977, *Learning to labour: how working class kids get working class jobs*, Saxon House, London.

Willis, P 1978, *Profane culture*, Routledge and Kegan Paul, London.

Winlow, S 2001, *Badfellas: crime, violence and new masculinities*, Berg, Oxford.

Winlow, S, Hobbs, D, Lister, S, & Hadfield, P 2001, 'Get ready to duck: bouncers and the realities of ethnographic research on violent groups', *British Journal of Criminology*, vol. 41, pp. 536-548.

Winick, C 1962, 'Maturing out of narcotic addiction', *Bulletin on Narcotics*, vol. 14., no. 1. pp. 1-7.

Winstock, AR, Wolff, K & Ramsey, J 2001, 'Ecstasy pill testing: harm minimization gone too far?' *Addiction*, vol. 96, pp. 1139-1148.

Wolfgang, M & Ferracuti, F 1967, *The subculture of violence*, Tavistock, London.

Wong, S 2005, 'For some chronic pain sufferers, 'Special K' may be the answer', *The Philadelphia Inquirer*, 26 August.

Wright, MA 1998, 'The great British ecstasy revolution', in G McKay (ed.), *DIY culture: party and protest in nineties Britain*, Verso, London, pp. 228-242.

Wu, ZH, Berenson, AB, & Wiemann, CM 2003, 'A profile of adolescent females with a history of sexual assault in texas: familial enviornment, risk behaviors, and health status', *Journal of Pediatric and Adolescent Gynecology*, vol. 16, no. 4, pp. 207-216.

Yablonsky, L 1968, *The hippie trip: a firsthand account of the beliefs, drug use and sexual patterns of young drop-outs in America*, Pegasus, New York.

Yacoubian, GS Jr., Arria, AM, Fost, E, & Wish, ED 2002, 'Estimating the prevalence of Ecstasy use among juvenile offenders', *Journal of Psychoactive Drugs*, vol. 34, no. 2, pp. 209-213.

Yacoubian, Jr. GS, Boyle, C, Hardin, CA & Loftus, EA 2003, 'It's a rave new world: estimating the prevalence and perceived harm of ecstasy and other drug use, among club rave attendees', *Journal of Drug Education*, vol. 33, pp. 187-197.

Yamaguchi, K & Kandel, D 1997, 'The influence of spouses' behavior and marital dissolution on marijuana use: causation or selection', *Journal of Marriage and Family*, vol. 59, pp. 22-36.

Young, J 1971, *The drug takers: the social meaning of drug use*, MacGibbon & Kee, London.

Young, J 1999, *The exclusive society: social exclusion, crime and difference in late modernity*, Sage, London.

Zealot 2005, 'Synthesis of ketamine-complete', viewed 15 July 2005, <http://designer-drugs.com/pte/12.162.180.114/dcd/chemistry/ketamine2.html>

Zemishlany, Z, Aizenberg, D & Weizman, A 2001, 'Subjective effects of MDMA ("Ecstasy") on human sexual function', *European Psychiatry*, vol. 16, no. 2, pp. 127-130.

Zinberg, NE 1984, *Drug, set, and setting: the basis for controlled intoxicant use*, Yale University Press, New Haven.

Subject Index

Author Index

Spare, KE 67
Spence, RT 31, 48
Staff of The Measurement Group 91
Stajic, M 62, 78, 86
Stall, R 67
Stanley, C 122, 127, 145
Stanley, L 17, 18, 38
Steffey, DM 31, 48
Steinber 88
Stelfox, P 149
Sternbach, H 56
Stewart, J 81
Stirratt, M 67
Stoddard, AM 67
Strathdee, SA 105
Strauss, A 69
Substance Abuse and Mental Health
    Services Administration (SAMHSA)
    5, 53, 88, 92, 104, 111, 112
Sullivan, G 88
Sunley, R 2
Sutherland, EH 33
Swann, A 88
Swartzwelder, S 42, 45
Sykes, G 137
Syme, SL xii

Taylor, I 149
Te YT 83
Teal, D 74
Temko, N 22
Temple, MT 56
Ter Bogt, T 27, 28, 31, 33, 35, 37, 38, 45,
    46, 48
Tewksbury, R 72, 75, 76
Thiede, H 67
Thomas, SH 89
Thompson, T 148
Thomson, R 6
Thornberry, TP 45
Thornton, S 2, 3, 5, 6, 8, 15, 16, 18, 33, 36,
    37, 38, 107, 108, 122, 127, 128, 144
Tildesley, E 90, 105
Tomlinson, L 2, 7
Topp, L 5, 56, 81, 82, 85, 89, 104
Tori, SP 80
Tortu, S 4, 77, 79, 81, 83, 85, 87
Traver, H 109, 112, 115, 116, 117
Travill, RA 55

Travis, A 82
Tuchtenhagen, F 88
Turner, DM 86
Turner, JJD 88, 90, 95
Turner, RJ 106

Urberg, KA 90, 105

Van de Ven, P 67
van de Wijngaart, RB 27, 31, 37, 48
van der Rijt, G 27, 34
van Straten, P 27, 34
Van Wel, F 27, 28, 31, 35, 37, 38, 45, 46, 48
Veblen, T 27, 36
Venkatesh, SA 123, 138
Verbraeck, H 107
Verhagen, S 27, 28, 31, 35, 37, 38, 45, 46,
    48
Verheyden, SL 46, 89, 90, 105
Vieira, L 86, 87
Viscount Ullswater 141
Vlahov, D 31, 48, 54, 80
Vollenweider, FX 89, 90, 105
von Sydow, K 88, 89

Waldorf, D 35, 45, 46, 49
Walker, AK 78
Walsh, P 149
Wang, J 54
Warner, J 27, 34
Warner, M 76
Warr, M 39
Watters, JK 69
Webster, R 1, 3, 10, 14, 122
Weil, A 77
Weinberg, M 75
Weiner, AL 86, 87
Weir, E 88
Weiss, RD 104
Weizman, A 56, 89, 90
Welle, D xii, 5, 105
West, B 2, 4
West, LJ 79, 82
Westcott, K 78, 86
Westenhouse, J. 67
Whalley, G 1, 3, 10, 14, 122
Wibberley, C 23
Wiemann, CM 90
Wijngaart, G 107